GANGA

what we must do to connect the river back to society; to the city that it flows through and to the wisdom that will ensure that Ganga is pristine once again.

Sunita Narain, DG, Centre for Science and Environment

Transforming, rejuvenating and reconnecting, this very engaging book that takes one through the various stages and challenges the team faced as they set out to restore the Ganga.

Mike H. Pandey, conservationist and winner of three Green Oscars

Through the National Mission for Clean Ganga, the river Ganga has now become an emblem for all the river ecosystems in the country, and this truly remarkable book will enable other readers across many countries to know the story of Ganga, and draw lessons from it.

Professor Edmund Penning-Rowsell, OBE, Distinguished Research Associate, Oxford University Centre for the Environment

There are very few people whose impact will be felt for a long time to come. Rajiv Ranjan Mishra, through his leadership of Namami Gange Mission is one of them. This book is an inspiration for those who would follow his example of turning the seemingly impossible dreams into tangible reality.

Christopher Gasson, Head and Publisher, Global Water Intelligence

The authors take us on a remarkable journey of discovery as they share their experiences navigating the complexity and diversity of the human connection with the waters of the Ganga. In a world where leaders grapple with the challenge of righting the wrongs of past water mismanagement whilst grappling with the emerging challenges from climate change, this book serves as an important reference of the enormity of the task and the importance of putting people at the heart of rebuilding our waterways so future generations can also prosper from their bounty.

Karlene Maywald, South Australian Water Ambassador

This book highlights the importance of the quality of the process, and the need for involving people in the efforts, capturing diverse values of rivers that often goes unrecognized (social, cultural, spiritual, recreational), providing a clear aspirational long-term vision for the river.

Dr Alejandro Jimenez, Director, Water and Sanitation Department,
Stockholm International Water Institute, Sweden

I have always believed that the uninterrupted flow of the river Ganga is not merely a matter of resources, but of clear, determined and persistent efforts. A journey of such efforts breathes through this book.

Abhay Mishra, author of *Dar Dar Gange* and
Mati Manas Choon and conservationist

This is an inspiring book that provides detail on the many and impressive efforts to rejuvenate the river. This book shows sensitivity to this cultural perspective of Ganga being incorruptible with its spiritual origins and also shows how modern scientific advances also have their place in the new world and are imperative if the Ganga is to continue providing the abundant benefits to the society that it supports.

Dr Chris Dickens, Principal Researcher, Ecosystems,
International Water Management Institute, Sri Lanka

This book is a timely initiative with most important feature being its intention to cover all issues right from culture to commerce to conservation. This highlights Ganga more as a living system.

Dr Anil Prakash Joshi, Founder, Himalayan Environmental Studies
and Conservation Organization (HESCO); Padma Bhushan awardee

As a child the Ganges was one of those rivers that captured my imagination. Few great rivers have such a powerful connection to people. This book is a story about saving this river.

Dr Guillermo Mendoza, International Programme Manager,
Institute for Water Resources, US Army Corps of Engineers, USA

I think sharing the successes and difficulties of undertaking such a complex and important project will be of great interest to so many people in India and beyond.

Dr Anthony Acciavatti, School of Architecture,
Yale University; author of *Ganges Water Machine:*
Designing New India's Ancient River

The book vividly describes the attempt, the efforts and the concrete action steps to achieve rejuvenation and thus salvation of the river Ma Ganga. The book is a reminder to all of us and a call to concrete action.

Dr Andreas Haarstrick, Professor, Systems Engineering, Technical University of Braunschweig, Germany

This book documents the challenges of restoring the eco-hydrology of one of the most complex watershed systems in the world.

Mr Eric Falt, Director and UNESCO Representative for Bangladesh, Bhutan, India, Nepal, the Maldives, and Sri Lanka

The book describes a transformative and transdisciplinary approach used for river management that goes beyond engineering solutions. The book is a great success story and the approach narrated has merit to solve other wicked problems we face.

Dr Basant Maheshwari, Professor, Life Sciences, Western Sydney University, Australia

The book tells a captivating story of how the Namami Gange mission unfolded.

Dr Mukand Babel, Professor, Water Engineering and Management, Asian Institute of Technology, Thailand

This important book highlights the institutional and governance challenges in river rejuvenation in India. I sincerely hope that this inspires us all to better value our rivers.

Stuart Orr, Freshwater Leader, WWF International

GANGA

REimagining
REjuvenating
REconnecting

RAJIV RANJAN MISHRA
and PUSKAL UPADHYAY

RUPA

Published by
Rupa Publications India Pvt. Ltd 2021
7/16, Ansari Road, Daryaganj
New Delhi 110002

Sales centres:
Allahabad Bengaluru Chennai
Hyderabad Jaipur Kathmandu
Kolkata Mumbai

ISBN: 978-93-5520-199-7

First impression 2021

10 9 8 7 6 5 4 3 2 1

The moral right of the authors has been asserted.

To Ma Ganga
Our lifeline and the door to divinity

Contents

Foreword

Books have been written on the Ganga. Eric Newby floated *Slowly Down the Ganges*. Steven Darian wrote a book on *The Ganges in Myth and History*. Ganga features prominently in Diana Eck's book on India's sacred geography. There are books by Giulio Di Sturco and Victor Mallet. Ganga fascinates. Ganga is that kind of river. It is not the case that Ganga only fascinates those from the Occident, though that's also a function of the language one has in mind. In the English language, there a book by Sudipta Sen and another, with lovely photographs, by Raghubir Singh. This book by Rajiv Ranjan Mishra and Puskal Upadhyay is the latest addition to the corpus.

The Ganga corpus precedes the evolution of English as a language. There is a beautiful description of Ganga in *Valmiki Ramayana*. She is the divine river, with three flows in heaven, on earth and the nether regions. Adi Shankaracharya's Ganga stotram is familiar to most Indians, as is the invocation, '*O Ganga, Yamuna, Godavari, Sarasvati, Narmada, Sindhu, Kaveri! Please be present in this water.*' After the advent of settled agriculture, civilization evolved along the banks and plains of rivers. India is no different from that general principle and in India's wealth of rivers, Ganga is foremost— as she is in that list of seven. History is woven into the flow of the river. She resides on Shankara's head. She originated from Hari's feet. She is Jahnu's daughter and that of Bhagiratha. She is Bhisma's mother and Shantanu's wife. She cuts across India and Bangladesh, from the Himalayas to the confluence with the ocean in the Bay of Bengal, where the sage Kapila's rage reduced Bhagiratha's ancestors to ashes.

Ganga is a long river. Depending on how the river and its tributaries are defined, it is around 2,600 km long. The geographical description of Ganga's progress on earth is given in some parts of *Brahma Vaivarta Purana*. That was hundreds of years ago. Hundreds of years later, Ganga's progress is marked out by cities—Badrinath, Haridwar, New Delhi, Agra, Prayagraj, Kanpur, Jaunpur, Varanasi, Mathura, Mirzapur, Auraiya, Etawah, Farrukhabad, Fatehgarh, Kannauj, Gorakhpur, Lucknow, Bhagalpur, Patna, Gaya, Munger, Baranagar, Kolkata, Murshidabad and many more. 600 million people, in 11 States, live in Ganga's basin and that basin, and people who live in that basin, are estimated to contribute 40% of India's GDP.

Rivers mean urbanization, civilization and development. Rivers mean life and at least 50 cities, with population sizes more than 50,000, are along Ganga's banks. But for this to be sustainable, the river has to remain alive and it is anything but that. Urban centres draw water from Ganga and dump waste and waste water into the river. All too often people assume it is the government's job to clean up raw sewage and industrial waste from the river. That can't work, not alone. Many people may not have heard of Kashi Ganga Prasadini Sabha, established by concerned citizens of Varanasi in 1886. The Sabha's objective was to introduce drainage and clean up the river, objectives we are still struggling with today.

To that end, there is a National Mission for Clean Ganga (NMCG). What does NMCG do? What has NMCG done so far and what does it propose to do? What have been the struggles and successes? Most people will have heard of NMCG, but probably no more than vaguely. Rajiv Ranjan Mishra and Puskal Upadhyay are insiders, with a vested interest in the cleaning up of Ganges, and rightly so. They do work for the government, but the book doesn't read like a boring government handout. While it isn't a biography of Ganga, it reads like an autobiography of NMCG. Nothing succeeds like success and there are success stories from Uttarakhand, Kanpur, Prayagraj, Varanasi, Bihar, Jharkhand and the Sunderbans. The most important chapter, in my view, is the last one. It is like an Epilogue and is a letter to readers. As citizens of a country where rivers like Ganga have given us life, the Ganga's future depends on what we, the readers, do and don't do.

Bibek Debroy
26 November 2021

Acknowledgements

Inspiration initiates a process; blessings make it happen. For this book, both inspiration and blessings came from Ma Ganga. Getting assigned to this job was a pure chance for both of us. But once initiated, our connection has only become more profound, and the result is the book in your hands.

This book is a product of the collective experience and efforts of the NMCG team. But for their resolve, commitment and work beyond their call of duty, we would have had no story to tell. Each team member and their leaders have made this possible, and so did those in the Ministry of Environment, Forests and Climate Change and the Ministry of Jal Shakti. We acknowledge their commitment and zeal to rise to the occasion. We also recognise the leadership of the captains of this team, Mission Director(s) and Director(s) General, who kept them going.

We thank Vasudha Mishra, wife of Rajiv Ranjan Mishra, for her encouragement and constructive feedback to make this book happen and Nishnat, her son, for expanding our horizon. Mother Yadeshwari Sharma, a lifelong teacher by nature, always supported and inspired her children to do better.

Nishtha, the wife of Puskal Upadhyay, was always there to support us and daughters Netri and Paavani, who deserve special thanks for sharing their fresh thoughts and bright ideas, enriching the environment in which the writings took place. Netri often helped, with her great literary sense, improve the readability of the book. His mother Sharda Upadhyaya inculcated in him a love for reading and writing in his childhood.

Jyoti Verma has been the team's backbone with her strong sense of research, creativity and urge to do more and more to improve the book. She, in the process, has acquired immense knowledge and insight into this subject. Her bright ideas made a tremendous contribution in helping us take the book to its final level.

Rupa Publications and their team led by Dibakar Ghosh made this book possible in a limited time and added tremendous value with their inputs and edits.

Most of all, we acknowledge the contribution of hundreds and thousands of the people who participated in the initiatives of Namami Gange, carrying the mission and vision both far and wide, nationally and internationally. We are conscious that many more are already conducting cleaning drives on the banks in thousands and millions. They are not only participating in the Namami Gange activities but running their own, contributing to Clean Ganga Fund, celebrating Ganga Utsav and making it a people's mission in a true sense. We are privileged to get to work for Ganga at taxpayers' cost, which is nothing in comparison to the selfless service they give in anticipation for a clean Ganga. They are Bhagirath of Ganga in their sphere, even if their names are not known in public memory. Ganga herself will remember them for sure.

Author's Note

Not many countries have set themselves to the agenda of cleaning their rivers and make them sustainable at par with their basic needs like hunger, health, and employment. India has done so. Rivers are fundamental to us and mean much more than just a resource. Since the establishment of NMCG in 2011 and the launch of Namami Gange in 2014, significant efforts have been made. The challenge of Nirmal Ganga has been primarily addressed by creating needed sewage treatment capacity in cities along the river apart from tackling other sources of pollution. Many other facets of rejuvenation like clean villages, ghats and crematoriums, improving ecology and flow, biodiversity and wetland conservation, plantation, strengthening People-River connect, research, knowledge dissemination, and public participation have been initiated with holistic approach. These efforts aim to make the river not just clean but also rejuvenated, a concept still new to many countries.

This achievement is phenomenal for any river conservation project in modern India, especially by an entity that grew and continued with the programme. In the process, its human capital, i.e., its employees, kept growing and produced tangible outcomes and laid the foundation of a model for other rivers. It makes an exciting story of aspiration, struggle and zeal, deriving lessons in management, project execution and planning. It also signifies the emergence of a new India, conscious of its natural assets and its drive to make them sustainable forever.

This story needs to be told. We owe it to our current and future generations. That is why we decided to put our thoughts and experience together and bring this book to you. Our tenures in NMCG were not concurrent, except for slightly more than one and a half years. But this was a very critical period of laying foundation of a long journey. Puskal had been working in the mission in the initial days even before Rajiv joined as Mission Director and both worked together having a first-hand experience of events before the launch of Namami Gange and seeing through the transition and conceptualization of Namami Gange. Puskal continued beyond our common tenure and experienced the exciting phase of the design and launch of the Namami Gange Programme, the new institutional structure and the Hybrid Annuity Model. Rajiv had the privilege of getting a second opportunity, elevated as the Director General, looking after the full-fledged programme implementation till date and getting a chance to see through several ideas conceptualized earlier while formulating the contours of the mission. He contributed towards activating the mission's multiple dimensions, forging several defining collaborative partnerships including much strengthened community participation, improving governance and scaling up activities and opening new possibilities.

This posed some challenges for us in the writing of this book. We wanted to bring up our experience, feelings, insights, and knowledge of the issue, but the non-contiguity of the tenures kept interrupting the flow. Finally, we decided to keep it, as it all happened and as the thoughts kept flowing, taking up chapters sometimes individually and sometimes together and penning them down accordingly. Narratives at some places have spontaneously changed from third to first person. We hope this will give the readers a more realistic feel of the entire gamut of things. We have indicated in the chapter itself whose experience the same pertains to. Readers are requested to take a note of the same for a better feel. The book is best read in sequence, but individual chapters will also make a good read for those who have a fair idea of the subject. The photographs at the end are a story in themselves, adding feel to the overall narrative and providing a fitting conclusion to the saga. This book is a collection of our personal experiences and insights throughout the project.

We have explored numerous formal and informal sources to add statistics and statements; however, this book only represents a select few. We encourage our readers to take a look at the bibliography for the sources we explored if they wish to further their knowledge on the topics mentioned.

We hope you'll enjoy reading this book as much as we did writing it.

Rajiv Ranjan Mishra
Puskal Upadhyay

'Had the old methods been adopted, the situation would have been equally bad today. But we moved forward with new approach and new thinking. We have not limited the Namami Gange mission to only cleaning of River Ganga, but also made it the largest and most comprehensive river rejuvenation program in the country.'

—Narendra Modi, Prime Minister of India

1

The Call of Ma Ganga

'I bow to Mother Ganga,
every morning after waking, I repeat your name,
I fold both my hands and, having seen you, I bow to you...
Mother Ganga, you have supported us, for ages and ages,
and you liberate us from the ocean of sorrow,
not just the world, but heaven too bows at your feet;
I, too, meditate at your feet.
Chorus together: Victory to Mother Ganga
(Jaya Jaya Gange! Namami Gange!)'

Sometimes, I feel that the umbilical cord that tied me to Ma Ganga from my very childhood has never really broken. Like a strong, invisible gravitational force, it keeps pulling me into its folds every day, teaching me new meanings of life, their varied interpretations and philosophies. This also keeps reminding me of the need to adopt a more humane and balanced approach towards life. After all, the river's ebb and flow does mimic our own ups and downs in life as we struggle to achieve our much-desired goals, quite similar to the river's journey to unite with the sea.

These strong bonds between the river and humans began developing at my birthplace and continued uninterrupted during my several years of academic life, and only grew stronger during my professional life as a bureaucrat. It is impossible to ignore the call of Ma Ganga, and even when circumstances force a change of scene, other circumstances and coincidences drag you back into her fold. That's the power of her calling.

Born in the historical city of Patna that resides along the banks of the Ganga, I grew up in a family that revered the river and its contributions to Indian civilization. Even my father's office was located on the bank of the river, and hence, some of that family reverence must have rubbed off on me from my early childhood. I have many fond memories of visiting the river for various rituals and during festivals, sometimes with the family and sometimes alone.

One of my earliest memories of the river is not a comforting one. I had gone to see the river in its full spate in 1975, and I remember racing back to my house as the river breached its banks and invaded our home. For the next two days, our house was completely flooded. This incident provided me with a glimpse of the might and power of the river and the havoc it can cause if not managed properly.

After leaving school, I joined the Science College in Patna, where the river flowed past our backyard. It is hardly surprising that many of my pleasant evenings were spent walking along its banks with friends in tow. However, those happy, carefree days came to a sudden halt when the first tragedy struck our family with the untimely demise of my mother. Even today, I remember vividly the image of her being consigned to the flames at Bansghat, on the banks of the river.

The very next year, I left Patna to pursue my graduation in engineering from the prestigious Indian Institute of Technology (IIT), Kanpur. Even when confined mostly to the IIT campus, I enjoyed my trips to the historical ghats of Kanpur and Bithoor along the Ganga during my free time. I also had a chance to visit Prayagraj with friends during the summer break, where I witnessed the holy Sangam. The river has never left my side.

Even during my training at Mussoorie after being selected for the Indian Administrative Services (IAS), I found myself joining a trekking group destined for Gangotri and Gaumukh, the birthplace of Ma Ganga. There I decided to trek to Tapovan, some kilometres away from Gaumukh, and was struck by the pristine beauty of the place. Those images of snow-clad mountains, green forests and steep valleys remain permanently etched in my memory.

After more than 10 years, during my posting in Mussoorie, I had another opportunity to visit Gangotri, along with visits to several other religious sites like Kedarnath and Badrinath. Then my job took me to Andhra Pradesh, a state located kilometres away from the course of the Ganga. But it was Ma Ganga's powerful force of attraction that brought me back to its banks when I decided to organize some rituals on my son's first birthday in Patna, despite him being born in Visakhapatnam.

When I returned to the Central government on deputation in 2013, I was immediately assigned the task of cleaning Ganga as part of the Clean Ganga Mission at the level of a joint secretary. It was a critical moment in my life because I had suddenly been assigned the onerous task of saving Ma Ganga, whose benevolence to the country remains unparalleled. My job—from revamping the World Bank project to seeing the launch of Namami Gange mission—was fulfilling and rewarding at the same time.

While working in Andhra Pradesh, I got a chance to work in the irrigation sector and had a fruitful experience of constructing projects on harnessing river waters, mainly for agricultural purposes. Our sole purpose was to understand how we could use the river water in the most productive way. These measures gave me the confidence to construct projects, rehabilitate displaced families with a humane approach and deal with multiple stakeholders. These skills came in handy while steering the Namami Gange mission projects. Now I realize that my understanding of rivers was minimal. I soon understood that a river has a life of its own, water of its own, land of its own and performs an important ecosystem service for our survival.

Later, I worked in the housing and urban development sector and kept my date with the water sector in urban areas. At a personal level, I went for a holiday to Gangasagar—the last stretch of the Ganga before it unites with the sea—on my marriage anniversary in

December 2015. My fascination with the river had not diminished one bit, even after several years.

It is uncommon in government services to return to the same assignment, and I consider it providence and a blessing that I received a second opportunity to rejuvenate the great river again. This time, as the Director General of Namami Gange mission in which my role was to plan, execute and expand several novel ideas.

My association with this mission has helped me grow as a person, changed my worldview and made me realize that rivers are not just water sources but entire ecosystems. Rejuvenating a river is like rejuvenating a whole civilization. It involves dealing with misunderstandings, misconceptions, ignorance and behavioural patterns of people, society and decision-makers. It also involves balancing of scientific principles and technologies on one hand and culture, traditions, and human beliefs on the other.

As a student of science, I am familiar with constants and variables in an equation that are meant to represent a real phenomenon. But while working on Ganga Rejuvenation, I soon realized that even the constants could become a function of something quite dynamic, and in a sense, everything can become a variable. It only underscored the challenges of river rejuvenation.

Working on such a massive and complex project can be an extremely humbling experience, and this project made me come to terms with my limitations, frailties and sometimes, moments of utter helplessness and despair. While preparing for the Kumbh Mela in Haridwar in 2021, we had completed all our projects on pollution abatement and riverfront developments well before time; the river, along with Haridwar and other cities impacted by the religious congregation, had been kept clean, but it did not produce the desired outcome. Danger came from pilgrims, victims of the pandemic and large congregations, only making matters worse. In parts of Uttar Pradesh and Bihar, the Ganga bore the brunt, and the local health infrastructure was soon overwhelmed.

These experiences have not only improved my knowledge but also moderated my worldview. Ganga teaches us to treat everyone with equal respect and to never discriminate on the basis of one's caste, creed, colour and religion, just as its water does not discriminate. It tells us to be equal in our approach to everyone. It is the greatest unifier in our country. The Ganga is mighty as well as the most benevolent. If we can follow the same approach in our lives, we can have a better society.

During my long stint at NMCG as Director General, I had a chance to meet and interact with people from different walks of life, including spiritual leaders, academics, scholars, authors, practitioners, activists and common people, all dependant on the Ganga for their livelihoods; I met both young children playing and the elderly seeking 'moksha', on its banks. All of them want to see a pristine and healthy Ganga and are anxiously awaiting the results. But there is little clarity on what needs to be done. Many of them have their own solutions. Can there be one singular solution?

This book is an attempt to share some details about the rejuvenation of India's holiest of holy rivers and an explanation of the approach we took. I can say with pride that I did achieve some success in this mammoth journey during my five-year tenure. My enthusiastic team managed to implement 159 sewage treatment plants (STPs) in 100 odd Ganga basin cities creating an additional treatment capacity of 4,916.05 million litres per day (MLD).

This includes capacity creation of 185 MLD in Uttarakhand, 623.5 MLD in Uttar Pradesh and 620 MLD in Bihar. A strong foundation has been forged, but the real challenge is to accelerate that change or at least to keep the momentum going.

For the more scientifically minded, the improvement in water quality too has been substantial. The dissolved oxygen (DO) level, i.e. the amount of oxygen present in the water, has improved in 27 locations, the biological oxygen demand (BOD) levels—the amount of oxygen consumed by bacteria and other microorganisms—has improved at 42 locations and quantity of faecal coliform in the water has been reduced in 21 locations. The important parameter to be met, keeping DO more than 5 mg/l, has now been successfully achieved and attained throughout the 2,525-km-long river, which is proof of improving river water quality. The BOD level is also under the set standards, i.e. 3 mg/l, except at two stretches of the river, where it is just exceeding the limit ranging from three to five.

This book also attempts to envision the future, the tasks and challenges along the way and offers some suggestions too. It is an attempt to continue this journey of learning through trials and tribulations. I hope it gets clearly established that we need to come together and unify to save the greatest gift of nature to India and to entire humanity for posterity. In fact, we have no choice but to do so.

'I hope to live on your banks, to drink your water, to be lulled by your currents, to remember your name in prayer and to gaze upon you until the day I die.'

(English translation of lines from *Gangashtakam*, composed by Adikavi Valmiki, writer of Ramayana)

Rajiv Ranjan Mishra

2

Why Ganga Matters? Am I a Believer?

Are you a believer? The question was sharp and concise, but I was hardly prepared to consider it, let alone answer. The problem lay in its addressee. It came from my boss, soon after my joining and being given a new assignment. After completing about 13 years of service, I had just opted for the Central Staffing Scheme for appointment in ministries of Central government and had been posted to the Ministry of Environment and Forests. After the usual wait, along with the uncertainty of job allocation and the hassle of getting a room, I was finally assigned to National River Conservation Directorate, specifically National Mission for Clean Ganga (NMCG).

Considering my past experience, it was not difficult to understand that this allocation was not a prized assignment, at least in the eyes of my colleagues and new-found co-workers. And then arrived this question, straight from the Mission Director himself. It was perplexing. It was clear that he did not expect an answer, and he quickly moved to other mundane issues. On asking, he clarified that most officials could be classified into two groups—one comprising people who believed that the Ganga was special, had unique properties and thus needed special treatment and a dedicated mission; and then there were others who believed it to be an overblown project for a river, no different from many others and was not designed to be successful, as already shown by the past.

I welcomed the digression, but it left me wondering: which group did I belong to?

I had been born and brought up in a middle-class family in Bihar with the traditional dose of Gangajal sprinkled on occasion, along with chants of '*Omapavitrah pavitro va, Sarvavastham gatopi va, yah smaret pundarikaksham sah bahyabhyantarah shuchi.*' As a child, I found the ritual convenient because it relieved us from the burden of taking bath on a cold winter day. It seemed to be the ultimate panacea, and so, the shloka indicated whether pure or impure, having gone into any state, with this sprinkling and remembrance of Lord Vishnu, one became purified, internally and externally. Such was the power of Gangajal, and of course, I had no reason to doubt.

At school swearing in the name of Ganga was the test of ultimate authenticity, the movie *Ganga Ki Saugandh* still had its hold on the popular imagination.

Later, I went to Prayagraj to study for a short period of time and was exposed to the aura of Holy Sangam with the trinity of rivers, the Arddha Kumbha and the regular Magh Mela. There was no reason to not take a dip in the holy waters alongside millions of others, and I did; just before leaving, I volunteered to take a dip on the auspicious occasion of Mauni Amavasya in Magh Mela. It did not seem to have any impact on me, but for some strange reasons, the experience kept coming back to me in my later years after I had joined my engineering college.

The expectation of the holy dip hardly matched with the reality, handfuls of sand stuck in my hair, remnants of spit still floating in front of my eyes and an unidentified object, which to my unspectacled eyes, appeared to be a piece of some dead animal. I came back to my hostel and longed to take a bath, but one of the seniors, also from my native place, forbade me from doing so. It would be an insult to Holy Ganga, he said. I did not take a bath for quite some time, the conditioning had been so strong. Eventually, I gave in. I spent the night with a fresh feeling and underlying guilt. The memory gradually faded as I continued deepening of my daily spiritual practices.

So, which side did I belong to? Having spent the larger part of my life in an otherwise more than religious environment and adorned with a natural inclination towards sanatan practices, there was no doubt that the Ganga with its ally rivers remained holy for me; I had no doubt that it not only had special properties but deserved special attention too. Much later, with the launch of the Namami Gange Programme, the dilemma revisited me. The ministry was trying to consolidate its stand on such an ambitious project with such an unprecedented outlay and could ill afford to base it solely on belief and popular imagination.

So came the question: is Gangajal special? Does it have any special properties? And we tried to find out whether this had been considered scientifically. With more than 30 years of the Ganga Action Plan in progress, we thought something would be found, but to our disappointment, nothing came up. More than anybody else, I myself wanted to have the answer. Finally, it was decided that some research institution of repute should be asked to study the special properties of Ganga water. We identified and persuaded National Environmental Engineering Research Institute (NEERI) under the Council of Scientific and Industrial Research (CSIR) to take up the study.

That night, the question kept coming back to me. How do we scientifically establish the special properties of the water in a river? So far as belief is concerned, neither I nor anybody else had a doubt. But scientifically speaking, how do we establish it? There was no harm in taking up the study, I thought. For ages, science has been confirming what faith had already established. But with the remotest of possibilities, what if the results of the study were different, and it indicated that the water was only as good as it was in any other river? How would the people take it? NEERI may be doubted, the methodology could be questioned, but was I ready to face the result? How would it affect my 40 years of existence and the ethos that I have been brought up with and with which I am raising my children? We finally awarded the work to NEERI. I waited for the results to come, eagerly and apprehensively.

Indian scriptures and history are replete with examples of the unique properties and magical powers of Gangajal. The arrival of the Ganga, from being a celestial river, on earth, is attributed to the objective of bringing back to life the 60,000 sons of King Sagar, a result of the 'tapasya' of King Bhagirath. Mahabharata elaborately outlines the incident of Sage Vyasa calling the slain armies from the depths of the river for a final reunion. All arose, alive, without any malice or hatred, and they rejoiced together for the night. All made possible by Gangajal. Even the Jataka in Budddhist tradition recounts the tale of the parrot king who was rewarded by Sakka for his commitment to the withered tree of his beneficence by making the tree alive again, merely by sprinkling holy Gangajal.[1]

The Ganga and its waters historically became the centre of economic sustenance since the early Buddhist periods of the fifth and sixth century. The cities of Magadha and ports of Champa find mention in Buddhist literature as trading and commercial hubs. Jain texts recount Kampilya, Banaras and Champa; cities on its tributaries, like Vaishali on Gandak and Hastinapura on the Yamuna, are repeatedly mentioned as other trade centres.

Steven Darian calls them 'great port cities strung out along the river,' and adds that:

'Serving as entrepôts for an ever-widening hinterland, quickening the commercial and cultural life with their exchange of goods and their reports of new lands and people beyond the ocean. These cities ranged from Hastinapura, north of Delhi to Tamralipti on the Bay of Bengal. Ganga finds mention in the ancient text of Periplus too used for the river as well as the famous port on its banks. Since then, the river and its waters have been consistently mentioned in all historical accounts, including Gupta age and during Harsha's reign. Its involvement in the lives of people on its banks has only been on the rise since then.'

---

[1]Steven G. Darian, 'The Ganges in Myth and History', Motilal Banarsidass Publishers, 2001.

The social, cultural and religious lives of people are engrossed with the Ganga such that it appears unimaginable and inseparable from the land. Sanskrit and Bengali literature are full of references to the Ganga. There is no social custom or religious ceremony where Gangajal is not mentioned. But the culmination of this imagination is the ultimate desire to die with Gangajal in one's mouth, on the banks of the Ganga (if possible) and to be immersed in its waters, even after becoming ash. The belief is that it takes one directly to the feet of Vishnu, thus naming the river Vishnupaga as well. Surprisingly, this belief is not only present among those living on the banks of the Ganga but transcends to almost all Indians, including the diasporic.

In social life, the river has even transcended the religious divide and has proven to be the meeting ground of society irrespective of religion. The biggest example is found in the Ganga Festival at Berhampore, Murshidabad, essentially a Muslim festival famous as Bera celebration dedicated to Khwaja Khijr, the patron saint of water. The rituals are replete with Hindu symbols and are equally participated by Hindus. *Ganga Stotra*, a Sanskrit hymn has been written by Dharaf Khan and is still sung.

The medicinal and rejuvenating properties of Gangajal have been mentioned time and again. Akbar, the famous Mughal ruler, called it the 'water of immortality' and used it regularly on his expeditions. Even the British carried it on their voyage back to England. The non-putrefying nature and healing properties of the water had been an undisputed belief for thousands of years, certified by scriptures and felt in lore. In 1896 British physician, E. Hanbury Hankins, had scientifically established that cholera microbes died within three hours in gangajal even though it was able to survive in distilled water.[2]

Most of us have witnessed the non-putrefying nature of its water when kept in closed vessels for years. The rate of oxygen retention in the water has been found to be relatively much higher than that of any other river. The assessment of the pollution load in Ganga

---

[2]*Times of India*, 'Polluted Ganga River Can Treat Infections: Scientists', New Delhi, 3 October 2016.

indicates that in spite of very high levels of BOD and faecal coliform, the availability of dissolved oxygen (DO) remains within permissible limits at most of the places.

The Union Minister of Water Resources, River Development and Ganga Rejuvenation, speaking to the press in June 2016, stressed that it was not just puranic wisdom, *Brahmadravya* (divine liquid) was a property attached to the river from texts such as Akbarnama and contemporary scientists too.[3] General belief, emerging from semi-scientific studies in between, largely concluded the existence of bacteriophages—viruses that replicate within bacteria and are toxic to them—along with the existence of certain chemicals derived from medicinal plants in the upper reaches of Ganga, all of which together lead to self-healing properties.

The study by NEERI, along with two other sister institutions, Central Institute of Medicinal and Aromatic Plants, Lucknow, and Institute of Microbial Technology, Chandigarh, was a bold attempt to connect science and belief. The study was extensively conducted, and detailed samples were taken over a period of two years along the entire stretch of Ganga and analysed.

The study confirmed the existence of bacteriophages and novel viromes and also included unexplored double-stranded DNA viruses. Noting the presence of terpenes and related compounds/phytochemicals/secondary metabolites in the water samples, the study has recommended the protection of the medicinal herbs growing in sub-alpine and alpine regions near Gaumukh, Bhojbasa, Chidbasa, Gangotri and other adjoining areas. They noted a high and near saturation concentration of dissolved oxygen—a direct indicator of river health and biodiversity survival throughout the Ganga—in spite of the substantial organic load discharged into the river. Their conclusion is even more interesting: 'The Ganga finds its own way to survive despite unabated disposal of waste yet warranting an immediate attention to protect its special properties.'

It is now official and scientifically established that the river *does*

---

[3]Ministry, Jal Shakti, *Jal Manthan*, New Delhi, July 2017.

contain special properties. Of course, far deeper research would be required to understand its true nature, causative factors and who knows, maybe a divine connection too. Till then, my mind rests at peace and my beliefs strengthen, backed by science.

No other river in the world has such dominating presence, transcending the physical, capturing the imagination and resting in one's mind forever. Millions of Indians, thousands of kilometres away from the Ganga geographically, relive its presence with just a few drops of stored water or by the recitation of a verse alone. They long to be finally immersed in Ganga, and if that is not feasible, contend with its drops. The Ganga embodies the ultimate symbolism and stands for all other rivers. There are verses prescribing that by remembering the Ganga while taking a bath, any river water turns into Gangajal. Lord Krishna in the Bhagavad Gita proclaimed that He was the Ganga (Jahnavi) among all rivers while describing his prime standing. This is an amazing tribute to the river, as it is considered a benchmark to define the ultimate god. Putting aside the realm of belief and away from the divine and scriptural paradigm, for a government sponsored programme, the importance of Ganga needed to be rediscovered to justify the outlay of a thousand crores. This needed to matter to all Indians, each one of us, without reference to religion.

DOES THE GANGA MATTER IN THIS PARADIGM TOO?

The geographical beauty of Ganga is mesmerizing, its braided tributaries in upper reaches almost depicting the locks of Lord Shiva, and its pristine waters have been an inspiration, yearning for spirituality and beauty alike. Its vast expanse in its lower reaches has given its neighbouring population the feel of Sagar, as is mostly said for the Brahmaputra. As much as 2,525 kilometres of its length, though shorter than many other rivers of the world, has shaped the course of many civilizations. Its meandering nature has equally seen the many bends in the history of the Indian subcontinent. The river sustains thousands of lives and provides water to more than 37 per cent of the Indian population. (CWC and NRSC 2014)

The Ganga, along with its tributaries, has been a key factor in the formation of landmass across northern India with a sediment load of 1.84 billion tonnes, the highest in the world, carried by itself. The shaping of the landmass has been made possible by its equally forceful water carrying capacity, at the rate of 11,000 cubic metres per second, which again is one of the highest in the world. Add to these the contribution made by its other tributaries and sub-tributaries, and it can be accepted as the fount of our physical existence.[4]

The mainly agricultural basis of human existence in the northern part of India has been made possible by the waters of the Ganga and its tributaries alone. The usage of irrigation canals in the Gangetic belt has been evidenced in writings of major historians like Megasthenes in the fourth century BC. Since then, the Indian economy has continued to be predominantly agricultural. In 2018-19, nearly 40 per cent of the GDP (at current prices) was attributed to the Ganga river basin. Rainfed agriculture is the most extensive land use in the Ganga basin, covering 52 per cent of the basin with correspondingly higher water use, an annual average of 372,000 million cubic metres (mcm), almost 32 per cent of the total water used. (Bank, The National Ganga River Basin Project 2015) Agriculture continues to be the main economic activity, and Ganga is its prime driver.

The Ganga inspired the early settlers to venture through its long course, and inland navigation long remained the main mode of transport and mover of trade in both ancient and middle-ages; it led to the growth of many notable empires in history. It promoted trade and simultaneously aided war, in turn rewriting the history of its land and people. More than 1,000 kilometres of its stretch, from Prayag to Haldia, has been redeveloped with renewed interest in this cheap mode of transport. (SANDRP, Decoding the Economics of Ganga Waterway (National Waterways-1) 2019)

---

[4]Consortium, IIT, *Ganga River Basin Management Plan-2015*, New Delhi: National Mission For Clean Ganga.

The hydroelectric potential of the Ganga system has been estimated at some 51,700 to 128,700 megawatts (MW), with almost 40 per cent lying in India.[5] This potential is huge, though its exploitation has not found much favour with environmentalists. Fisheries in the Ganga have kept its biodiversity alive and provided food in the plates of Indians. But its uniqueness has been brought by the iconic species, the Gangetic Dolphin, scientifically known as the *Platinista Gangetica* and commonly called Susu. This mammalian river species is at the top of the food chain, and is now considered endangered.

For most of us, statistics makes us believers. Why Ganga matters can be understood by the fact that 26 per cent of the total landmass of India is formed by Ganga and its tributaries, creating 28 per cent of India's total water resources, sustaining not only 43 per cent of the Indian population but also providing habitat for 143 aquatic species. (Bank, The National Ganga River Basin Project 2015) The river itself is the twentieth longest river in Asia and the forty-first longest in the world. The largest delta in the world, Sunderbans, lies at its mouth, and thirteen million people directly get their livelihood from the rivers in the Ganga basin. For non-believers, the story continues further.

Culturally, the river has been a symbol of coexistence, the unique characteristic of Indian ethos dominant in the past commonly called as the 'Ganga-Jamuna sabhyata'. This characterizes the spirit of coexistence of diverse cultures like the clear-white water of Ganga and blue water of the Yamuna mixing and becoming one. The festivals on its banks, the people living and earning their livelihood transcend caste, creed and sometimes nationality. A large number of foreigners have been drawn to its waters, mesmerized by its charm and enigma from the ancient ages. Starting from Gangotri and Yamunotri to Kedarnath, Badrinath, Harki Pauri, Dev Prayag, Triveni Sangam, Kumbh Mela and Ganga Sagar, all of these signify its cultural heritage.

The existence of ancient cities like Varanasi, Pataliputra, Haridwar, Prayagraj, Kanpur and Kolkata are a testimony to its being the cradle

---

[5]Britannica, *Ganges River,* 6 March 2009.

of civilization. The river provides ample opportunity for boating and rafting in its scintillating waters and also yoga and meditation on its banks. Important ecological sites, like the Valley of Flowers, national parks like Jim Corbett, mangrove forests at Sunderbans and wonders of the world like the Taj Mahal are within its reach.

For many of us, the words and views of experts and renowned people matter. Starting with Lord Krishna in 'Bhagavad Gita', who proclaimed, 'I am the wind among things of purification, and among warriors I am Rama, the hero supreme. Of the fishes I am makara the wonderful and among all rivers the holy Ganges.' Even God had to signify his supremacy with the example of the Ganga. And later Bhagwan Shankaracharya prayed, 'Oh goddess Ganga, having come to your shores and taking nothing else but your waters and praying to see Krishna, my thirst for worldly objects has gone. Oh Ganga, remover of all stains, our ladder to heaven of delightful frolicking waves, oh goddess Ganga, be pleased with me.' This is an unqualified expression of faith in the river and ultimate submission to the eternal.

In relatively modern times, Sir William S. Meyer noted in the *Imperial Gazetteer of India*, 'There is not a river in the world which has influenced humanity or contributed to the growth of material civilization or of social ethics to such an extent as the Ganges. The wealth of India has been concentrated on its valley and beneath the shades of trees whose roots have been nourished by its waters, the profoundest doctrines of moral philosophy have been conceived, to be promulgated afar for the guidance of the world.'

Convinced by facts and figures, enchanted by the expressions of the great, with embedded doctrines and established by science, I emerge a believer in the concept of Ganga as the cornerstone of civilization, economy, culture and belief system of India.

Ganga matters.

Puskal Upadhyay

3

Solving a Wicked Problem: The Enormity of the Challenge

The critical importance and significance of this holy river, the Ganges, is best exemplified by a quote from India's first Prime Minister, Jawaharlal Nehru[6]: 'The Ganga, above all the rivers of India, has held India's heart captive and drawn uncounted millions in her banks since the dawn of history. The story of the Ganga from source to sea, from old times to new, is the story of India's civilization and culture, of the rise and fall of empires, of great and proud cities of the adventure of men and quest of the mind which has so occupied India's thinkers, of the richness and fulfilment of life as well as its denials and renunciations, of ups and downs of growth. This is evident from the mass gatherings and social assemblies taking place on the holy bank of River Ganga.'

While recognizing the river as the lifeline and symbol of the collective consciousness of India, its state and the enormity of the challenge of rejuvenating the Ganga is most aptly brought out by Sudipta Sen in his book *Ganga: The Many Pasts of a River.*

'Will the Ganga survive its burden of human and industrial contaminants? Will dams and barrages strangle its flow one

---

[6]K.N. Khandelwal, *Jawaharlal Nehru The Discovery of India,* Lakshmi Narain Agarwal, 2017.

day with an unbearable burden of slit and detritus? Will it go the way of the great Yellow River of China, which dried up in 1997, at a staggering distance of 400 miles inland from the delta, sacrificed in the pursuit of industrial progress and in the name of modernity? The physical death of the most cherished river of India would be unthinkable for most people in India, who, despite the evidence of its endangered environment and ecology, still find solace in the idea of the Ganga as the maternal spirit of their civilization. The river, with its water and its valley that have sustained the imaginative life, material culture and daily subsistence of millions of inhabitants of the subcontinent over so many centuries, is now, alas, facing its most daunting challenges.'

The uphill task for officials helming the NMCG was more than just rejuvenating the holy river but also restoring its wholesomeness and pristine quality as it existed in ancient times before the march of modern civilization started destroying the intrinsic goodness or healing quality of the river. It was also about maintaining the centuries-old traditions, culture, history and sanctity of the ecosystem around the river to ensure that it continued to be revered among rivers for millions of Indians.

'Give me a lever long enough and a fulcrum on which to place it, and I shall move the world,' said Archimedes indicating that there is no problem which does not have a solution, and only the ingredients need to be available. If a problem statement is clear, the solution comes in sight easily. What do you do for problems that are not transparent in terms of the nature of the challenge they pose? For NMCG, with the word 'clean' inherent in its name, it took a while to grasp the meaning of 'rejuvenation' which quickly became its mandate in no time. Restoring its wholesomeness and pristine quality is easier said than done. Where do we draw the line, where do we set the benchmark back in time to set the goals? The struggle started from there. Some problems are more than complex, and they are neither yes vs no, nor right vs wrong. They mostly form a situation of right vs more right and trick you into taking a call for which you can always be faulted. They are wicked.

Baffled by the plethora of options available and pressures from various stakeholders to take up one priority over the other, NMCG backed on the report of IITs, which also provided too many options to start and only added to the confusion. It took us a while to decide that we need to pick up the most visible and no-regret activities on priority. It was not difficult to pick up the Nirmal Ganga objective for immediate action thereafter, as was the opinion of technical experts and government officials in general. However, in the popular imagination and in the opinion of religious leaders, the issue of ensuring minimum water levels in Ganga was far more important. This issue had seen some political heat with fast unto death undertaken by Swami Sanand. That is the great debate of 'aviral vs nirmal' and the dilemma as to which side one should choose without offending the other stakeholders and bringing your credibility into question. NMCG realized quickly that if trapped into this, they will never be able to move and initiated steps for sewage treatment capacity generation, simultaneously moving on Aviral Ganga issues. It was clear that each of the stakeholders was equally concerned, only their approach was different, as seen in the story of the elephant and the blind. Being blind was something NMCG could ill afford and, in parallel, started building a knowledge base for the problem and its mitigation. Only that it hardly had any supporting mechanism, both the fulcrum and the lever were missing, even if the problem was as evident as moving the world. The challenge seemed more than tricky, it could bite from any side, and public patience had already run out, so was of the masters. The trickiest of the games could be seconded to this, and only it was for reality.

In our childhood, the ready-made pullovers had still not caught the fancy of smaller places; sweater weaving still was a major activity and skill set. In those days, entangled wool was a common situation, and children like us were mostly assigned the task of untangling the wool and make it into a neat ball. There was no standard operating procedure (SOP) for that, the only wisdom was to take one end, whichever was available and get started, solving each knot one by one. No wastage of time on predicting the problem and deliberating, just handle the problem as it comes. This experience came in handy, and we thanked our mothers again.

THE QUEST FOR A CLEAN GANGA

An ill-advised decision to construct numerous hydroelectric dams, beyond its sustainable capacity, on the fragile and seismic zones of the upper Himalayan reaches, indiscriminate and rapid industrialization without concern for the environment and haphazard urbanization without proper sewerage infrastructure over the years has virtually sounded the death knell of the river.

Even a report by the Central Pollution Control Board (CPCB) in 2012 pointed out that in the upper reaches of the river, where oxygenating abilities of the river are at their highest, there are growing signs of contamination, which suggests that even here, water withdrawal for hydroelectricity was endangering the health of the river. As the river reaches the plains, the water withdrawal peaks for irrigation and drinking water. In the stretch of the river from Rishikesh to Prayagraj during the winter and summer months, there is almost no water, and the river becomes dead and dry over long stretches until wastewater, effluents and sewers fall into the dry basin.

Compounding the existing crisis was the critical issue of over-extraction of water for irrigation, industrial usage and drinking water, which resulted in inadequate flows of the river for downstream cities and towns. The lack of effective coordination between various stakeholders like the Centre and the states, and between states and urban local bodies or municipal bodies, made the task even more complex.

'The Ganga is now no more life-giving, life-supporting river than it was. It has degenerated into a big sewer, one of the 10, the dirtiest of all rivers,' states the Committee of Estimates (2016-17) on Ganga Rejuvenation.

Adding to the enormity of the task at hand was the lack of any successful examples of either policy-making or its execution to fall back on. The track record of earlier attempts at cleaning the 2,525 km stretch of the Ganga and of providing livelihood to 43 per cent of the population did not inspire much confidence because it lacked proper institutions, management processes and monitoring systems.

Its lack of success in tackling the pollution problem was well articulated by the Ministry of Environment, Forests and Climate Change (MoEFCC) to the Committee on Estimates (2016-17) on Ganga Rejuvenation which was presented to the Lok Sabha on 11 May 2016. 'Pollution loads in the Ganga have been increasing over the years due to rapid urbanisation, industrialisation and increase in population.'

THE EVER-WIDENING GAP OF CLEAN GANGA CHALLENGE

So, where did the problem exist in allowing this situation to emerge when successive governments have been putting efforts in its cleaning for more than three decades. One of the more evident reasons is the ever-widening gap between the quantum of sewage being discharged into the river and the available treatment capacity. The need for the creation of treatment capacity had been more than obvious, but the slow pace of capacity creation and ignorance about the actual size of the problem caused the gap to continuously increase with the increase in population and urbanization.

Besides open defecation, cattle wallowing, garbage disposal, carcass dumping further aggravate the problem of pollution.

According to an estimate of NMCG, based on the mapping of cities with a population of over 50,000 located within 5 km from the riverbanks, the treatment capacity was just 900 MLD up till 2014 as against sewage generation of roughly over 2,900 MLD. Moreover, the STPs were plagued with various challenges, amongst which operation and maintenance were the primary cause of concern. A consortium of seven IITs, entrusted with the task of providing a comprehensive Ganga River Basin Management Plan (GRBMP) in 2009, presented a much more serious and larger picture of the entire basin covering 11 states. According to its calculations, the total sewage generation in the Ganga basin was 12,051 MLD, with 6,334 MLD flowing untreated into the river. Considering that the creation of about 900 MLD of capacity had taken more than three decades with no guarantee of performance. This challenge would be daunting, if not impossible. At the normal pace of functionning and increase in population, the gap will never be met.

If reining in raw domestic sewage from households was a daunting task, taking care of the industrial pollution was no cakewalk either. According to a MoEFCC study in 2014-15, there were 741 grossly polluting industries (GPI) such as tanneries, pulp and paper, sugar, textiles, chemicals, along the main stem of the river discharging more than 100 kilolitres per day (KLD) that were categorized as hazardous chemicals under the Manufacture, Storage and Import of Hazardous Chemicals Rules of 1989, within the Environment (Protection) Act, 1986.

A more detailed note by the CPCB to the Executive Committee of Namami Gange pointed out that 632 out of 764 GPI (seven in the UK, 590 in UP, 13 in Bihar, and 22 in West Bengal) were discharging 200 MLD of wastewater directly into the Ganga through drains, posing serious health hazards for humans and crops alike. The eleven Ganga basin states account for 45 per cent of the total chemical fertilizer consumption of 10 million tonnes per year. Such high consumption meant that the contamination of the Ganga with high levels of nitrogen and phosphorous through drains and other sources was inevitable. As per the CPCB's estimation, the run-off from arable lands constitutes up to 70 mg per litre of nitrogen and 0.05-1.1 mg per litre of phosphorous.

Untreated solid waste from households flowing directly into the river was only hastening the early demise of the river. According to the 2011 census, 33.64 lakh households in the five main states of the river did not have access to toilet facilities, of which 28.91 lakh households defecated in the open and the rest, 4.72 lakh, had access to community toilets only. Additionally, a large percentage of an estimated 14,000 metric tonnes per day of municipal solid waste generated from Class-I and Class-II cities and towns situated along the main river, too, was adding to the filth in the river. Domestic sewage accounts for 70 per cent of the pollution load, industrial wastewater 20 per cent, and the rest 10 per cent is due to non-point sources, like the run-off from agricultural fields. (MoHUA, Census of India 2011)

The overall situation of Ma Ganga in 2014–15, before the launch of Namami Gange was rather grim, to say the least. These figures were scary for an organization which was yet to find its feet and the expectations of its masters and the public at large. By no means the targets seemed achievable, and the word 'enormous' appeared modest in the face of this challenge. Even if the organization dared to face this challenge somehow, where were the funds for the purpose? The past experience of moderate fund availability and even slower absorption by the states was not encouraging by any means.

MAINTAINING THE ECOLOGICAL FLOW AND PROTECTING THE ECOLOGY

It is not deniable that the availability of sufficient water in the river can address the pollution issue to some extent. This leads to the popular notion that 'dilution is the solution to pollution'. However, it is easier said than done. Maintaining the ecological flow or a continuous current in the river was turning out to be an even bigger nightmare.

After damming the river at Tehri in Uttarakhand, much of the water descending into the plains is robbed by diversions through the Upper Ganga Canal at Haridwar, which limits the discharge to mere 15 billion cubic metres of water per year (one cubic metre is 1,000 litres of water), and then by the lower Ganga Canal near Aligarh. Such extraction means that in the dry season in downstream Kanpur, the discharge is as little as 90 to 386 cubic metres per second; at Prayagraj 279 to 997 cubic metres per second, and at Varanasi 278 to 1,160 cubic metres per second.

The development of irrigation systems dates back to more than 150 years with the Ganga canal system and has completely changed the landscape. The Ganga Basin is also the one with very high groundwater extraction along with the surface water. Anthony Acciavatti has done a detailed mapping of the engineered landscape of the Ganga Basin, which he presented in his book *Ganges Water Machine*, where he comments that 'Since 1854, when water from the Ganges River was first redirected into the Ganges Canal, irrigation has reshaped the built environment of the Ganges River Basin. Over the past 160 years, the main trunks and branches of colossal canals have been cut through cities and hamlets; brick lined water tanks were embedded deep in the ground to capture rainwater, and countless small diameter shallow tube wells have been connected to miniature engine-driven water pumps.'[7]

The challenges of improving flows in the river can not only be managed with notification and implementation of the flow regime but also needs strong demand side management, which is not very efficient across all sectors. The abstraction of water is maximum in the irrigation sector which also, unfortunately, has very low water use efficiency. Though we all know this, but it is really a daunting task to improve the situation, which needs solutions of a diverse nature, technical as well as stakeholder engagement. The irrigation sector has been struggling with low water use efficiency and poor standards of management and maintenance of infrastructure. The main causes of low irrigation efficiency—less than 40 per cent—can be attributed to the deficiencies in the water delivery system, losses during conveyance and distribution, inequitable and untimely delivery of water, poor on-farm development, inappropriate methods of field application, lack of drainage, etc. The other areas involve choice of proper cropping pattern, irrigation practice, etc.

Together with the popular notion that northern India in general and the Ganga basin, in particular, had plenty of water with so many rivers in the region, makes it further difficult to convince them to agree to restricted water usage. The farmers are used to liberal usage

[7]Anthony Acciavatti, *Ganges Water Machine: Designing New India's Ancient River,* Oro Editions, 2015. (Acciavatti, Ganges Water Machine: Designing New India's Ancient River 2015)

of water over generations, and changing an attitude will be more than a task. It would be more challenging to make people realize that these monsoon-fed rivers are actually water surplus only during rains, i.e. about 55 days a year, and during the rest of the year, the groundwater recharge replenishes the demand. In a developing country still grappling with challenges of hunger and employment, putting restrictions on drawing water from the river has serious implications. Not that it is impossible, but no one knows where to start. The size of the river also adds to the complications, its main stem itself passes through five different states, with different aspirations and economic needs and different political set-ups. Reaching an agreement or a single prescription is next to impossible.

The river is dotted with several wetlands in its basin, which also face severe challenges from encroachment for agriculture, construction activities as well as dumping of pollutants. The floodplains too suffer from such activities reducing the capacity of recharge of aquifers, and hence consequently, the base flow, which rejuvenates the river during the lean season, gets acutely impaired. The urban planning leaves much to be desired by way of their sensitivity towards rivers and water bodies. With the continuous loss of wetlands due to population pressures, the groundwater recharge is seriously affected, causing most of the monsoonal surplus to get drained directly to the oceans, creating an imbalance. The multiplicity of agencies, departments, stakeholders and influence groups convert the situation into a wicked problem in true sense.

A MATTER OF THE MIND

It was by chance that Puskal attended a lecture organized by GIZ India (German development organization) on social security by virtue of his previous experience in workers' pensions. Having tea later, he met a girl from France who was on a short visit to India. The moment she realized that he worked on the Ganga Cleaning programme, she asked for the possible causes of pollution in Ganga even though it was revered by all. By the time he had mastered the art of facing such questions, she cut him midway and remarked that she too had a take on that. He was amused and asked her to go ahead. He could not believe first what she said, 'Ganga is in this state because you Indians call her a mother and remember, mothers, are taken for granted across societies. You don't even look at her as a resource because if you did, you will dare not destroy her.' He was shocked, but with the passage of time, the reality dawned upon both of us. For long, a question had lingered in our mind, why Ganga was in this state when all of us revered and worshipped her. We started understanding our own minds. The problem was inside.

Earlier during a study carried out by John Hopkins Bloomberg School of Communications on communication needs for the Ganga for the NMCG, it had emerged that many of the surveyed citizens in the Ganga basin believed that the river had evolved to clean up our filth and as such could never be unclean herself. How do you convince such people to take measures for its cleaning and restrain their own behaviour by putting themselves at inconvenience? Stakeholder engagement in this condition is easier prescribed than undertaken.

And how do you convince such states to forego their power needs that do not have alternate power sources? How do you ask farmers to forego their irrigation needs in states which do not have alternate occupations or ask them to use superior irrigation methods which they cannot afford? Moreover, how can you convince a downstream state not to pollute the river that has to bear the pollution load of the upstream state? This would need a completely different type of public engagement—enforcement seems out of the question at first glance. The answers do not seem in sight. Maybe we can look elsewhere, the experience of other countries for a starting point.

WHOSE RIVER IS IT ANYWAY?

What if NMCG decided to move ahead and start engaging different stakeholders for stricter pollution management and water use efficiency. Who will issue necessary directions in this regard? Both at the Central and state level, different aspects of rivers are dealt with by different ministries and organizations. How to bring all of them on board?

Even the larger public, the conscious ones, are not of the same opinion. There are those who believe that this is only for the governments to handle. And there are those who believe that ensuring sufficient quantum of water in the river is the only solution. There is a significant number of educated mass who believe that controlling pollution is more than enough to bring the river back to its glory. The moment you take an effort in one direction, the other group starts raising voice in opposition. Most important are those who have permanent disbelief in any governmental effort and they are too happy to use any tool, including RTI, to ask questions at times enough to demoralize the strongest of the workers. Managing public expectations and keeping the morale at the same time is a bit tricky, and the problem remains wicked.

LOOKING BACK FOR LESSONS

A natural course of action in the face of a problem is to look for some way ahead from the past experiences. Ganga cleaning, having been initiated in 1985–86 had a lot to look back to, starting with the Ganga Action Plan (GAP-I) covering 25 towns of Ganga Main Stem, followed by Ganga Action Plan II (GAP-II) in 1993 extending GAP-I to some of the tributaries—Yamuna, Gomti, Damodar and Mahananda—in 60 towns. National River Conservation Plan (NRCP) was launched in 1995 to include other major rivers of the country subsuming the GAP-II, including eight rivers from the Ganga Basin (Ganga, Yamuna, Gomti, Damodar, Mahananda, Betwa, Mandakini and Ramganga). National Ganga River Basin Authority (NGRBA) was created as a separate authority for the Ganga in 2009 to promote a holistic and integrated river basin approach.

To declare the earlier attempts as being completely infructuous would not be entirely correct. The money spent under the GAP-I and GAP-II schemes did have a positive impact on reducing pollution levels in the Ganga. However, a report titled 'Report on Utilisation of Funds and Assets Created through Ganga Action Plan' in states published by the Ministry of Environment and Forests in May 2009 argued, 'Though a considerable sum of money has been spent on the programme and the impact of GAP and NRCP has been positive, it has been less than desired.'

In fact, in a detailed analysis, the report of the consortium of seven IITs highlighted some of the weaknesses of GAP-I and GAP-II. These included delays in programme implementation, confusion over funding, technological issues, lack of support for operation and maintenance of assets, monitoring and evaluation, lack of Centre-state coordination and state-urban local bodies, etc. 'The conflicting/overlapping roles of multiple institutions, especially at the local level warranted the development of suitable institutional mechanism for effective implementation. Inefficient implementation and the level of citizen's participation resulted in poor sustainability of the assets created,' the report added.

The total spending of ₹4,168.55 crore for 30 years between 1985 and 2015 in various schemes like creation and maintenance of assets was only one-fourth of the budget outlay of ₹20,000 crore sanctioned for the next five years under Namami Gange launched in 2015–16. The Central government's expenditure in GAP-I and GAP-II was ₹961 crore; for the Yamuna Action Plan I, II & III ₹1,256.4 crore only. Expenditure on other projects, like the Haryana (Yamuna) project, was around ₹121.54 crore; the Gomti Action Plan of ₹472.22 crore, Damodar Action Plan of ₹4.29 crore, Mahananda Action Plan ₹50.54 crore, and NGRBA of ₹1,032.51 crore—none of which had the necessary impact. (1 crore is 10 million)

Not satisfied with the outcome of GAP-I, II, NRCP and seriously concerned over the growing pollution levels in the Ganga, the Government of India in 2009 set up the NGRBA as a collaborative effort between the Centre and the states under the chairmanship of the Prime Minister. Along with granting Ganga the status of the national river, it also took recognition of the fact that the entire river basin needed to be the basis for planning and implementation and the importance of ecological flow at all times of the year. The NGRBA also created the NMCG in 2011, as the implementation arm of the parent organization. It also ensured that the five NGRBA programme states of Uttarakhand, Uttar Pradesh, Bihar, Jharkhand and West Bengal notified the State Ganga River Conversation Authorities (SGRCA), which was responsible for making policies and other decision-making structures at the state level.

Although the NGRBA had a limited number of meetings, its diverse discussions led to several benefits for the institutions and the river. Its interventions led to the discontinuation of three hydroelectric projects: Loharinag Pala (4x150=600 MW), Bhaironghati (381 MW), and Pala Maneri (480 MW) on Bhagirathi River. Subsequently, a fourth hydroelectric project, namely Kotli-Bhel on Alaknanda River (320 MW), was discontinued following orders from the National Environment Appellate Authority (NEAA). More importantly, Jairam Ramesh, the then Minister of State for Environment and Forests, awarded a contract to a consortium of seven IITs, with Kanpur IIT as the coordinator, to develop a comprehensive GRBMP for the revival of the Ganga River Basin in 2009.

The final voluminous report of the consortium, which was finally released in 2015, identified eight different missions and more than 80 different thematic reports for the rejuvenation of the Ganga. The restorative missions included Aviral Dhara (to ensure an adequate ecological flow of the river), Nirmal Dhara (to maintain the purity of the river), ecological restoration, sustainable agriculture, geological safeguarding, geomorphological upkeep of the basin, protection of basin against disasters, river hazard management and environment knowledge building and sensitization.

It also suggested a host of holistic solutions to clean and preserve the river across the eight themes, such as preparing a water resource plan for wetlands, forests and distributed groundwater, restrictions on riverbed farming, sand mining from riverbeds, drainage improvement of low-lying areas, stabilization of disturbed areas, assessment of soil salinity and its mitigation strategy, the need to build a comprehensive data bank to enable meaningful analysis and obtain qualitative indicators of the river basin.

THE REPORT AS LODESTAR

This report then became the lodestar for organization officials, as for the first time they had a scientific, evidence-based and comprehensive study with a strategic plan to carry out the twin objectives. It also gave them great insights into basin characteristics and concepts entered into the public domain. This was also very timely as the new ambitious 'Namami Gange' had been announced, and scheme formulation was an immediate task.

The study not only brought credibility to the project but also silenced a host of critics. During the study, the consortium consulted experts from more than 50 universities, concerned organizations and spiritual leaders for their inputs. Thus, they were able to mix traditional knowledge with modern technology and the latest developments in various sectors. The report even quotes Sanskrit scriptures, which talks of avoiding 13 types of human actions that polluted the river: defecation, throwing of used floral offerings, discarding garments, etc.

However, getting the seven IITs to come together on a project and complete it turned out to be yet another challenge. Every IIT is an expert institution and is unwilling to take orders or advice from others, and reaching a consensus was not easy. Moreover, they found it extremely difficult to cope with the government's bureaucracy. Soon, a war of words broke out with the government complaining about the project's lack of progress and the consortium hitting back by saying that it was the unwillingness of the government departments to share data that was actually delaying the report. No data analysis, they chorused, could be possible without enough data. The interim report of the GRBMP came out only in 2014, five years after the awarding of the project, and the final report only in 2015.

The very fact that the IIT report had identified eight distinct missions and more than 80 thematic areas made the assignment more complex. These areas are not independent ones to act upon; they are intricately connected as components of the ecosystem, and efforts, whether taken or not in any particular area, affect the outcomes in most others. This converts the problem, at least mathematically speaking, into a multivariate one, known for the complexity of its solutions because the problem itself keeps constantly evolving. Add to this the impact of climate change which is becoming more real every day with long-term impacts on the quantity of water in the river, and the problem becomes complex multifold.

NAMAMI GANGE: *YEH DIL MANGE MORE*

The mandate of Namami Gange went beyond just cleaning and looked at rejuvenating not only the Ganga but also its tributaries such as Ramganga, Gomti, Ghagra, Ghanda and Kosi in the north and the Yamuna and Son in the south. It also has to provide 100 per cent sanitation coverage to 1,657 gram panchayats along the river. Recognizing the multi-sectoral, multi-dimensional and multi-stakeholder nature of the challenge, many key ministries like the Ministry of Water Resources, River Development and Ganga Rejuvenation (MoWR, RD&GR), Ministry of Environment, Forests and Climate Change, Ministry of Shipping and Tourism, Urban Development, Drinking Water and Sanitation, Rural Development, Housing and Urban Affairs, Agriculture and Farmers' Welfare etc., were included in the project.

Such activities were to be supplemented with rural sanitation, riverfront development, management of solid waste and pious waste, sewerage network, setting up of a national Ganga monitoring system, GIS mapping and restoration of special properties of the Ganga. The pollution of the Ganga is caused by both point sources and non-point sources. Point sources include domestic and industrial wastewater, which contains harmful chemicals and non-point sources include agricultural run-off, solid waste dumping, open defecation, leftover religious material. All of this would have to be accounted for.

Moreover, biodiversity conservation, afforestation, habitat improvement, communication, public outreach activities and prevention of sand mining also fall within the key performance indicators of the organization. The organization was also expected to work on tributaries and sub-tributaries of Ganga, including the Yamuna, in a phased manner and approach Ganga rejuvenation in a way to set a model for rejuvenation of other rivers in India.

More perplexing for the NMCG was the massive allocation of ₹20,000 crore for Namami Gange with the limited absorption capacity of the implementation system. The reason was simple: they did not have a shelf or pipeline of projects to bid out. Secondly, the officials realized that it was important to bid out larger projects, and one needs to understand risks and develop a robust process for mitigating them. Thirdly, the team realized that they would have to live with the legacy of the earlier years of poor decision-making, implementation, operation and maintenance, as well as any shortcomings in the future. After all, as the funding agency for all Ganga-cleaning projects in the states, they would be hauled up for any negligence or time and cost overruns, despite the responsibility being in the hands of state agencies like Uttar Pradesh Jal Nigam, Uttarakhand Jal Nigam and so on.

WICKED AT ITS BEST—THE UNPREDICTIVENESS OF THE PROBLEM

Anthony Acciavatti, the author of *Ganges Water Machine*, has described the complexity of understanding the Ganga and the dynamic nature of the challenge in its rejuvenation as, 'Perceptions of the Ganges are constantly mediated, and these mediations produce artefacts like canals and water pumps that regulate the river's flow, alongside the temples and ghats (steps) that make up the ritual infrastructure.[8] Neither geography nor tradition, neither engineering nor ceremony, these sites together create a dynamic interplay of a changing river and its changing culture. Is the river shaping society and society reconfiguring the river? Are cause and effect distinguishable? The drama that unfolds does not progress in a linear narrative towards some over-arching conclusion. It is, rather, the cyclical replication of

---

[8]Infrastructure available alongside the rivers helping people perform different rituals.

a single spectacle: destruction always at the heels of creation, forever interlinked coevals.'

The wickedness of such problems is that they themselves are of an evolving nature. Mostly seen in the digital games today, the challenge keeps on refining itself and making it tougher depending on how you perform. In this case, you are playing not only against the computer but with thousands of others, and each one of them has the capacity to complicate your strategy. You are never sure where or from which sector the problem will emerge. The Ganga rejuvenation is a multi-stakeholder and multi-sector challenge, and this list is ever expanding—new stakeholders are continuously being added, and new sectors are emerging. The problem can emerge from any of them and mostly when you expect them the least. Many a time, they are not even directly relevant to you, at least not in your imagination and definitely not in your control. But the issue emerges, and you have no option but to respond. One mishandling and it has the potential to cause a serious dent to your hard-earned achievements and definitely the spirit of the team. I am reminded, here, of the nightmare we all faced in the wake of one of the greatest crises our country faced by COVID-19 this year.

FLOATING CORPSES: A RIVER DEFILED

As the number of bodies swelled and multiplied because of the COVID-19 pandemic, overwhelming district administrations and stretching the functional limits of crematoria and burning ghats of UP and Bihar, the Ganga became an easy dumping ground for the dead.

I was recuperating from a severe COVID-19 attack in the Gurugram-based Medanta, a super-speciality hospital when I heard about the unclaimed, half-burnt and swollen corpses floating in the holy Ganga in early May. Television channels, magazines, newspapers and social media sites were awash with macabre images and stories of bodies being dumped unceremoniously into the river.

It was a traumatic and heart-breaking experience for me. As the Director General of the NMCG, my job is to be the custodian of the health of the Ganga, to rejuvenate its flow, ensure its return to its pristine purity and to ensure the same for its tributaries after years of neglect. Five years of intense work to save the river seemed to be coming undone in a matter of days.

Like the holy river itself, I was the victim of an unknown virus, an unprecedented epidemic that had snowballed into a national crisis. I was now being asked to take responsibility for the rejuvenation of a river that had been further polluted and defiled by the breakdown in health services and the inability of the local bodies to manage the crisis. Poor management of funeral services, miscreants taking advantage of the situation to dump bodies into the river instead of cremating them, and adverse publicity from the media only added to our discomfort and helplessness.

Adding to our woes was the fact that the NMCG has no direct power or authority to punish miscreants or to initiate action against those disposing of the dead in the river or burying them on the riverbanks. Our power lay in giving directives, but we are dependent on the state authorities to maintain law and order. In religious congregations as well, our job is to ensure the health and safety of the river. Even during the recent Kumbh Mela at Haridwar, it was not the river that had led to any health hazard. In fact, the water quality in Haridwar was of the highest level, i.e., Class-A.

Floating corpses or the dead being buried on the banks are not an unusual spectacle for those living in close quarters near the river. After all, poverty, along with the inherent belief in the curative power and religious significance of the river, propels many. Burying the dead on the banks is also a tradition and religious practice among some communities in Uttar Pradesh, especially in certain months of the year when cremation is disallowed. This was an argument that even the Allahabad High Court used in a recent case.

However, the swelling numbers and the macabre images accentuated the enormity of the crisis. This proved to be a major challenge for NMCG officials. It was during my stay at the hospital that I realized the urgency of the matter.

FIGHTING A DIFFERENT PANDEMIC

After much pleading and persuasion, the doctors agreed to discharge me on 9 May 2021 at 9.30 p.m. I was still reeling under the after-effects of the pandemic. Through the powers granted under the Contravention of the River Ganga (Rejuvenation, Protection and Management) Authorities Order, 2016, I issued a direction on May 11 to dispose of the bodies of suspected Covid victims according to the Government of India guidelines on immediate management of COVID-19 dead bodies, and ensured strict vigilance along the length of the river. District magistrates presented voluminous action reports of their work, including a 34-page report by the district magistrate of Ballia, UP.

I also realized that mere use of force was not going to do the trick due to the ignorance of the rural populace about COVID-19 cremation protocol and no access to oximeters and testing facilities. Moreover, poverty-stricken people who had used up all their money on doctor's fees and medicines to fight COVID-19 were in no position to pay the enhanced cremation charges, nearly trebled within days. I authorized the district authorities to use the funds from the District Ganga Committee to fund dignified cremations in case needed. This also triggered action by the state to support such cases with financial help.

And on 11 May, I issued a direction and virtually contacted the district magistrates and senior officials of Bihar and Uttar Pradesh and a follow-up meeting on 15 May along with Shri. Pankaj Kumar, Secretary of Ministry with the senior officials of UP and Bihar to put an immediate stop to the disposal of bodies in the river and to check probable contamination of water quality of the river water and sewage.

I stressed on establishing a proper mechanism to ensure regular and verifiable information on the issue and more frequent monitoring by CPCB. It emerged that the water quality was being monitored and analysed in 11 stations in 27 districts of UP every 10 days, and CPCB ruled out the survival of the virus in the drinking water of these states because of chlorination and other disinfectant measures. Water quality monitoring data did not show much variation in terms of biological parameters, even with the disposal of COVID-19 bodies into the river. All doubts were set to rest with a World Health Organisation (WHO) study, which categorically stated that the virus does not spread through water and therefore could not even infect the sewage system.

This information was a godsend. All our efforts at cleaning and rejuvenating the Ganga had not gone to waste. Yet, to be doubly sure, the NMCG appointed the Council of Scientific and Industrial Research-Indian Institute of Toxicology Research (IITR), Lucknow, to carry out an objective study and create a database to identify possible contamination of the river with SARS-Cov-2 virus (COVID-19) due to the disposal of bodies in the river and its tributaries. The scope of the study included two or three rounds of sampling near the burial sites of Kannauj, Unnao, Kanpur, Prayagraj and Ghazipur district in UP, Buxar and Saran district in Bihar, barrages/dams in the stretch from Kannuaj (UP) to Farraka (West Bengal) and other hotspots where bodies were found floating or had accumulated. We also asked an agency to conduct bioremediation within a radius of 3 to 4 km in many of these hotspots.

After reading the reports of various district magistrates and panchayat committees, I realized that the number of bodies dumped into the river was no more than 300 (definitely not the 1,000 plus reported by a section of the media). The problem, moreover, was confined only to UP (between Kannauj and Ballia), and the bodies found in Bihar were those floating from UP. Today, the UP government has deployed the State Disaster Response Force and Provincial Armed Constabulary along the river and water bodies and has also alerted panchayats and urban local bodies that no such dumping occurs hereafter. The state government has also launched a massive drive to dissuade people from such actions, where the municipal corporations will bear the cost of cremations and funerals with a maximum amount of ₹5,000 per cremation. Similar provisions were also made in rural areas.

As we return to normal, it is time to take a critical and radical look at some of our traditions and behaviours if we are to sustain and rejuvenate the physical form of the Ganges. Burdened by the sins of those who bathe in her, she, too, needs some kind of commitment from her devotees so that such incidents are never repeated. The ancient scriptures mention 13 practices we should avoid while bathing in the river. The time has come to follow those practices in letter and spirit. These prohibited human actions include defecation, gargling, throwing of used floral offerings, rubbing of filth, flowing bodies (human or animal), frolicking, acceptance of donations, obscenity, considering other shrines to be superior, praising other shrines, discarding garments, bathing and making noise. (Consortium, Ganga River Basin Management Plan 2015)

गंगां पुण्यजलां प्राप्य त्रयोदश विवर्जयेत्। शौचमाचमनं सकं निर्माल्यं मलघर्षणम्। गात्रसंवाहनं क्रीडां प्रतिग्रहमयोरतिम्। अन्यतीर्थरतिश्चैव: अन्यतीर्थ प्रशंसनम्। वस्त्रत्यागामथाघातं सन्तारंच विशेषत:

We faced a problem which did not have anything to do with the programme or the NMCG. We had no option but to respond because even the normal things for which not even an eyebrow will be raised otherwise become a major concern the moment it gets connected to Ganga, even indirectly. Such is the impact of the river in public imagination. The challenge to respond to such issues is daunting, and many a time, we think of extricating ourselves. But the sense of a fiduciary responsibility towards the river and to the people keeps us going. The challenges will not cease to come, nor will our resolve to respond to them.

Ganga rejuvenation is far more complex than it sounds. No wonder it took a Bhagiratha to bring Ganga to this earth, and it will take no less an effort again to bring it back to its pristine state as is the national expectation. The country believes in the idea of the Ganga, revers it as a goddess and loves it as a mother. This is the epitome of astha (belief). To rejuvenate the Ganga and return its lost glory, we need to get reminded of our kartavya (duties) towards it and transform our astha into kartavya. Only then will this effort be successful. In this age, there cannot be a single Bhagiratha. Each one of us will have to believe and turn into a Bhagiratha. Only then will the wickedness of this problem be tamed.

4

From Vision to Mission: The Ebb and Flow of a Start-up Journey

Like the holy Ganga that helps conceive, nurture, sustain and protect by breathing life into its various headstreams (including the two main ones, Bhagirathi and Alaknanda), the NMCG owes its origin to the confluence of many initiatives and programmes launched by earlier governments. Every initiative, however piecemeal, poorly designed or inadequately executed, had one thing in common: they were all designed to save, protect and rejuvenate the health of the mighty river, which had not only become highly polluted but toxic too.

The alarm bells had been ringing for years. Despite many announcements, significant expenditure from Central and state governments and many claims, there was little progress on the ground—both in the quality and quantity of the water. What was needed was a radical, transformative and revolutionary change in the functioning of the new institution to tackle this massive challenge, which was acknowledged even by the top officials in government, but unfortunately, never acted upon it.

In its early years, unfortunately, the NMCG and the cause of the mission was held hostage to traditional thinking in policymaking and funding. The resources tied to the apron strings of the ministry were made worse by the continuation of a not-so-successful implementation strategy of earlier governments.

Continuation with the existing architecture of the Ganga rejuvenation project seemed impossible given the mood of mistrust, helplessness and resignation that had enveloped the public as they stood mute witnesses to the deteriorating health of the river every passing day. A sculpture is as good as its artist and the tool. This mission cried for a new vehicle and novel techniques to drive through the web of challenges.

Repeated attempts by the governments to clean the rivers (first under the Ganga Project Directorate in 1986 and the National River Conservation Directorate in 1995, which expanded the scope of the project by including tributaries of Ganga) did not yield much, at least not as much as expected. Then came the NGRBA in 2009. It was a basin-centric, ecosystem-led approach that ultimately led to the creation of the NMCG in 2011.

Simultaneously, the sanctioning of a loan of $1 billion by the World Bank for Ganga clean-up made the operationalization of NMCG mandatory for the project. The multilateral funding agency had demanded the establishment of an independent organization to carry out this complex and humungous task. NMCG, set up in 2011 by the Ministry of Environment and Forests (now Ministry of Environment, Forests and Climate Change), was different from its preceding institutions, both in terms of its constitution and its functioning. It was registered as a society under the Societies Registration Act, had its own governing body with provision for its delegation of powers and internal processes. The entire concept had developed under Rajiv Gauba, the then Joint Secretary in the Ministry of Environment and Forests (MoEF). NMCG continued with MoEF till mid-2014 when it was transferred, along with its officials, to the MoWR, RD&GR now reorganized as Ministry of Jal Shakti.

While the NMCG was still struggling to find its own independent identity, after more than a year of its coming into being, the World Bank, deeply involved in the clean-up initiative, was not just ruthless in monitoring the progress of its funded projects but was equally critical about its functioning. By mid-2013, a situation had emerged where the World Bank and the Department of Economic Affairs seriously discussed the partial cancellation of the project, which proved to be a challenging and existential situation for an institution that was still trying to find its bearing.

BUILDING THE INSTITUTION

NMCG began functioning in earnest only after the appointment of a full-time Mission Director, Dr Rajiv Sharma and later, Puskal Upadhyay, as the Director of Finance by early 2012. There was also the skeletal staff of about six, hired initially on a contractual basis for project preparation and some National River Conservation Directorate (NRCD) officials on an additional charge basis. The team functioned out of a small, about 2,000 sq ft office in the National Building Construction Corporation (NBCC) complex at Lodhi Road, New Delhi.

For the team, it felt like the launch of a new start-up with a vision, mission and challenges that few entrepreneurs had ever attempted. It entailed cleaning the 2,525-km-long meandering course of the Ganga, passing through five states—11 with its tributaries—and developments of the ghats, crematoria and other structures that surrounded it while also rejuvenating the water bodies, carrying out afforestation activities at the same time. In short, they needed to rejuvenate the Ganga's entire ecosystem and everything in between. Baggage of the past comprising poor project execution record and allegations of misappropriations only added to the challenge.

The fact that the functioning of NMCG involved dealing with and convincing officials of various ministries and departments in basin states to prioritize Ganga rejuvenation projects only added to the confusion. The mission's functioning was also hampered by the constant interference by some officials in the administrative ministry, who were only too happy to throw the rule book to scuttle any project.

One of the accepted practices used by many of the government officials is the 'look behind, move ahead' approach, better known in Hindi as '*peechhe dekh, aage chal*'. It meant that one had to play safe by following practices and precedence followed for years. Such a strategy insulated the implementing official from any adverse government action, and in case the project failed, the concerned officials had a ready excuse. For NMCG, the task was much more challenging because many critical decisions had to be taken at the spur of the moment and in very trying conditions, which had no mention either in official rulebooks or in training academies. 'Amongst ourselves, we agreed that the situation was extraordinary and logically warranted a unique solution. However, first, we needed to be sure of the problem,' said Puskal.

However, before coming to a solution, it was critical that the umbilical cord that had tied the mission to the MoEF, requiring permissions for every new project and seeking funds for every new proposal, had been cut. Major decision-making powers still rested with the MoEF, hampering speedy implementation of projects, which incidentally is the hallmark or defining feature of a start-up compared to a larger and traditional organization. By March 2012, despite heavy odds, the NMCG's start-up operations had started making progress. It was allocating funds to complete ongoing projects (sanctioned by earlier governments and those funded and monitored by the World Bank) such as the riverfront project at Patna and STP and sewerage projects in Prayagraj and Kanpur. Moreover, the organization was smart enough to realize that it did not have the necessary resources to monitor existing projects or take up new ones. Hence, the topmost priority was to induct more professionals into the team and create enough bandwidth.

FORTUNE FAVOURS THE BRAVE

Fortunately for the organization, the original six-member team appointed by the NRCD was intact, though their contracts would have lapsed within a few days. To ensure their continuation, the NMCG decided to engage them directly on a long-term basis. However, the migration from one governmental organization to another was not the norm and proved to be a major roadblock. The challenge was soon overcome by seeking approval of MoEF itself and leveraging the fact that NMCG was an integral part of it.

Despite having a dedicated Director of Finance, all financial proposals were scrutinized and cleared by the MoEF. Such a procedure created its own set of problems. For instance, ministry officials had competing priorities, and this was mostly the lowest among many. Ground-level implementation issues are also not well understood due to limited exposure. After much persuasion and arguments, the MoEF agreed not to insist on scrutinizing individual proposals on file and deliberate only through the Empowered Steering Committee (ESC), where the Financial Advisor of the ministry was a member. The ESC got activated in its true spirit due to support from the then Financial Advisor, Mr Sudhanshu Shekhar Mohanty.

It was the beginning of the start-up's tryst with independence and its final destiny. However, the success was short-lived. The MoEF soon raised objections about the use of external consultants in its financial decisions. Clearly, the independent identity needed to be further strengthened. Nothing could be better than a tangible office and the power to hire its team of professionals to take care of project appraisals, its management and the implementation of issues and procedures.

With the support of the World Bank, M/s. ABC consultants, a leading HR consulting agency, was brought on board. That was one of the best things that could happen for the mission. The deployment of an amazing all-women team, comprising six bright young experts, Naeha Sharma and Namrata Jatana noteworthy among them, helped NMCG in more ways than one. While the recruitments were on track, discussions with them led to the crystallization of some basic ideas and tenets of the mission. The ABC team was initially hesitant to accept the assignment, their experience indicating that government recruitments mostly landed in controversies and in many cases, the interviews were inordinately delayed. This affected their financials, which they could ill afford. As a bold step, NMCG agreed to pay the applicable fee even if no interviews were conducted within 45 days, owning up the responsibility based on sheer resolve. This did not come easy, but it set the tone for a new and accountable work culture.

It was their team leader, Veenu Nehru, who first inquired about the vision and mission for the organization as an initial step towards understanding their assignment to plan a proper recruitment policy. The idea emerged: 'NMCG should be for river cleaning what Delhi Metro is for the rapid mass transport'. Persuaded by the ABC team with some support from the World Bank, the MoEF agreed to pay relatively higher salaries to the professionals (despite some heartburn among officials), and the recruitment process finally kicked off. Team ABC agreed to shortlist eight to ten candidates for each position, of whom NMCG could select a single candidate based on interviews. The entire process was expedited under the backing of Shashi Shekhar, the then Additional Secretary leading NRCD, who later became Secretary, MoWR, RD&GR and oversaw NMCG operations, briefly as its Mission Director as well. He led the formulation of both the implementation strategy and the new institutional structure of NMCG as Secretary of the Ministry.

Keeping the past track record in view, NMCG was committed to avoid controversies and remain transparent at any cost. To prevent pre-interview pressures, the main cause of the complications later, NMCG adopted the strategy to move fast and protect information. The composition of interview boards was closely guarded, and results of the interview were invariably published the same day. Shortlisting process done by the ABC team was already insulated from pressure. The process did not encounter any roadblock, and the first leg was completed smoothly by August 2013, a rare feat in the government setup. In the meantime, a new premise at New Delhi's CGO complex, the MTNL building, was identified and refitted to meet the organization's needs. In fact, most of the interviews were conducted in the partially completed new premise. To ensure its financial and organizational independence, the mission decided to put a new governing structure in place, with enhanced delegated powers to the Mission Director for incurring expenditure, making appointments and other administrative decisions. They then approached the Governing

Council, the highest tier of decision-making in NMCG and custodian of all powers, financial and administrative. To the surprise of NMCG, the proposal went through without a hitch, which made NMCG feel that the clean Ganga mission was no less important to the officials and the people. That realization only grew more powerful as more and more people started to associate themselves with the mission, and support for its cause started to surge across states. By August 2013, the identity crisis had been addressed to a large extent, and its future prospects looked better than before. The organization was finally finding its feet after surviving its first existential crisis.

In May 2013, the Department of Economic Affairs (DEA), Government of India, after scrutinizing the projects and pressure from World Bank, argued that the loan size should be curtailed by half, if not cancelled. It was a testing time. Earlier Mission Director (MD), had recently moved, and the new incumbent, Mr Rajiv Ranjan Mishra, was yet to join. The new MD had to prepone his joining date to take care of the so-called vacuum and attended the meetings within two days of taking over.

The Ministry (DEA) was almost ruthless in its approach, considering the non-starter state of the mission at that moment. At one point, Rajiv Ranjan Mishra almost stood up to leave the meeting, arguing that he saw no need to continue with the discussions since a decision seemed to have been made already. This sudden outburst took others by surprise and earned the mission another six months of probation. He offered the ministry to fast-track the recruitments and review the project preparation and appraisal process. The projects were being prepared under an NGRBA framework adopted for the World Bank project by that time, which necessitated a four-stage documentation concept note, feasibility report, detailed project report and the bid document, each to be prepared in sequence. These documents needed to be approved at each stage by four different entities, Executing Agency, State Programme Management Group (SPMG), then NMCG and the concerned ministry. This effectively made the approval process a 4x4 matrix, notwithstanding the multiple channels within the same organization through which the project had to move and made the approval process a never-ending one. Cutting down the approval stages was a necessity, not an option. Both ministries were finally convinced to allow the DPRs to proceed with FR as a component and not as a separate step. Bid document preparation was also to start simultaneously with the DPR preparation. The need for concept notes was also rationalized, considering that the indicative list of eligible cities was already a part of the government approval sought for the World Bank project. This rationalizing drastically reduced the processing time and facilitated the states to leverage some work already completed on the ground. The effect was visible immediately. The experience encouraged the NMCG and provided it with the insight to continuously review their implementation methods and test their efficacy for results as a strategy. This formed the basis of the Agile Model that gradually evolved.

Mishra soon realized that the 'business as usual approach would not hold, and to ensure a holistic approach for the project, NMCG needed to outsource some work to other agencies. The organization lacked the necessary bandwidth in terms of employees and expertise. It did what most start-ups do: they adopted an expertise-oriented outsourcing model to survive. It entered into long-term institutional partnerships with organizations like the Survey of India, Consortium of IITs, Centre for Environment Education, WWF India, among others, where the NMCG only acted as a centre for ideas and the anchoring platform defining the main objectives and funding, while the implementation was left to these bodies, considered the best in their sector. While the Survey of India took on the work of GIS mapping and the Centre for Environment Education initiated a campaign for the Gangetic Dolphins, the Consortium of IITs continued to develop and refine the GRBMP. This strategy, they hoped, would not only help the institution in scaling up faster but would also bring in technology and management practices to deliver the projects on time. It would also help the institution in capacity building in various sectors.

Easy access to the top management, faster exchange of information and working in teams with a focus on collaboration was adopted, advocated and encouraged at the NMCG as the new work paradigm. Such work culture is not commonplace in governmental setup, and to bring it in, the new and conducive genetic material needed to be infused. It was a conscious decision to recruit and encourage a younger, skilled workforce to foster a culture of innovation.

Hence, the NMCG came up with a strategy for the appointment of research officers, young talents with less than a year of experience. Unsurprisingly, the move faced much resistance and only got the go-ahead when the number of recruits was scaled down to four. The selected candidates, Lochan Alagh and Neeraj Gahlawat were postgraduates in river management from IIT Roorkee, Lolia Mary was a postgraduate in urban planning from the School of Planning and Architecture while Ruchi Verma was a Geographic Information Systems (GIS) expert. Later Shravan Kota too joined and continues to contribute to mission championing the industrial pollution control aspects. They later went on to become the mainstay of the mission, especially when innovations and redesigning of existing programmes became a priority to make the Namami Gange projects that much more effective. Bhawna Badola initially recruited as a GIS expert, soon evolved as the natural team leader of this young squad facilitating quality research, their participation in high-level deliberations, countering their fears and handholding them in the face of disappointment.

Like any fledgling start-up, the mission, too, was always in a state of a crisis, fighting one emergency after another with little or no time for project preparation. 'The concept of lead time for project preparation was unheard of in those days,' says Mishra. Review meetings were conducted on the premises itself, and new appointees were asked to join the day after receiving their employment letters. Barriers of designations and expertise were kept aside, and an all-hands-on-deck approach was adopted to ensure monitoring of existing projects and preparation of newer ones simultaneously. When the need arose, the mission directors themselves typed notes and made presentations, finance people reviewed projects, and often, clerks coordinated with state machinery on project assignments. Puskal also took up the responsibility of acting as the Additional Mission Director in addition to being the Director of Finance. The spirit of a mission had started emerging, and it was geared to take up its assigned and challenging role of cleaning the entire stretch of the Ganga.

PUTTING A STRATEGY IN PLACE

Soon after assuming office, the Narendra Modi-led National Democratic Alliance government at the Centre transferred the entire Ganga-related work to the newly created MoWR, RD&GR through an amendment to Allocation of Business Rules dated 6 August 2014. It was clear that Ganga clean-up and rejuvenation had taken centre stage. The government's renewed focus came with shock and awe for Puskal Upadhyay, the then Director Finance in the mission, who had already spent two years on the Ganga clean-up programme. He mentioned feeling fear and apprehension regarding the future challenges and responsibilities and happiness and contentment that Ma Ganga was finally getting what she deserved.

If further proof was required, it came via the Union budget of 2014–15 presented on 6 July 2014, with three paragraphs under the title 'Sacred Rivers'. The first was an unequivocal admission that substantial amounts had been invested in cleaning the river without the desired results. Secondly, it announced the setting up of Namami Gange Mission with an initial allocation of ₹2,037 crore. Another ₹100 crore was dedicated to the development of the ghats and riverfronts at Kedarnath, Haridwar, Kanpur, Prayagraj, Varanasi, Patna and Delhi. 'We wondered how we were going to handle the mega-budget and the mega attention, but more importantly the mega expectation and fulfilling the mega responsibilities,' Puskal adds.

The launch of the Namami Gange Programme in 2014 injected much-needed political backing and re-ignited the public imagination. 'In the first few months, we were inundated with thousands of suggestions from Indian public routed through the Prime Minister's office obligating us to respond to each one of them,' remembers Puskal.

NMCG also had to deal with compliance issues of earlier years, over which it neither had any control nor any ready solutions. Everyone wanted to know why so little was achieved in the project even after thirty years and expenditure of thousands of crores. The first few months were spent on taking stock of the existing situation and making repeated presentations at different forums about the Ganga programme.

'Once the dust had settled on the past, public leaders and experts wanted to know our next steps, create a magic wand to sweep away all the shortcomings of the earlier regimes in one go. Tragically, we did not have any such magic charm,' says Puskal.

From the beginning, it was clear that the country and its leaders wanted a concrete plan and a promising innovative strategy to convince the citizens that it was no longer 'business as usual.' They needed a radically different approach to the problem. The challenge was that the problem had never been understood in its entirety, neither in terms of its size and nature nor in terms of the complexity of the challenge involved.

'We decided to make the most of this opportunity to redesign the whole programme and address the problems already in sight notwithstanding our limited capacity and heightened scrutiny, treating it as an advantage,' Puskal recalls. Namami Gange needed a holistic and lasting strategy that identified the targets and the methods to achieve them. Its current design amply reflects the same.

Fortunately, the idea of Ganga Manthan, the first-ever national dialogue on the Ganga, emerged in one of the discussions with the then Union Minister for Water Resources, River Development and Ganga Rejuvenation, Uma Bharti, who was in charge of the project. The plan was to hold consultations with major stakeholders, including scientists, researchers, academics, politicians, administrators, and religious and spiritual leaders. The idea of holding discussions with religious leaders over such a sensitive issue saw deep divisions within the organization because such an initiative had never been attempted before and seemed fraught with dangers.

'But our eagerness to understand the larger issues and the

confidence to deal with such personalities helped us take up the challenge. The fact that our minister was herself seen as a sanyasi helped matters too,' says Puskal. Ganga Manthan was finally held on 7 July 2014, at Vigyan Bhawan, New Delhi, with more than 500 delegates from various sectors, while several hundred had to make do with a live telecast. 'The discussions not only made our resolve to find a solution for Ma Ganga stronger but also helped us to see the problem in a different light,' Puskal recalls.

Ganga Manthan deliberations identified that a holistic approach to the solution included maintaining an adequate environmental flow (e-flow) downstream of hydroelectric projects[9], zero discharge into the Ganga, the guarantee of a 100 per cent formula of reuse and recycling of treated water, effective monitoring of the water quality and river flow by the Central Pollution Control Board, etc. Other suggestions included innovative financial models for running STPs, regulating development activities on banks of the river, conservation of the Ganga and its tributaries, focusing not just on the quality of the water but also on the ecosystem, which involves conservation of biodiversity and aquatic life and promotion of organic farming, among others. It also highlighted that there is a need to bring together all the stakeholders to take the responsibility of restoring the Ganga, building the capacity of Urban Local Bodies (ULBs) and learn from the successful international experiences of restoring a river and elements of rejuvenation of aquatic life as a measure of success.

To find a long-lasting solution for Ganga rejuvenation, the NMCG had earlier asked a consortium of seven IITs to prepare a draft report on the GRBMP. The voluminous report, running thousands of pages, did not prescribe any clear-cut action, but it did specify various aspects of river conservation and basin management, which soon became the bedrock of the implementation strategy of the organization. For the first time, the concepts of Nirmal, a pollution-

---

[9]Environmental flow describes the quantity, timing and quality of water flows required to sustain freshwater, estuarine ecosystems and the human livelihoods that depend on this ecosystem.

free river and Aviral Ganga, ensuring adequate availability of water, took centre stage in all discussions.

Availability of water in the river is a major concern, especially in the upper stretches, where at many places, entire water is diverted to allow generation of hydroelectricity, and thereafter in the plains, where huge quantities are abstracted for irrigation purposes. Additionally, the dumping of domestic sewage and the discharge of industrial waste from factories into the river makes certain stretches of the river extremely polluted. This is complicated further by the lack of water availability.

The challenge set before the officials is best understood from a 2015 CPCB report, which stated that despite three decades of the Ganga programme, almost 30 per cent of the STPs monitored in the four states of Uttarakhand, Uttar Pradesh, Bihar and West Bengal were not operational, and 94 per cent of them did not comply with the prescribed effluent standards. Of the 11,000 MLD treatment gap of untreated sewage being discharged into the river in the Ganga basin states, only 1,000 MLD had been created by 2014.

Hence, Nirmal Ganga could not be achieved just by ensuring adequate flow or ecological flow and needed immediate solutions. Setting up STPs, tapping drains, cleaning and maintaining ghats became the organization's focus, while Aviral Ganga became its long-term objective. The other two aspects highlighted by the GRBMP report—ensuring longitudinal connectivity and geological integrity of the river—completed the spectrum of river conservation. These two aspects were included in the priority list but did not have any specific budget allocations.

In parallel, the government had constituted a Committee of Secretaries to suggest an action plan for the Ganga, making recommendations, sometimes drawing arguments from Ganga Manthan deliberations. 'We were privileged to regularly get reviewed and guided by another group of ministers comprising Union Minister(s) of Environment, Shipping, Tourism and Urban Development. The scrutiny and frequent presentations unnerved us at times, but their relevance became clear much later,' says Puskal.

Rarely had any government programme or scheme witnessed such widespread consultations and discussions like Ganga rejuvenation, which only added to the quality of the outcome.

One of the aspects ignored before was the sewage and solid waste coming from the rural areas. A study by NMCG in consultation with the Ministry of Drinking Water and Sanitation in charge of rural areas showed that the pollution emanated from open defecation and cases of half-burnt bodies being dumped into the main stem of the river by some 5,000 villages located on its banks. While preventing open defecation was the responsibility of the Swatch Bharat Mission (SBM), the NMCG officials stepped in to stop this particular source of pollution. This approach led to the concept of Ganga Grams (model villages), which sustainably managed their waste and did not pollute the river. The mission took up the programme through the Ministry of Drinking Water and Sanitation, already implementing SBM in rural areas.

The outlay on repair and construction of ghats and crematoria on the banks of the Ganga was significantly increased as they are the primary interface between citizens and the river and are often a major site of solid waste disposal. Institutional development, capacity building of ground institutions (especially ULBs), and setting up the National Ganga Monitoring Centre and another Centre of Excellence for Ganga Studies make up the support mechanisms for the programme.

A dedicated component of research studies, innovative pilots, model interventions for non-point pollution mitigation, agricultural run-off, GIS-based data mapping and spatial analysis, assessment of special properties of Ganga water, the study of communities and their livelihood, guidelines for sand mining, etc., were also included in the programme's design.

Ecological sustainability is also being ensured through a separate component for the conservation of aquatic life. Protection of dolphins, turtles and ghariyals, measures for afforestation and conservation of wetlands, habitat improvement programmes like amenities for Char Dham yatra, and safe disposal of flowers and puja material contribute to making it an actual 360-degree programme. Public participation has been emphasized in a serious manner, including the population as an equal stakeholder.

But the real game-changer under the programme had been the formulation of the Hybrid Annuity Model (HAM) to create and maintain sewage treatment infrastructure, including networks and STPs, moving beyond the 'business as usual' form. NMCG team had realized that in more than three decades, the sewerage capacity created was too less than the situation warranted. To top it all, most of the STPs created were not operational due to funding and operational issues, and nobody could still be held accountable. It was clear that those who set up the plant had to be responsible for their operation over the long term and had a built-in stake for the entire duration. HAM had been introduced in the transportation sector and other sectors before with mixed results, but its usage in the wastewater sector, where revenue generation was almost unheard of, was more than bold. The idea was to build a long-term stake for developers in construction and its operations for 10–15 years to ensure accountability and continuity of the operation. The scheme provides for construction-linked payments up to 40 per cent of the project cost, while the rest would be paid over the contract period (10–15 years) in annuities based on compliance to performance standards with built-in incentives for performance and efficiency. There were not many takers, but with some support from the World Bank, the scheme went through in 2016. The NMCG team followed up the projects with lingering anticipation, keeping their fingers crossed. The HAM model has not looked back thereafter, starting with Jagjeetpur STP in Haridwar and followed by Mathura and Ramana STP in Varanasi.

Now all major projects are being awarded based on this model. Much to everyone's surprise, it is witnessing the participation of more bidders compared to engineering, procurement and construction (EPC) and other traditional modes. Together with the concept of 'One City, One Operator', market reform of the wastewater treatment sector has been achieved in a very subtle manner. NMCG has received accolades and awards for this model, even the prestigious award of a Global Water Summit. Hitesh S. Makwana, Executive Director (Projects), took up the challenge of operationalizing the scheme on the ground in addition to developing necessary documentation and coordinating with concerned agencies.

Drafting the scheme for Namami Gange was an enlightening exercise. As we got deeper into its aspects, we started seeing its connection with other ecological and economic aspects. It was not just an onion with its multiple sheaths; it appeared to be like multiple onions that were inter-twined. This may be the cause why earlier attempts had not yielded results since they addressed only one dimension at a time and were inadequate in terms of size.

The institutional structure for any organization is of great importance because it establishes the credibility of the institution's programmes. However, the realization soon dawned that NMCG alone was not capable of delivering on the increased demands and required a similar approach from other organizations, especially those directly linked to the noble task. After all, the organization was required to work in tandem with state government's departments.

Initially, the NGRBA framework was envisaged as a three-tier structure—a broad policymaking body under the prime minister, state coordination for projects under a steering committee headed by the Finance Minister, and NMCG as its implementing and funding special purpose vehicle (SPV). The NGRBA started on a grand note on its inception in 2009, closing down a few hydroelectric plants, declaring the upper Bhagirathi region as a protected area and designating Ganga as a national river. However, until 2012, the NGRBA could only meet thrice. The third meeting was organized almost under compulsion on demand of Swami Gyan Swaroop Sanand, a saint, who had undertaken a fast-unto-death pledge to ensure rejuvenation of the Ganges. The framework also envisaged the creation of State Ganga River Conservation Authorities (SGRCAs) in five major Ganga basin states. These were to be the mirror images of the NGRBA in the states. Similarly, State Programme Management Groups (SPMG) had been set up as SPVs for the construction of sewerage infrastructure and other Ganga clean-up activities, except in Jharkhand, where it worked through a dedicated cell under the government. Though the SGRCAs were constituted and notified, they could not establish their separate identities or meet their intended goals to be part of the state machinery. SPMGs too faltered to conduct the necessary recruitment of officials and could take up various projects.

While the 'SPMGs as SPV' model was useful in insulating NMCG funds from being part of the state budget, no meaningful support came from organizations like the SGRCA. And, by the time the NMCG had created a pipeline of appraised projects for World Bank funding and monitoring, the realization soon dawned that there was no choice but to work with state-run implementing agencies like the UP Jal Nigam, Uttarakhand Jal Nigam, Bihar Urban Infrastructure Development Corporation and Kolkata Metropolitan Development Agency.

Since these institutions were riddled with archaic rules and procedures and suffered from slow decision-making, they were unable to cope with the expectations of NGRBA's framework. Saddled with more pressing priorities, Ganga's cleanliness was never accorded enough time and resources. Even roping in the urban local bodies did not provide much help as most of these bodies lacked resources to carry out major tasks.

The riverfront development (RFD) project in Patna was a classic example. The NMCG had to handhold the SPMG and Bihar Urban Infrastructure Development Corporation (BUIDCO) at every step of the journey, including identifying consultants for rigorous environmental sustainability framework, crowd modelling and biodiversity impact assessment. The detailed project report of the RFD was analyzed, and NMCG's suggestion was incorporated in the plan to meet World Bank's stringent conditions. The project finally achieved closure from the Finance Ministry after deliberations and discussions, which had lasted for months. Today, after completion, it has achieved an iconic status in Bihar.

Once the Namami Gange Programme was announced and its work was transferred to a new ministry, the NMCG team realized that it was a once-in-a-lifetime opportunity to seek changes in the organization's functioning. It was also an opportune moment to remove the roadblocks that had been hampering their functioning. Subsequent interactions with the new set of political leaders and others helped the organization expand its scope, powers and financial muscle. While the Namami Gange Programme and its phenomenal ₹20,000 crore funding were cleared by the Cabinet in 2015, its new institutional structure consolidating the objectives, mandate and institutional framework was approved by the government only in October 2016. The new institutional structure was significant for the growth of the organization.

First, it upgraded the NMCG to an authority under the Environment Protection Act, 1986, while retaining its structure as a registered society, keeping its governance simple and at the same time adding some regulatory powers to it. Since its inception, NMCG had been mainly a policymaking and funding agency with no real teeth, lacking enforcing powers. NMCG now had powers to issue directives not only to the state and district agencies under its framework but other entities as well. Secondly, while retaining the policymaking framework (National Ganga Council under the prime minister)—a Union minister-led review structure at the Centre and corresponding structure at the state level—it also introduced for the first time, a District Ganga Committee at the district level, which really crystallized the 'DM to PM' connection.

The District Ganga Committees (DGC) were not only vested with powers to recommend projects, review its local implementation but also to issue directives. But the most significant reform was the enhanced financial power of its CEO, now titled the Director General, who could now sanction projects worth ₹1,000 crore post appraisal by the Executive Committee, which otherwise would have required approval of the Finance Minister together with the administrative minister. This ensured that even large-sized projects could be approved at the institution level. Further, the approval process was simplified through a much smaller executive committee for project approvals comprising nine members, six of whom were from the mission itself—including the Director General. Undoubtedly, the NMCG is administratively the most empowered organization under the Government of India. U.P. Singh, Additional Secretary in the ministry who became the first Director General, effectively operationalized the new structure and continued to support the same as Secretary of the Ministry.

NMCG has been evolving in terms of its structure and business model simultaneously. Initially, there were regrets that the institutional processes had not been well thought out, but now, in hindsight, it appears beneficial because it allowed the organization to experiment and identify the bottlenecks through appropriate pilot projects and arrive at the right mix at the right time. Today when the IT business models talk about agile solutions, the approach adopted by NMCG appears to be the same—solutions worked out while the development takes place—in a practical mode. This saves the time taken in policymaking and adds to the ability to implement measures based on the ground experience. The mission's spirit has been supported with the agility of its body, making it a unique mix for the unique challenge.

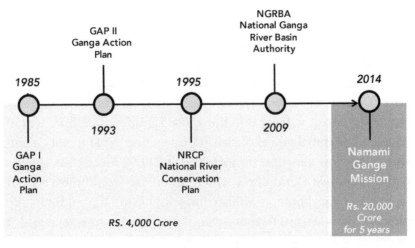

Towards a Comprehensive Basin Approach

This agile model helps NMCG scale up to new roles as its business model keeps evolving in times to come. With most of the infrastructure projects already lined up for the next five years, the focus will now remain on project monitoring and, gradually, the regulatory roles like e-flow management. Functions like water allocations, alternate usages, salinity management, etc., will evolve. Accordingly, the organizational structure will have to evolve in line with River Basin Organizations (RBO) like the Murray Darling Basin Authority or Rhine and Danube authorities. At the moment, the NMCG seems to have developed the right genetic material to adapt and evolve in a sustainable manner so as to become the final word on river rejuvenation in both India and abroad.

5

Uttarakhand: The Sweet Scent of Success

GANGA CLEAN-UP: HOW THE BATTLE FOR UTTARAKHAND WAS WON

It is indeed difficult, if not impossible, to control the gamut of emotions as one witnesses the origin of the Bhagirathi, as it surges from underneath the cow-shaped mouth of a Himalayan icy glacier, the Gaumukh, in the temple town of Gangotri in Uttarakhand, only to see it plunge a few hundred kilometres from the steep mountainous slopes as it enters the floodplains of northern India.

After all, Bhagirathi, along with Alaknanda, which too has its origin in the glaciers of the mighty Himalayas in Badrinath, forms the two main headstreams whose confluence at Devprayag results in the birth of India's most sacred, most revered, most productive and most important river of the country, Mother Ganga. Incidentally, according to mythology, there is another river, Saraswati, that belongs to this confluence which originates from Mana near Badrinath.

However, it would not be correct to accord full credit to just Bhagirathi and Alaknanda for giving birth to India's holiest of holy rivers. The volume and flow of these two rivers are regularly rejuvenated and strengthened by a host of small streams at various points in their journey, culminating in their union at Devprayag. The pride of place for strengthening Alaknanda should go to five such prayags or locations, where these streams merge with this headstream to create the Ganga as we know it today. These include the likes of Vishnuprayag, Rudraprayag, Karnaprayag, Nandprayag and Devprayag.

There is near-unanimity about the Ganga's birthplace; difference exists on the exact origin of the river among believers and experts. While Hindu mythology traces the source of the Ganga to the Bhagirathi, geographers and other experts maintain that Alaknanda should be declared as the true source because of its long journey and the greater volume of water carried by it. Thankfully, there is complete unanimity on its crucial role, significance and importance—not just in the daily life of Indian citizens but also with respect to the country's economy. After all, 43 per cent of the Indian population resides in the Ganga basin and are directly or indirectly impacted by the river's water quality.

There is also unanimity on the urgent need to cleanse the polluted river of its impurities and ensure its return it to a pristine state, although disagreements and debates over the methods, processes and technologies for accomplishing this complex and challenging task still rages on. Many experts even go to the extent to say that there is no need to stop the pollution from entering the river; the river's health can be restored simply by increasing the flow of the water. This is noted in the aviral (increasing the flow) versus the nirmal (cleaning the river) debate. However, for most people, witnessing a clean and pristine Ganga (as it existed some 300 years ago) within their lifetime is like a distant dream, a near impossibility that is unlikely to be achieved even in the distant future.

Yet, most people can hardly be blamed for their pessimism. For years, they have fed on the governments' grandiose plans—huge investments in such projects for improvements of the water quality of the rivers, modernizing the crematoria and hundreds of decade-old bathing ghats that dot the river banks—only to return disappointed because of the absence of any movement on the ground. Despite so many announcements and funding stories by successive governments over the past 35 years, the river and its tributaries' health only deteriorated over the years, sometimes even raising doubts on the proper utilization of funds for the clean-up.

In 1985, former Prime Minister late Rajiv Gandhi announced the first Ganga Action Plan. It was followed by Second Ganga Action Plan, the Yamuna Action Plan and the Yamuna Action Plan Phase II. Even these did not yield any visible signs of improvement, either in the river's water quality or its banks. The Manmohan Singh-led United Progressive Alliance established the NGRBA in 2009 and the NMCG two years later and ensured that five Ganga basin states each have a State Ganga River Conservation Authority. Yet, to allege that thousands of crores have been siphoned off in the name of Ganga will be patently wrong, because over a period of 30 years—from 1985 to 2015—only about ₹4,000 crore had been sanctioned, which is a slight change with respect to the enormity of the task. Not only was the amount too little and thinly spread over decades, but it was also very narrowly focused. It only focused on setting up STPs in selected cities/towns to prevent untreated waste from entering the river. No holistic approach was taken.

Any attempt to clean a massive river like the Ganga broadly calls for taking three main steps: collecting data on the river basin, quality of water and flow of the river at any time of the year; secondly, it involves preparing policies and projects customized to suit the specific needs of a particular stretch of the river depending on the nature and quantity of pollutants that enter the river, and finally, ensuring that those specific policies and projects are also implemented in time. In the absence of such a holistic approach for the clean-up process, it is hardly surprising that most of the projects never took off.

It was a historical occasion when Prime Minister Narendra Modi had on 29 September 2020 unveiled dedicated measures for the development of major STPs in Uttarakhand, especially the ones in the Haridwar-Rishikesh zone, as well as in other parts of the state such as at holy Badrinath. This marked the complete coverage of STPs required along Ganga towns in Uttarakhand. It was also an occasion that marked the opening of the first Ganga Museum at Chandi ghat in Haridwar. The Prime Minister remarked, 'Had the old methods been adopted, the situation would have been equally bad today.

But we moved forward with a new approach and new thinking. We have not limited the Namami Gange mission to only cleaning of the Ganga, but also made it the largest and most comprehensive river rejuvenation program in the country.' It was a matter of satisfaction and pride for the Namami Gange team. At this point, memories of my personal journey as the Director General of NMCG—which I found challenging yet rewarding—over the past few years flashed before my eyes. It dawned on me how my experience with mission Ganga and Uttarakhand, in particular, has changed and matured my understanding of the river and environment; everything that was done to meet the challenges and finally execute an all-round rejuvenation effort in this mission and particularly in Uttarakhand felt important.

It was in the last week of May 2013 when I had joined as Joint Secretary and Mission Director of NMCG. My first challenge was to revive the World Bank assisted project, which had not taken off in the last two years. We were on borrowed time. We had to show progress regarding the construction of pollution abatement projects and sewage treatment capacities.

Just after a few days, a major calamity struck Uttarakhand in the form of heavy floods in Kedarnath and other parts. This national disaster had wide-ranging ramifications and shook the entire nation. Thousands of people died or were declared missing, and severe damage to property and infrastructure was recorded. The immediate challenge that we faced was the damage to several old projects in the state and having to undertake their reconstruction. But it was also a trigger to think about the more significant issues of the ecological impact of human interventions.

In August 2013, Supreme Court ordered the Ministry of Environment and Forests to do a detailed study on the impact of the hydro-electric projects (HEPs) on the ecology and their relation with this disaster. This started a long series of consultations and several decisions in future. It was also a time when discussions on the determinations of environmental flow were underway in the light of Chaturvedi Committee recommendations[10] and in reference to the long-term decisions based on the GRBMP being developed by the consortium of IITs, which was in progress since 2010. These helped me broaden my perspective, following which I realized that while we need to aggressively move towards the construction of pollution abatement infrastructure along the river, we also needed to address long-term ecological issues for the rejuvenation of the river. The first obvious challenge was to expedite the GRBMP. I started interacting with IITs and also went to IIT Kanpur (after decades) for in-depth understanding and to bring about a sense of urgency among the experts. It took efforts to coordinate and help the group of experts arrive at a conclusion. Finally, we started a draft in 2014, which became helpful in conceptualizing and developing the contours of the Namami Gange Programme. This came very handy when the new government took over. We could then brainstorm and conduct stakeholder consultations such as 'Ganga Manthan' for formulating the contours of a new approach for the Ganga Rejuvenation Mission. GRBMP could have become available in June 2015.

However, when the Narendra Modi-led government National Democratic Alliance assumed power at the Centre in 2014 with a thumping majority, it was clear that it was unlikely to repeat past mistakes and thus adopt a more holistic and integrated approach in its critical mission of cleaning the Ganga. The vision for the Ganga rejuvenation constitutes restoring the wholesomeness of the river defined in terms of ensuring Aviral Dhara, Nirmal Dhara, geological and ecological integrity. In simple terms, it was no longer just about setting up STPs to ensure a clean Ganga—free of all pollutants—but also about having an Aviral Ganga—which could ensure a constant flow of water even during the dry seasons. Additionally, it was also about maintaining the geological and ecological integrity of the river. In the context of Uttarakhand, we had to address the pollution problem arising from towns and villages along Ganga while tackling

---

[10]An inter-ministerial group chaired by Shri B.K. Choudhary, Member, Planning Commission on issues related to river Ganga, that specifically recommended determination of e-flows

the larger problems of disturbance to the continuity of the flow because of HEPs, maintaining the e-flow, biodiversity conservation and protection and development of catchment area forestry, springs and wetlands.

We also had to work towards riverfront development, which includes modernizing and constructing state-of-the-art ghats and crematoria to ensure that the burnt or half-burnt bodies are not dumped into the river. It also meant reviving flora and fauna, which were once integral to the river's life, protecting the river basin from disasters. But most importantly, it was about changing the mindset of people and providing hope to millions that the impossible task of cleaning the river can be possible, making them active partners in this noble mission of saving and rejuvenating a dying river.

After winning the elections from the holy city of Varanasi, in Uttar Pradesh, an important Ganga state, the Prime Minister resolved to save and rejuvenate the Ganga. In a major shift, the work of Ganga cleaning was transferred from MoEF to MoWR, now represented as Ministry of Water Resources, River Development and Ganga Rejuvenation, bearing the name of the river itself. He also launched the Namami Gange (obeisance to the Ganga), which was a national mission. Under it, the central government took more responsibility for the river clean-up, providing the entire funding of the project. It also announced a dedicated five-year budget allocation (2014–15 to 2019–20) of ₹20,000 crore, which is likely to be enhanced in view of long-term commitment of 15 years for operation and maintenance (O&M) of projects taken up in the mission.

The programme has been split into three parts: starting with quick wins for an immediate visible impact, including the collection of plastic waste, rural sanitation to cut the sewage flow, construction of crematoria and the beautification of the bathing ghats. Then in the medium term (over five years), the government plans to build additional sewage treatment plants with a capacity of 2.5 billion litres a day and to enforce industrial effluent controls, protect wildlife, plant 30,000 hectares of forests in the watershed to reduce erosion and install 113 water monitoring systems. In the longer term, a 10-year period that would extend into the next government's mandate, the current government will ensure adequate water flow (environmental flow) in the river and improve irrigation efficiency to reduce the use of water in agriculture.

Additionally, an example of how the NMCG has been implemented successfully is the state of Uttarakhand, described as the abode of the gods—Devbhumi. The pollution abatement strategies and interventions are discussed first. The Haridwar-Rishikesh zone accounts for almost 70 per cent of the pollution from Ganga towns. To address this issue on a war footing, a strategic decision was taken to keep aside the earlier strategy of connecting every house in Haridwar to a sewerage network. Instead, the focus was put on different points of pollution. The sewage flowing out of drains is intercepted and diverted to an STP so that not a single drop of untreated waste enters the river. Connecting every house to the sewer network would have meant digging up many parts of the city, which would take decades apart from causing traffic jams and other civic problems in the densely-populated town. The solution would come at a huge price, which successive governments may not be able to sustain. In the meantime, untreated sewage would have continued to flow into the Ganga. This approach was river-centric and a game-changer for the city because tapping the drains—diverting the outflow of the city's untreated sewage flowing from its numerous drains and connecting it to an STP—was not only a faster and easier option but also a much more cost-effective exercise. The long-term network construction can take place later, if necessary, as it is not a suitable option for *all* habitations or towns. Incidentally, such projects have subsequently been planned with the assistance of KfW, a German financing agency.[11]

Today, 35 STPs of about 185 MLD capacity have been created. About 121 small and large drains have been intercepted and treated, and about 14 crore litre sewage is being treated per day in the Ganga

---

[11]https://www.kfw-entwicklungsbank.de/International-financing/KfW-Development-Bank/Local-presence/Asia/India/.

basin towns. Even the earlier STPs have been modernized and their capacity enhanced. Today, Haridwar officials can thump their chest and declare that not a single drop of untreated sewage waste enters the Ganga, returning it to its pristine form.

However, to understand the enormity of the task and sincere efforts made by the team to make this mission a success, one has to understand the complexity of the task. The challenging task of building over three dozen STPs on the steep and earthquake-prone upper reaches of the Ganga and constructing state-of-the-art treatment plants at Haridwar and Rishikesh are a few examples. A special mention must be given to the 68-MLD STP at Jagjeetpur, Haridwar, the biggest STP plant of the state, that takes care of 80 to 85 per cent of the domestic discharge of the city (coming from five of the six different zones in which the city has been divided). Constructed on a plot of two hectares, the Jagjeetpur STP plant commenced operation from February 2020 using the latest Sequence Batch Reactor (SBR) treatment technology to treat the domestic discharge, not just to meet the standards laid down by the National Green Tribunal (NGT)—an independent body—but also those set by other international bodies. Today, the treated effluent out of the STPs in Haridwar meets the minimum prescribed criteria indicated by biochemical oxygen demand (BOD)[12], chemical oxygen demand (COD)[13] and the total suspended solids (TSS)[14]. Similarly, the phosphorous and nitrogen content has been brought down within permissible limits.

While the use of the SBR technology itself may not be a novelty, the fact is that the public-private partnership project was completed in 18 months, well ahead of the deadline of two years and at least a year in advance of the time taken by projects of such size and complexity before. This achievement is not small. Moreover, the 68-MLD plant has been built keeping in mind the city's future needs—at least till

---

[12]BOD is the amount of oxygen needed by aerobic biological organisms to break down organic material present in the water.

[13]COD is a test that measures the amount of oxygen required to oxidize the organic material and inorganic nutrients chemically.

[14]TSS refers to the dry-weight of suspended solids in water.

2028, when the demand is expected to touch the 68 MLD milestone. Currently, the plant treats only 50 MLD of domestic sewage.

More importantly, this plant has many firsts in its list of achievements. First, it was built on a new financing model with suitable modifications—the Hybrid Annuity Model (HAM) that was earlier initiated in road projects with mixed experiences—that articulated that the same company carrying out the construction activity will take full responsibility for its O&M for the next 10–15 years. It is a model that ensures complete accountability and removes major drawbacks in many of the pre-existing projects, where both the O&M player and the project developer would blame each other for the malfunctioning or the inefficient functioning of the plant. The project with two STPs—68 MLD at Jagjeetpur and 14 MLD at Sarai— was bid out on HAM model through a transparent bidding process on the basis of life-cycle costs, which included not just the cost of construction of the STP but also the cost of its O&M; it also included the land cost since acquiring land is a major challenge in these hilly and densely populated areas.

Under this scheme (which has been discussed in greater detail in the chapter titled 'Sustainability'), only 40 per cent of the total construction cost is paid to the private operator in several tranches, depending on when the construction is completed. The remaining 60 per cent of the cost is paid over a period of 15 years with interest, along with the O&M charges, which are paid as long as the builders meet the stringent standards laid down in the bidding document.

The STP plant at Jagjeetpur uses a three-stage cleansing process, where the untreated domestic discharge first goes through a primary separation process, then passes through a biological treatment chamber and finally, undergoes a chlorination process to disinfect the clean water before it is either released to the farms through a canal for irrigation purposes or sent back to the Ganga to contribute to its 'aviral' flow. The primary treatment units, which receive water from pumping stations, separates sand particles, heavy metals, small stones, unwanted floating matter like polythene bags and wrappers. Different mechanical and automated screens have been set up to separate the floating debris from the untreated sewage; the heavier materials are allowed to sink to the ground from where they are first swept to a corner through a sweeper system and then removed through the use of a rotating screw conveyor belt. The untreated sewage then enters biological treatment chambers, where it first goes through a process of de-nitrification before it can be sent to the six aeration chambers for the bacterial decomposition of the sludge. These six chambers have a diffused aeration system, where oxygen from six blowers (three extra blowers are always kept ready for emergency) keep injecting oxygen to activate the bacteria in the sludge itself. These invigorated bacteria then devour the sludge, grow in size and sink to the bottom of the tank, thereby ensuring that the water is free from all pollutants. The treated water is then allowed to settle for half an hour before being taken out through a separate channel. This process is called the decantation process.

The water is then sent to the chlorination chamber for disinfection. The leftover sludge that has settled at the bottom of the tank is now taken to a centrifugal chamber to remove any traces of water that might have remained and sent back for retreatment—a process called slug thickener. The dry sludge is then collected and given out as free fertilizers to farmers. The whole process is automated and runs for 24 hours, seven days a week in a perfect three-stage sequence without any human intervention.

What is even more remarkable is that these biological treatment chambers are fitted with sensors connected to the main control panel of the plant to measure the quality of the input, the efficiency of the processing units and the quality of the output. Hence, when the chambers achieve the optimum oxygen level, the blowers are automatically switched off, saving a lot of electricity. The plant uses 1,200 KW of electricity every hour, and hence, any shutdown of power means higher profits. Every STP also has a central monitoring system that provides real-time data on pollution parameters in the water sample and even generates information about the state of the plant and which parts need replacement.

Under the mission in Haridwar, more than 20 drains have been tapped, a new STP of 82 MLD has been constructed, and one of 45 MLD capacity has been renovated, bringing the total sewage treatment capacity to 145 MLD. The 68-MLD plant in Jagjeetpur, built at the cost of ₹99.3 crore, along with another newly constructed 14-MLD STP (₹44.3 crore) at Sarai, use the same SBR technology. All these STPs are enough to take care of the entire domestic sewage of Haridwar and serve as great examples of turning an impossible task into possible. Now more than 11 crore litres of contaminated water is being cleaned every day in Haridwar, due to which the quality of Ganga water has improved significantly. Thus, the Namami Gange project has come a long way in the last five to six years—from 2014 onwards—when this holy city only had a 45-MLD STP. The Jagjeetpur project of Haridwar is the first sewerage project in the country completed in HAM.

However, converting the impossible into the possible meant overcoming on-site construction and logistic challenges in the hilly terrains of the state and clearing surrounding areas and convincing the citizens to join in this noble cause. This was especially necessary when the task was to tap many of the drains in the middle of the city, disrupting traffic and creating inconvenience. For instance, tapping the Kasavan or Kasavanala or drain on the river ghat and setting up a new STP there was a huge challenge not just because of the size of the drain, which was discharging some 8.8 MLD of untreated domestic sewage into the river, but also because a new STP had to be constructed right in the middle of encroachments. Officials had to spend nearly six months clearing the encroachments and then building a bridge over the upper Ganga canal to carry the untreated waste (because the drain could not be blocked at one go). Finally, 11 months after the project was sanctioned, the infamous drain was tapped, a small STP constructed, and the ghat was given a makeover. The newly-constructed steps of the ghat have become a major tourist attraction today.

Keeping in mind the growing urbanization of the city, the rush of tourists during festivals like the Kumbh Mela, and the pressure of tourists on the existing Har ki Pauri ghat, the mission has financed the setting up of a new state-of-the-art 41,872 sq m Chandi bathing ghat.

Under the mission's riverfront development plan, it also includes a new, improved eco-friendly crematorium and a Ganga museum, known as the Ganga Interpretation Centre. Named after the famous Chandi temple of the city, it is located on the other side of the Har ki Pauri ghat, a kilometre downstream from the Bhimgoda barrage, and can accommodate 10,000 people at any given point of time. Developed by Water and Power Consultancy Services (WAPCOS) under the public-private-partnership model, the ghat boasts of a toilet block, kiosks, cafeteria, railings, a ramp for the differently-abled to reach the river and also a small STP to tap all the untreated sewage of the ghat. The museum captures the rich history, biodiversity (which had been lost over the years and is now making a comeback) and various measures taken under the Namami Gange to return the river to its original form. It is run by the Ganga Praharis trained by the Wildlife Institute of India (WII) to create awareness among the local populace and the tourists who will again throng this ghat once the threat of COVID-19 is over.

On similar lines, another Ganga Museum is coming up at Triveni Ghat in Rishikesh which is a very popular spot for thousands of tourists and pilgrims visiting to see the Ganga aarti performed every day.

The issue of industrial pollutants in Haridwar and Rishikesh's twin cities has been resolved. Industrial sewage coming from the limited industrial belt in Haridwar has been tapped and dispatched to a Common Effluent Treatment Plant (CETP), ensuring that not even a single drop of untreated industrial waste enters the river. One of the project's major achievements was to ensure that the river remains spotlessly clean, even in the upper reaches of the Ganga basin and before it enters the town of Rishikesh. Although these areas are sparsely populated, have limited pollutants entering the city and present several roadblocks including high cost and various challenges related to the construction of STPs in such high-altitude and inaccessible areas, more than three dozen small STPs have been constructed in these upper reaches of the state like Gangotri, Badrinath Joshimath, etc.

Overcoming the challenges of constructing STPs in these earthquake-prone, steeply inclined hills on either side of the river should be considered an art in itself. There are many stories about how STPs had to be rebuilt after landslides had destroyed them. Moreover, even if a suitable site is found, bringing men and material to the site can be a logistical nightmare, not to mention the seven or eight bitter winter months when many of the cities are in complete lockdown. A case in point was the construction of two STPs of 1 MLD capacity and another of 0.1 MLD capacity in Badrinath. Though the distance between the two STPs was only 300 meters, they had to be built on the two sides of a turbulent river, adding to the construction challenges. While the size of these treatment plants may seem relatively small, their constructions took more effort and sacrifices than those required even to construct a 50-MLD plant.

The other polluting industry in these holy towns is the hotel industry, which has proliferated with the rising tide of tourists. Today, hotels with more than 20 rooms either have to construct their own STPs or connect their discharge to the state government's sewerage network. The temple town of Badrinath is open only from April to October, which also coincides with its tourist or yatra season. The heavy traffic inflow makes it extremely difficult to move construction materials, heavy machinery and equipment to the site, which anyway have to be lugged from the plains because no material is available in the hills. The problem of storing these items only compounds the challenge.

Moreover, since the construction sites were located in inaccessible areas, the building materials had to be first transported by trucks over a certain distance, then hauled by taxis to the point where the road gave way to the dirt road, and finally, had to be transported by human beings during the last leg of the journey. Not only did all this add to the construction cost, but it also extended the time frame for completing the project. A far more daunting task was to convince the private players to bid for these projects because none of the reputed players would be willing to work in such extreme conditions—the STP had to be constructed at the height of 10,000 feet—and that too for such small capacity projects. After much persuasion, a Gurgaon-based company called Aastha Engineering agreed to build the STP.

In order to take advantage of those four to five months during which the town remains open, the Namami Gange team in Uttarakhand not only completed the STP design but also secured the government's permission to move truckloads of materials and equipment to a place, some 60 kilometres south of Badrinath during the lockdown period. Once the lockdown ended, the team quickly moved the equipment to the site before the tourist trickle could turn into a deluge for the yatra. With little or no network for communication in such high altitudes—mobiles hardly work there—a Namami Gange team had to be permanently stationed at the site to resolve any day-to-day problems and to procure immediate engineering and technical solutions affecting the construction of the STP. Having a team stationed in such inhospitable and harsh conditions also meant ensuring a regular supply of food from the plains and heating arrangements. To add to these difficulties, the constant threats of accidents and roadblocks from falling debris and avalanches were unending.

However, the real engineering feat was the construction of these STPs; not being able to find the right-sized patch of 250 sq m for the 1 MLD plant meant changing the design so that the wider parts of the plant could be fitted on the larger platforms and the smaller parts on the smaller ledges. Since the structure had to be protected from flooding by the river first, a reinforced concrete boundary was built from the bed rising above the river, which later became the platform for the STP. Such engineering innovations are rarely found in textbooks and call for lateral and imaginative thinking by those on the ground. Once it starts snowing and the water freezes, the concrete refuses to harden, making these structures fragile. The only solution is to cover the structure with plastic during the winter months and hope that the concrete will harden when the weather improves. However, thanks to the team's efforts, the project, which started in November 2017 was completed in nine months at a cost of ₹1 crore. However, the effort and the cost has paid dividends because the river in the upper reaches is nearly as pure as it was a hundred years ago. Ma Ganga has been returned to its earlier, beautiful avatar.

While engineering and technical innovations have been the

hallmark of many STPs, the pride of place must go to the 7.5-MLD Muni ki Reti plant in Rishikesh. An urgency awaited its construction since in 2018, a video of the Chandreshwar Nala draining its polluted water into the Ganga at Laxman Jhula in Rishikesh went viral. Newspapers and local media picked up the news, and it soon became a talking point for the city, as infamous as the Sisamau Nala of Kanpur.[15] It was not that the NMCG officials were not cognizant about the issue, but constructing an STP on such a limited space was fraught with many dangers. There was not enough space to set up a treatment facility to tap the drain and treat the wastewater simultaneously. More importantly, the drain had to be tapped in the midst of a residential area surrounded by other buildings.

After many consultations with experts from IIT Roorkee and other top institutes, a new solution was proposed: the construction of a four-storeyed sewerage treatment plant for the first time in India. A plant that would otherwise have required 3,750 sq m of land was to be now constructed in almost a quarter of that area—around 936 sq m—by building a four-storeyed STP. It was a critical innovation, especially for a densely-populated country like India, where land is at a premium, and the motto is to do more with less. Keeping in mind the land constraint, the equalization tank of the STP was constructed below the ground level not just to collect the untreated sewage flowing out from the various drains but also to remove the grit and floating debris from the water. This is then pumped through pipes into reactors or the treatment chambers located on the top floor. To accommodate the blowers, office and the genset, a platform was created on the second floor. The first floor housed the clarifier or the sedimentation tank, where water is allowed to settle after being cleaned in the reactors before it is fed into the chlorine tank for disinfection. However, unlike the Jagjeetpur plant, this STP uses the moving bed biofilm reactor (MBBR) process in the reactors. The

---

[15]The Sisamau Nala, often referred to as the largest drain in Asia, has been used as a sewage conveyance channel since the 1890s, discharging more than 140 MLD of domestic sewage and untreated wastewater from slaughterhouses. The drain was also an eyesore with its dirty water falling into Ganga in public view.

reactor is filled with thousands of small plastic chips, called media or carriers, that allows the sludge or the biofilm to grow on them, which then sinks to the bottom of the tank. There is also a small lift at the back to carry materials to the four-storeyed building. Interestingly enough, all these STPs are technology agnostic—the officials do not want to be wedded to any particular technology—and are willing to give the project to any player as long as they meet the financial and water quality parameters set out in the bidding document.

There is also the example of a 26 MLD STP plant in Lakkarghat, Rishikesh, and 5 MLD STP at Chorpani, built at the edge of the forest. The permission to construct the STP came after the Namami Gange officials accepted a host of conditions from the forest department, including closing the plant at night not to disturb the animals. Similarly, there is a double-walled boundary wall to keep away the elephants from the Chorpani site. More importantly, there is a plan to convert the dry sludge from the wastewater treatment plant into pellets that can be used for the construction of road or buildings. Again, these pellets have a high calorific value, which can be used in various industries to generate heat.

However, for the twin cities of Haridwar and Rishikesh, the second phase of the Ganga cleaning project is already a work in progress and has been in force since March 2021. The state-owned German development bank KfW has promised to invest €120 million to ensure that every house in Haridwar and Rishikesh is connected to a sewerage line. Since connecting every house will mean digging up the main roads, crowded lanes, resulting in traffic and chaos, the plan has been tweaked. Now, every house will have a pithead constructed by the NMCG, whose upkeep will be the responsibility of the house owners. The domestic waste coming out of these houses will be discharged into these pitheads, which in turn, will be connected to the existing sewerage network and then taken to an STP. While it may not be possible to connect every single house, the plan is to make sure that 97 to 98 per cent of the houses are connected. This five-year project has already been formulated and will take off once the appointed project management consultant validates the project report.

The drive to maintain and regularly clean the Ganges is not an easy task. As the states urbanize, it places increasing pressure on its infrastructure and the facilities provided. But it is not an impossible task, as Uttarakhand has already proven. However, regular monitoring of the quality of the water by the NGT, CPCB and third-party independent players, and Central and state-level executives keeping close tabs on the status of different projects have gone a long way in keeping the Ganga in its pristine form. That is a true reflection of the success of the Namami Gange mission and the solution to a wicked problem. The sincerity, hard work and willingness of the team to go the extra mile to achieve their targets, the active participation of the citizens in the noble cause, adequate funding by the Centre and multilateral agencies make the task easier to achieve.

Apart from these successful initiatives towards pollution abatement for Nirmal Ganga, Uttarakhand also has been at the forefront of improving ecology and flow or Aviral Ganga within Namami Gange mission with several historic decisions.

As the source state of Ganga and all its headstreams, Uttarakhand has a special responsibility to ensure the pristine and continuous flow of the river. There is a history of demands from environmentalists and spiritual leaders that this is ensured. However, the state's developmental needs to harness the river's potential and generate hydroelectric power have been in conflict with these demands. These issues were also very seriously debated during the construction of the Tehri dam and the submergence and relocation of the revered Dhari Devi temple. GRBMP developed a scientific framework for e-flow. In the meantime, the Chaturvedi committee also made interim recommendations for e-flow. Several expert committees were formed, and a final decision was taken to notify the e-flow for a stretch of the Ganga, including all headstreams of Ganga up to Unnao in Uttar Pradesh. This historic notification issued by NMCG in October 2018 prescribes minimum flows to be maintained at all HEPs in Uttarakhand and at barrages at Bhimgoda, Bijnore, Narora and Kanpur.

For the first time, this delivered an official recognition of the river's right over its own water to enable it to survive and perform its ecological functions. As prescribed in this notification, the Central Water Commission is the monitoring agency that submits periodical reports to NMCG. As of now, the measure/policy has been implemented and is being further improved via automation, which is aimed at enhancing effectiveness. Another significant development that took place earlier was the declaration of the Bhagirathi Eco-Sensitive Zone between Gangotri and Uttarkashi and the cancellation of three HEPs at an advanced stage by NGRBA in 2009.

A big challenge to protect ecological integrity has also come from the HEPs. Often, they are justified for their non-consumptive use of water in typical engineering parlance, but an ecological understanding of the river goes beyond these factors. HEPs affect the connectedness of the river and also the aquatic biodiversity. Ganga vanishes into a series of tunnels close to the river's source, which has been a cause of concern. The cumulative impact of these needed to be taken into account, which the Supreme Court ordered to be studied by an expert body in the aftermath of the 2013 Kedarnath disaster. In August 2013, it asked the MoEF and state government to refrain from providing any further clearances. The Supreme Court order said, 'The cumulative impact of the various projects in place and which are under construction on the river basins have not been properly examined or assessed, which requires a detailed technical and scientific study.'

The Expert Body-I was formed in October 2013, headed by Professor Ravi Chopra, which provided certain guidelines and did not recommend construction work in 23 of the 24 HEPs. It laid down that the HEPs that fall in any of the following conditions should not be approved for construction.

- Proposed HEPs that fall inside wildlife protected areas such as national parks and wildlife sanctuaries
- Proposed HEPs that fall within the Gangotri Eco-Sensitive Zone
- Proposed HEPs that fall above 2,500 metres and encompass critical wildlife habitats, high biological diversity, movement

corridors and are fragile in nature due to unpredictable glacial and paraglacial activities

- Proposed HEPs that fall within 10 km from the boundary of protected areas and have not obtained clearance from the National Board for Wildlife

However, the recommendations of the Expert Body-I were not unanimous as the Ministry of Power and Central Water Commission both recorded their dissent.

An Expert Body-II was formed by MoEF&CC, which modified the earlier order. By now, Ganga rejuvenation was part of a different ministry. A view has finally been communicated to MoEF&CC in 2019 that apart from seven HEPs at an advanced stage of construction, all other HEPs and future proposals should not be considered. The matter remains unresolved and is currently under consideration at the Supreme Court.

Uttarakhand has witnessed several disasters due to the nature of geo-climatic conditions and the fragility of the young Himalayan ecology. Landslides, cloudbursts, glacial bursts, floods and earthquakes cause damage. Between 1894 and 2021, the Uttarakhand Himalaya region has witnessed at least 16 major disasters such as flash floods, landslides and earthquakes. At times, these HEPs also have borne the brunt of these disasters. There is a history of frequent and repeated damages to some of them. The latest was on 7 February 2021 when a catastrophic mass flow descended on Ronti Gad, Rishiganga and Dhauliganga valleys in Chamoli, Uttarakhand, causing widespread devastation and severely damaging two hydropower projects in the valleys. More than 200 people were killed or went missing. Analysis of satellite imagery, seismic records, numerical model results and eyewitness videos reveal that large quantities of rock and glacier ice collapsed from the steep north face of Ronti Peak. The rock and ice avalanche rapidly transformed into an extraordinarily large and mobile debris flow that transported boulders greater than 20 metres in diameter and scoured the valley walls up to 220 metres above the valley floor.

The intersection of the hazard cascade with down valley infrastructure resulted in a disaster. This enables us to highlight critical questions about adequate monitoring and sustainable development in the Himalayas and other remote, high-mountain environments. The impacts can be in distant sites as well; the drinking water supply to Delhi was impacted for a few days, and high levels of sediments were found in the water.

The Chamoli event again raises questions about clean energy development, climate change adaptation, disaster governance, conservation, environmental justice and sustainable development in the Himalayas and other high-mountain environments. This stresses on the need for a better understanding of the cause and effect of mountainous hazards that lead to large-scale disasters. The Chamoli disaster tragically revealed the risks associated with the rapid expansion of hydropower infrastructure into increasingly unstable territory. Enhancing inclusive dialogues among governments, local stakeholders and communities, the private sector, and the scientific community could help assess, minimize and prepare for existing risks. The disaster indicates that the long-term sustainability of planned hydroelectric power projects must account for both current and future social and environmental conditions while mitigating risks to infrastructure, personnel and downstream communities.

In Uttarakhand, NMCG ventured into new initiatives, earlier ignored but now a part of the Namami Gange mission to make it a real comprehensive rejuvenation programme. Any possible misuse or encroachment cannot be regulated in the absence of an authentic demarcation of the flood plains. It is needed even for effectively ensuring river-sensitive city planning. Sensing the same in advance, the survey to identify the boundaries of the flood plain and its notification has been taken up. For the stretch from Haridwar to Sultanpur, floodplain has been demarcated after carrying out a detailed survey on the ground by the Irrigation Department.

Sand mining is another challenge. Using its powers as an authority under the Environment (Protection) Act, directions were issued by NMCG to local authorities in Haridwar for its ban/regulation.

Complaints are varied and numerous regarding this issue—several of which have been flagged by spiritual leaders. NMCG has set up a comprehensive study with the help of IIT Kanpur to analyse hotspots along the Ganga to develop a scientific framework. The Namami Gange mission is implementing a scientific plan for afforestation prepared by the Forest Research Institute. This covers natural, urban and agricultural riverscapes to restore traditionally rich and natural medicinal plants that contribute towards the special properties inherent in the Ganga waters. The mission is assisting in regenerating forest cover in the catchment area, and in turn, improving river flow and recharging groundwater, strengthening floodplain stability and providing natural resources including herbal, medicinal plants, fuel and fodder for the communities. Rudraksha plantation has been taken up in the mid-hills of Uttarakhand in collaboration with the Indian National Trust for Art and Cultural Heritage (INTACH). This is a form of catchment treatment, and as the trees mature, the Rudraksha beads will provide supplemental income to the villages in whose gram sabha lands the plantation is undertaken.

Mountain springs are the primary source of water for rural households in the Himalayan region. As per a rough estimate, there are nearly three million springs in the Indian Himalayan Region (IHR) which has a population of around fifty million. (Ayog 2017) Spring recharge is reported to be declining due to increased water demand, land-use change and ecological degradation. NMCG considered a study into a suitable intervention for the rejuvenation of springs and took up pilot projects to assess the impact of land use—land cover changes or impact of natural and anthropogenic precipitation variability. One such project is in the Tehri Garhwal district, conducted with the Survey of India for systematic mapping for the inventory of springs, ground-truthing and delineation of spring sheds using drone-based Light Detection and Ranging (LIDAR). This will help in the identification of different types of springs and their recharge zones and the selection of feasible sites for recharge structures and rainwater harvesting. Another project has been taken up with IIT Roorkee and other institutions in the Takoli

Gad catchment area to study such impacts and identify the frequency of structural attributes to enhance permeability, recharge zone and flow path for drying springs using isotopes and other techniques. The project also aims to develop SOPs and strengthen local water governance and participatory spring shed management.

The two projects sanctioned by NMCG are of high significance and may help in increasing flow in Ganga and its tributaries. The projects are also in line with the recommendations of the Working Group on 'Inventory and Revival of Springs in the Himalayas for Water Security' constituted by NITI Aayog.

The Uttarakhand chapter of the Namami Gange project thus prioritizes completing pollution abatement infrastructure along the Ganga and seeing the successes take shape in the form of purity of flow. At the same time, this is also a saga of several path-breaking decisions, which will have an impact on protecting the ecology and also on improving the flow of Mother Ganga. Devbhumi Uttarakhand gives hope to other states in the basin to proceed on such a challenging journey. This is a journey each one of us is responsible for and has a stake in our own survival.

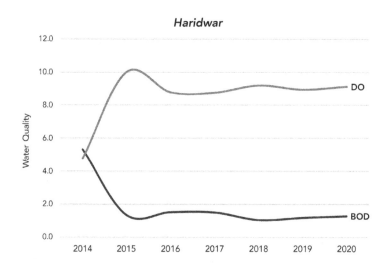

DO–Dissolved Oxygen; BOD–Biological Oxygen Demand. Increased DO and decreased BOD levels improved the health of River Ganga at Haridwar.

6

Rebuilding Kanpur for Ma Ganga

Even a few years ago, visiting Kanpur—Cawnpore as it was once called—was like a journey to hell, like travelling in a time machine to Dickensian Britain with all its filth, squalor and poverty. As you enter what was once described as the 'Manchester of India', famous for its century-old textile mills and other industries, your senses will be overwhelmed by an extremely odious smell originating from the tanneries, mixed with pollutants from other industries. It was nauseating, to say the least.

Visually too, there was no relief to be found in Uttar Pradesh's main industrial city. Mule-drawn carts carrying buffalo hides to the tanneries for treatment crossed the path; household tanneries spewing toxic pollutants openly into the drains marred the sight and women washing clothes in dirty drains with children and dogs bathing in them only added to the gloom and made the visit even more depressing.

There is absolutely no reason for things to have come to such a pass. After all, Kanpur's commercial and historical importance has been well acknowledged. It is impossible to ignore the city's crucial role in the First War of Independence of 1857 and other freedom struggles. Even today, it remains the commercial capital of Uttar Pradesh, manufacturing nearly 90 per cent of the total leather produced in the country, specializing in boots and saddles. That specialization was critical even during the nineteenth century when the city was famous for providing saddles and leather boots to English soldiers. According to historical records, the first government tannery factory began operations in 1869, and by 1880, a company known as Cooper Allen & Co. had reputedly become the world's largest leather company.

Personally, as Director General of NMCG, Kanpur holds a special place in my heart because I spent some of my best years there as a mechanical engineering student at IIT. Even today, I fondly remember those long evening walks along the banks of the Ganga with my friends, happily dissecting scientific theories and other philosophical issues. A visit to the historic town of Bithoor and its beautiful and architecturally unique ghats is still fresh in my memory. Bithoor has witnessed many important events throughout the country's history— ancient, medieval and modern. Right from the time Brahma created this world and the Brahmavrat Ghat, the Valmiki Ashram during the Ramayana period, the Sita Rasoi and the saga of Luv and Kush during Lord Rama's times, to the first battle of India's independence with heroes like Nana Saheb and Tatya Tope, all enrich the history of Bithoor in Kanpur.

When I returned to Kanpur in 2013 on official work with my team (relatively small at that time) to attend a consultative meeting to prepare the GRBMP, I could not resist the temptation of visiting my hostel room within the college campus. When I entered the hostel room, I found a young man furiously playing online games, unaware of my presence, but I was flooded with memories of my college days. My long association with the holy river and my desire to save the river had found a new meaning here. I wasted no time in pleading, cajoling and arguing with the IIT professors to complete the task as early as possible. After a gap of more than two decades, this visit was the beginning of a series of subsequent visits, some in 2014 to get the GRBMP in shape and later in connection with various projects.

My alma mater is now host to cGanga, a unique collaborative platform and repository of knowledge on the Ganga, facilitating interactions among a pool of institutions and other stakeholders, researches and documentation of learnings in dealing with the subject of river rejuvenation, a first of its kind, maintaining its tradition.

By 2018, when I re-joined this mission, the NMCG officials were fortunate to be present at the inauguration of some ghats in Kanpur and Bithoor. Some were new, while others had been renovated, like the Sarsayya Ghat by the Union Minister Nitin Gadkari and the Chief Minister of UP, Yogi Adityanath. It was also an occasion to formally launch the innovative Ganga Task Force, a battalion raised out of the ex-servicemen and deployed for Ganga rejuvenation activities such as afforestation, bank protection, conservation of water bodies, public outreach, etc.

While we had conceptualized the idea of a Ganga Task Force in 2015 as part of the Namami Gange mission, it had to weather opposition and criticism before it could be launched in the presence of the Chief Minister and the Union Minister. The force is currently deployed in Kanpur, Prayagraj and Varanasi, comprising an important stretch of the river.

Another important occasion in this regard was the laying of the foundation stone by Prime Minister Narendra Modi in 2019 for the construction of a 20 MLD state-of-the-art Common Effluent Treatment Plant (CETP) to find a lasting solution for the long-pending and vexing problem of pollution because of the tanneries in Jajmau, Kanpur. He also inaugurated the beautiful new Atal Ghat at Kanpur, which has become one of the main attractions in Kanpur. The Prime Minister also inaugurated a major sewage project in Kanpur along the Ganga. Kanpur saw another landmark event on 14 December 2019 when the Prime Minister held the first-ever historical meeting of the National Ganga Council in the city to deliberate on the progress of the Ganga rejuvenation mission and other long-term policy issues.

When I went to the helipad area to receive the Prime Minister, I noticed that all three officers waiting there were IIT Kanpur alumni: Secretary, Department of Water Resources, U.P. Singh, District Magistrate of Kanpur, Vijay Vishwas Pant and myself. It was a joyous and proud moment for all of us.

A RIVER-CENTRIC APPROACH TO PLANNING

The meeting, chaired by Prime Minister Narendra Modi, and attended by several Union ministers and chief ministers, overshot the scheduled time and was very thought-provoking, informative and interactive. It reinforced the importance of a 'Ganga-centric' approach for all departments of the concerned states and Central ministries.

The Prime Minister emphasized on the need for a 'Jan Andolan' or a people's movement led by citizens as the need of the hour to ensure a Nirmal Ganga. In the first council meeting, four major concepts of Ganga Rejuvenation emerged: a special approach to planning for river cities and preparation of Urban River Management Plan (URMP), promoting sustainable agriculture with an organic corridor along Ganga, dolphin and wetland conservation and a model for sustainable economic development called Arth Ganga that linked river conservation and livelihood generation. 'The Namami Gange mission should lead and transform into a model for sustainable economic development—Arth Ganga—to integrate people in the basin with Ganga rejuvenation. The key role here needs to be played by sectors such as agriculture, tourism, water and energy. The attempt should be made to develop it in a way, to harness 3 per cent of GDP from Arth Ganga,' the Prime Minister stated.

Underscoring the need for new thought on 'river cities', the Prime Minister argued that there is a need for the residents of those cities to ask what they can do for the rivers? 'Learning from the experience of Namami Gange, there is a need for new river-centric thinking in planning for cities on the banks of rivers; the city master plan, at present, does not adequately address this. River health needs to be mainstreamed into the urban planning process by the development of Urban River Management Plans. Cities should be responsible for rejuvenating their rivers. It has to be done not just with the regulatory mindset but also with development and facilitatory outlook,' he added.

Saving the Gangetic dolphin through a special conservation programme by NMCG and the Ministry of Environment, Forest and

Climate Change called 'Project Dolphin' was announced on 15 August 2020 in line with the Prime Minister's vision of conserving a national aquatic animal that was facing extinction on various accounts. The Prime Minister also stressed the need for organic farming, where farmers should engage in sustainable agriculture practices, including zero budget farming, planting fruit trees and building plant nurseries on the banks of the Ganga. Priority could be given to women self-help groups (SHGs) and ex-servicemen organizations for these programs.

After the meeting, the Prime Minister took a boat ride from the newly constructed Atal Ghat. Today, people use the ghat for organizing functions, including pre-wedding shoots. For youths in Kanpur, it is a major recreational spot that also binds them to the Ganga. The Prime Minister also inspected the successfully cleaned Sisamau Nala and was briefed on the efforts made to clean the Ganga in Kanpur.

THE KANPUR CHALLENGE: FIGHTING THE MONSTROUS POLLUTION OF JAJMAU AND SISAMAU

Kanpur became a symbolic site of Ganga's pollution as two monstrous causes existed here: century-old roaring drains, Sisamau nala (and several others) and toxic industrial waste from the tannery cluster at Jajmau. It is also rather intriguing that nothing effective had been done despite realizing and acknowledging the seriousness of the problem at hand. Ironically, while sewage treatment capacity had been created, poor management resulted in gross underutilization of facilities resulting in major discharge of untreated sewage into the Ganga in spite of available treatment capacity. Similarly, few attempts had been made to prevent the untreated toxic discharge from the tanneries, causing bad health for the people of the state. NMCG decided to take the bull by the horns, addressing these vexed issues comprehensively.

While the number of tanners in the city has gone down over the years, the intensity of pollution has only increased. Today, there are nearly 400 tanneries, with only 50 of them being large enough to export to other countries of the world. More than 300 of them are poor, running their tiny businesses from their houses and located in the narrow and crowded by-lanes of the old city. However, for the 400-odd tanners—both big and small—the city had only a 27 MLD STP plant, with a separate 9 MLD CETP as part of the STP, to treat the highly toxic and chemical wastes spewing out from the tanneries. This treatment plant was highly inadequate to clean the 15 MLD of untreated waste flowing out of the tanneries. Compounding the problem was the dilapidated state of the STP. Constructed during the 1980s, successive governments made little or no effort to maintain this plant. Thus, a substantial amount of toxic waste and raw sewage from the tanneries and other industries were going untreated into the river. In fact, 80 per cent of the industrial wastewater flowing into the Ganges came from Kanpur. (Print 2018) But the biggest eyesore in Uttar Pradesh's most populated city was the sight of the huge drain, Sisamau, discharging some 140 million litres a day of toxic effluents and untreated waste into the holy Ganga, apart from 15 other drains bringing in their own share of pollutants into the river.

It was a sure-fire way of killing a river through mismanagement, despite its importance to the state's economy and the high self-rejuvenating power of the river. Such was the infamous attraction of this nullah that many foreign tourists, including celebrities, would take the time for a boat ride on the river to witness from a safe distance the spectacular waterfall of untreated waste polluting the Ma Ganga—a spectacle that they could not witness anywhere else in the world.

It was not that the concerned officials at the Centre or in the state had little or no inkling about the deteriorating health of the river, which was not just from tannery effluents but also from other industries that manufactured paint, dyes, pharmaceuticals, electroplating, etc. Moreover, the near absence of a sewerage network in the city—only 20 per cent of households, around 92,000 houses—meant that much of the domestic waste was going untreated into the river. Especially alarming was the rise in the level of carcinogenic chemicals, called hexavalent chromium, from the tanneries in the river, responsible for causing lung cancer, liver failure and premature dementia. Moreover, extreme pollution was not just destroying the geology, flora, fauna of the river and the land around it but was also contaminating the crops because farmers were using water that had a deadly combination of sewage and untreated tannery wastes, which could affect the health of the nearly 3.01 million residents of Kanpur.

The reason for such indifference and apathy can be attributed to a host of factors: a lack of political will to disturb a community predominantly engaged in the tannery business because they represented a strong electoral group, lack of adequate and timely funds for the Ganga rejuvenation—30 per cent of the total funds had to come from the state exchequer—and a disjointed approach to the whole problem comprising different agencies with different mandates, sometimes working at cross purposes. It was like the left hand not knowing what the right was doing. But the biggest roadblock in the clean-up of wastes from the tanneries since the 2000s was one issue: who will pay for the construction of the new CETP? While the government wanted the tanners to pay (under the concept of 'polluter pays'), the tanners were both unwilling and unable to do so.

Under the earlier system, 40 per cent of the funding had to come from the Centre, 40 per cent from the states, and 20 per cent from the tanners. The problem was finally resolved when the NMCG decided to fund the construction of a 20 MLD CETP in that area while making some arrangements for O&M through the tanneries' association. The foundation stone for the Jajmau CETP was the hard-earned victory and milestone for NMCG because it involved a long battle with different stakeholders and different levels of government.

Puskal and I still recollect our encounter with the Jajmau tannery issue during 2012–13. Though the issue had been festering for the past few years and the Allahabad High Court was aware of this problem, it had directed the state government to develop a comprehensive DPR. The state, in turn, had approached the Central Leather Research Institute to prepare a concept note for a 50 MLD CETP for the Jajmau tannery cluster in April 2012. Later, the concept paper was submitted to NMCG on 21 May 2013 by the state. While supporting the state government in preparing the DPR, several suggestions were deliberated upon in the ministry (Namami Gange was then under the MoEF), including a study of tannery clusters in Tamil Nadu and their experience of opting for a zero liquid discharge (ZLD) approach. The Tamil Nadu model was taken up as the best solution when the NMCG was moved into a new ministry.

The NMCG gave an advance of ₹4 crore in September 2015 to the state, subject to its fulfilling certain conditions like compliance with the High Court order, adopting the ZLD approach in DPR, forming a SPV, ensuring that the O&M charges would be borne by the SPV, which had nothing to do with the Jajmau Tanneries Association. The state government was also asked to prepare and send a time-bound action plan.

The UP Jal Nigam then submitted a proposal for a 25-MLD primary treatment (only) but this was not accepted because a team of experts deemed it costly, and it did not meet the accepted norms of reduction of total dissolved solids (TDS) in the discharged sewage. Also, the proposal had not suggested any mechanism for the disposal of recovered salt.

After detailed analysis, several site visits and consultations with senior officials of various stakeholders including Central and state ministries, pollution control boards, experts and others, it was decided that a 20 MLD CETP with appropriate design and technical parameters would be adequate for the Jajmau tannery cluster. NMCG then engaged Tamil Nadu Water Investment Company to prepare a DPR for the 20 MLD ZLD-based CETP in January 2016. The technology proposed by TWIC was discussed with the Central Pollution Control Board, the Central Leather Research Institute (CLRI), and the UP Jal Nigam in February 2016, and a consensus was achieved at with certain modifications. This matter was also under consideration of the NGT, which issued an order on 13 July 2017 in the case of M.C. Mehta vs the Union of India, saying: 'The CETP for Jajmau tannery cluster should have physio-chemical treatment before the primary treatment, biological treatment and tertiary treatment (R.O. System).' (NGT, M.C. Mehta vs Union of India 2017) The NGT further added that the discharge of the treated effluent from the CETP should be subjected to dilution by the treated sewage from the STPs in Jajmau itself. 'Such diluted effluent discharged from the CETP should be recycled, reused for industrial units at Jajmau, agriculture or horticulture activity in that area or nearby areas and for cooling purpose of the power plants located in close vicinity,' the NGT contended.

The proposed DPR of TWIC for setting up a 20 MLD ZLD-based CETP at Jajmau was agreed upon by the tannery associations in the TEC meeting held by the Uttar Pradesh Pollution Control Board Lucknow, under the condition that the DPR may be modified as per NGT order. A commitment was also given that the tanneries will adopt cleaner technology to reduce the TDS load to CETP.

STARTING THE CLEAN-UP

To put an end to the uncertainty, the NMCG took the entire responsibility for financing and implementing this critical project. In June 2018, it finally sanctioned ₹554 crore and gave all the necessary clearances for the project. The project was conceptualized as a state-of-the-art solution with provisions for primary treatment for individual units, conveyance network to bring effluent from individual tanneries to CETP, complete treatment up to tertiary level, provide for chrome recovery plant, odour control and a pilot ZLD unit with polishing facility and treated sewage at Jajmau tannery cluster, Kanpur.

The Jajmau Tannery Effluent Treatment Association (JTETA), too, had committed to contribute ₹25 crore towards the implementation of CETP and ₹137 crore for the upgradation of the pre-treatment units. We also expedited the tendering process, conducted market analysis to ensure a good response, facilitated all statutory clearances, and ensured that the work was awarded. The DM of Kanpur was made chairman of the board for providing oversight and support, and representatives from the NMCG and the state were made directors on the board. The JTETA is still a work in progress, and we expect the new CETP to be completed by 2022 to rid Ma Ganga of the curse of pollution from tanneries. The project of CETP at Jajmau is complex, with technological as well as managerial challenges. It needs close monitoring and swift decisions to ensure a steady pace of work, and a special team from NMCG is addressing such challenges under the supervision of DP Mathuria, Executive Director (Technical).

The approach to facilitate and support industries to end pollution by the tanneries was also supported by stricter enforcement norms. Unauthorized capacity created by tanners were destroyed after a detailed survey, and several units were also closed till they complied with the established standards. The industries are also being supported through international agencies like Solidaridad from the Netherlands (under Indo-Dutch Ganga forum), and a centre of excellence has been established to promote greener process technology, reduce water consumption, effluent discharge and recycle, all of which are of great help to these industries. The CETPs at the adjoining tannery clusters in Banther and Unnao are also being upgraded with NMCG support.

This Jajmau experience, however, does not tell the complete story of the Kanpur clean-up. The untreated sewage flow into the Ganga needed a complete solution, and the city's STPs had to run efficiently for the CEPT in tanneries to show the desired results. But there was no early solution in sight. More shocking was the fact that the state continued to suffer despite having a large number of operational STPs, benefitting from the earlier Ganga clean-up projects like the Ganga Action Plan and the Jawaharlal Nehru National Urban Renewal Mission (JNNURM), and a few others conducted by the state government from funds sanctioned by the Centre.

In fact, a visit to Kanpur by Lok Sabha's Committee on Estimates (2016–17) on Ganga Rejuvenation found that treatment capacity of 162 MLD of domestic sewage and 9 MLD of tannery wastewater was created during 1989, 1994 and 1999 under the Ganga Action Plan I and II. However, the real tragedy was that most of these treatment plants either did not function and, even when they did, worked only at 25 to 30 per cent of their full capacity. For instance, while the Sisamau nullah was discharging 140 MLD of untreated sewage directly into the river, the STPs of Binagawan and Jajmau were treating only 55 and 65 MLD of the flow while they had installed capacities of 210 and 135 MLD, respectively.

But the excess treatment capacity turned out to be a boon for the officials of Namami Gange because they now had a rickety but ready infrastructure network to begin their arduous journey of cleaning up the entire stretch of the river and its tributaries. However, cleaning the 16-km Kanpur stretch, the most polluted portion of the river, turned out to be an extremely challenging and complex task. It not only required a multidisciplinary and integrated approach to address the problem, but it also required complete cooperation between the state administration and Central government. It also called for major technological and process innovation to ensure that the outflow from the CEPTs for treating toxic wastes from the tanneries was clean and odour-free.

UNLEASHING THE ENTIRE RANGE OF REFORMS

Moreover, given the scale and magnitude of the challenge, the NMCG was required to unleash its entire set of solutions and approaches to ensure unpolluted (nirmal) and continuous flow (aviral), ecological restoration, the construction of a city-wide sewage network to connect every house through pipes to different STPs, the conservation of ecology, biodiversity and connect people with the river. Hence, Kanpur became a crucible for testing and experimenting with all the processes and strategies in the arsenal of Namami Gange.

With the support and active participation of the state government, a comprehensive plan to rebuild Kanpur—from domestic sanitation to abatement of industrial wastes from flowing into the Ganga—began in earnest from 2014 onwards. And in doing so, the NMCG developed a detailed master plan of the city, which provided a true status and exact locations of the water bodies, drains, different kinds of encroachments on government land, and wetlands. All this information helped in rationalizing the available sewerage infrastructure for better utilization, development of new sewerage infrastructure, rehabilitation of existing infrastructure to boost industrial pollution abatement and their O&M. For better utilization of the existing STPs and to connect the core city of Kanpur with the sewer network, a 30-km-long sewer network project along with rehabilitation of old trunk sewer lines was initiated at a cost of ₹430.49 crore.

For the 92,000-odd families in the city using septic tanks to take care of their domestic sewage, the organization has deployed 15 de-sludgers, with vehicles having a capacity of three to four kilolitres per day, to carry the faecal sludge and septage to the 210 MLD treatment plant at Binagawan for co-treatment. It also took care of the recycling and reusing of treated wastewater by signing a memorandum of understanding with the Ministry of Power to provide treated water to thermal plants within a 50-km radius. Real-time water quality monitoring, redevelopment of the dilapidated ghats—nearly 20, for Kanpur-Bithoor area, including a spanking new and beautiful Atal Ghat—and crematoria, LIDAR mapping (or detailed aerial mapping of everything within a radius of 5 kilometres of the river) and wetland conservation were used to transform Kanpur.

Other measures included biodiversity conservation, small river rejuvenation (like the River Pandu rejuvenation by setting up an STP), urban river management plan, building people-river connections to take care of the current discharge of 375 MLD of untreated sewage and create enough treatment capacity for the future—460 MLD by 2035. Under the LIDAR mapping project, Kanpur and its surrounding areas have been mapped out, which will help in further planning and monitoring of different aspects of Ganga cleaning and rejuvenation. In fact, this conditional assessment of the city's requirement produced some shocking insights. Not only were most STPs functioning way below their capacity and were poorly maintained, but there was also an example of an STP (Sajari of 42 MLD, Baniyapurwa of 15 MLD), which did not even have an electrical connection—not connected to any power source—and had not functioned even for a single day. It had been created under the JNURRM initiative. Similarly, in another case, an STP had been constructed (Bhingawan of 210 MLD) without connecting it to an adequate sewerage line, making it grossly underutilized. As a result of overall city-wide monitoring, several of these could be rectified.

THE NEW STATE-OF-THE-ART STP PLANT

The NMCG is also working with reputed national institutions like the Central Leather Research Institute, National Environmental Engineering Research Institute, Indian Institute of Technology-BHU, IIT-Kanpur and Malviya National Institute of Technology and international organizations like the United Nations Industrial Development Organization and the German chemical giant, BASF, to make further innovations in technologies and processes to improve the functioning of STPs. It is also working with the National Geophysical Research Institute (NGRI), Hyderabad, to identify new aquifers from Kanpur to Kausambi.

To tap the city's biggest drain, it was decided that Sisamau, Jajmau and Bingawan would be converted into a single project, creating a pipeline of ₹30 crore. This was considered since it was not possible to shift the entire 140 MLD of untreated sewerage from Sisamau and treat it at a single STP. Secondly, the presence of an underutilized 200 STP MLD plant in Binagawan, though located on the other side of the city, helped in the making of that decision. Thus it was decided that the flow of untreated waste from Sisamau would be cut midway, taking 80 MLD to the Binagawan STP, while the rest of the 60 MLD would be diverted to Jajmau for a clean-up.

While the NMCG performed the surgical operation, cutting and connecting the discharge from Sisamau to both Bingawan and Jajmau, the O&M of 15 years of these two old STPs and associated infrastructure was assigned to one corporate concessionaire under the 'One City, One Operator' model. This model envisages bringing the entire city under one concessionaire entrusted with the task of constructing new STPs to bridge the gap in treatment capacity, rehabilitation and upgradation of old plants as required, operation and maintenance of all assets (new and old) under HAM with a performance-based approach. This approach was developed in 2018, and now we have implemented it in several cities and towns along the Ganga.

Leaving the O&M to a single operator had its advantages. First, it was a cost-saving exercise because the whole sewage load of 140 MLD was no longer required to be carried across the city to the Binagawan STP. Secondly, it resulted in higher capacity utilization of the 200-MLD plant and ensured that some spare capacity was left for future use to take care of the untreated waste coming from the yet-to-be constructed new housing societies, which would come up as population increased. The absence of spare capacity would force the next generation to dump their untreated waste into the nearby the Pandu river, a tributary of the Ganges that unites with it some 30 km downstream. Similarly, the decision to divert 60 MLD of untreated waste to Jajmau was a practical decision. That area already had a cluster of functioning STPs, a 36 MLD, a 135 MLD and even a smaller one of just 7 MLD. Most of these STPs had been created during the earlier programmes and programmes, including those by the state governments (209 MLD). Successive governments had used the sanctioned funds to construct STPs, but their O&M left much to be desired.

The rationale for an integrated approach stemmed from the fact that each of these STPs functioned independently, and was handled by different departments and engineers and was given funding from different accounts. It was important to bring all the different projects under one roof because it was no longer just about saving the river but creating a complete urban development plan by designing a new master plan.

Today, the capacity of the six existing STPs in Kanpur is 457 MLD, and the 18 MLD of waste generated from Unnao, Shuklaganj and Pankha (outside Kanpur) is also being managed by the concessionaire Shapoorji Pallonji group under the 'One City, One Operator' concept. The company is constructing a 15 MLD plant in Unnao, another 5 MLD in Shuklaganj and a 30 MLD plant in Pankha near the Pandu, thereby innovatively expanding the scope from 'One City, One operator' to a 'One Cluster, One Operator' approach. Where the organization has failed to provide the necessary sewerage network, it has decided to provide every household with a septic tank for the collection of untreated waste. This waste can be collected, aggregated and carried to the Bingawan STP for treatment by private operators. Septic tanks carry out core treatment, where the sewage is allowed to settle long enough for the solid particles to settle at the bottom while allowing the grease and oil to float on the top, and thereby making it easier to dispose of such waste.

Awarding the contract to a single entity came with its own set of challenges. First, many of the operators were reluctant to take up the project because they had no mechanical drawings or detailed plans of the STPs that had been constructed over the years. They argued that they could not be expected to repair, maintain or even to increase the capacity if they had no idea of the existing construction plan. After much coaxing (and several threats of dismissal), the state government officials were finally able to recover the documents. Unearthing the documents not only helped Shapoorji Pallonji make up their mind but also helped in the documentation of the city's various landmarks and projects, which helped the NMCG to develop a sewerage master plan for the city. The institution is now able to develop a proper sanitation plan, not just to work with piecemeal initiatives but also to go a long way in converting Kanpur into a future smart city.

'ONE CITY, ONE OPERATOR'

The 'One City, One Operator' based on HAM offered many advantages to the city and the NMCG. Since the operator had to maintain a certain quality of water throughout the 15-year concession period to receive the annuity payments, it had to take the additional responsibility of repairing, restarting and constructing new STPs. In fact, under the concession agreement, the operator had to construct a new treatment plant in the nearby cities of Unnao and Gangaghat (Shuklaganj) to maintain the purity of the river.

Today, Kanpur has a sewage treatment capacity of 400 MLD, which is enough to take care of its current needs, and all its twenty drains are completely mapped. The authorities have also realized that cleaning and rejuvenating the Ganga stretch of Kanpur means taking care of 'greater Kanpur', thereby including towns like Unnao, Shuklaganj and Bithoor in the list. The plan is to create zero discharge tanneries in the future as well.

Furthermore, a trash skinner had been earlier deployed at a strategic location in Kanpur for three years (2016–19) to cleanse the river from floating garbage. Apart from these efforts, regular cleaning of ghats in Varanasi, Bithoor, Kanpur, Prayagraj and Mathura, Vrindavan has currently been taken up. The 39 ghats in Kanpur and Bithoor are also being cleaned daily. All the 16 drains of Kanpur, which have outfall in the Ganga, have been tapped and screens ensure that floating garbage does not enter the river. Regular follow-ups have also resulted in improvements in municipal capacity utilization from 30 per cent to 80 per cent. These initiatives have led to Kanpur securing the second position in the Swachh Survey, 2020, in the category of the cleanest Ganga town.

All these measures have resulted in the improved quality of water, making even the Kanpur stretch of the river fit for bathing. For instance, an important parameter for measuring the river's health is the presence of DO in the river. That number, too, has risen significantly to more than 5 mg/litre throughout the length (2,525 km) of the river, including the Kanpur stretch. There is also a significant improvement in the biological oxygen demand standard. To ensure the quality of the river, the CPCB monitors the water through 97 manual water quality stations and 36 real-time water quality stations along the length of the river.

Today, after performing a few major surgical operations in STPs and CETPs and injecting massive doses of antibiotics into the sewerage system in the city of Kanpur, the Ganga is finally out of the ICU (intensive care unit). Now, it is up to the state governments and other implementing agencies to nurture and monitor its progress and ensure that the river and the ecosystem around it continue to thrive and grow. There are lessons for all of us here.

We should not endanger the Ganga because it has enough resilience to take care of itself if left alone. Personally, a project that is well begun is half done, and I remain supremely confident that Kanpur residents, having once tasted the benefits of a clean environment, will no longer tolerate an unhealthy and filthy Kanpur. But their real journey has just begun.

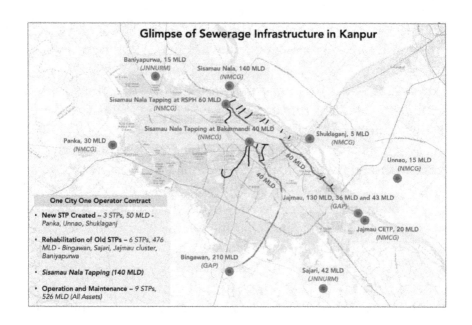

Glimpse of Sewerage Infrastructure in Kanpur

Baniyapurwa, 15 MLD
(JNNURM)

Sisamau Nala, 140 MLD
(NMCG)

Sisamau Nala Tapping at RSPH 60 MLD
(NMCG)

Sisamau Nala Tapping at Bakarmandi 40 MLD
(NMCG)

Panka, 30 MLD
(NMCG)

Shuklaganj, 5 MLD
(NMCG)

Unnao, 15 MLD
(NMCG)

60 MLD

40 MLD

Jajmau, 130 MLD, 36 MLD and 43 MLD
(GAP)

One City One Operator Contract

- **New STP Created** – 3 STPs, 50 MLD - Panka, Unnao, Shuklaganj

- **Rehabilitation of Old STPs** – 6 STPs, 476 MLD - Bingawan, Sajari, Jajmau cluster, Baniyapurwa

- **Sisamau Nala Tapping (140 MLD)**

- **Operation and Maintenance** – 9 STPs, 526 MLD (All Assets)

Jajmau CETP, 20 MLD
(NMCG)

Bingawan, 210 MLD
(GAP)

Sajari, 42 MLD
(JNNURM)

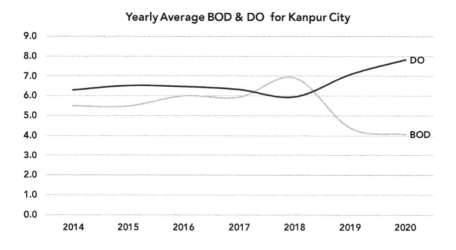

Yearly Average BOD & DO for Kanpur City

DO

BOD

2014 2015 2016 2017 2018 2019 2020

DO–Dissolved Oxygen, BOD–Biological Oxygen Demand. Increased DO and decreased BOD levels at Kanpur is a direct result of the sewage infrastructure creation and tapping of infamous Sisamau Nalla.

Source: NMCG

7

Prayagraj and World's Largest Ephemeral City

Standing on the ramparts of Prayagraj Fort in 1906, Sir Sidney Low, well-known British journalist, historian and essayist, called the sprawling human settlement of two million souls at Sangam living in tents as a 'town', although only a temporary one. Yet, he argued that as long as the event lasted, 'it is one of the world's great cities, more populous than Peking or Vienna.' He was obviously, referring to the extravagant spectacle of the great Kumbh Mela, or the 'Festival of the Urn' organized every twelfth year in the holy city of Prayagraj (earlier Allahabad). (Low 1975)

Low, however, was not the only foreign traveller fascinated, amazed and appalled by the sights and sounds of this grand congregation, which featured not only the rich and the famous with all their colours and pageantry but also throngs of beggars, destitute, half-clad sadhus and bathers lining up for a dip in the holy river. Mark Twain, celebrated American writer, humourist, entrepreneur and publisher, while touring the city in 1895, was moved to write: 'Two million of natives arrive at the fair every day. How many start and die on the road, from age, fatigue and disease and scanty nourishment, and how many die on the return, from the same causes no one knows, but the tale is great, one may say enormous. Every twelfth year is held to be a year of peculiar grace, a greatly augmented volume of pilgrims result then.' (Twain and Clemens, 2008)

The year of grace that Twain described so eloquently is the modern-day Kumbh Mela. It is a religious congregation like no other in the world. It attracts crores of devotees and millions of tourists to a vast and magnificent temporary tent city, with all its modern attendant facilities, suddenly springing up on the confluence of the shifting floodplains of the Ganga, Yamuna and the mythical Saraswati rivers. It was a 55-day-long event in 2019, but this time span can change depending on the auspicious dates of the event. But irrespective of its duration, it holds the world in thrall as they watch with disbelief the parade of holy men lining up to bathe in the river on the six 'auspicious' (holiest) days of the year. Visions of densely packed pilgrims pressing towards the riverbank, taking dips in the river and then cupping the water in hand and putting it back as an offering to the gods and the ancestors, are forever etched in one's memories. Images of flowers and oil lamps floating down the river and lighting up the river, evening aartis (a ceremony in which lights are lit and offered to gods) performed on the riverbanks by pujaris (priests) accentuate the spiritual experience of the Kumbh Mela.

Yet, this largest gathering in the world is far more than just a religious extravaganza. The audacious job of constructing a temporary, vast and complex infrastructure on 3,200 hectares of 'Kumbh City' floodplains in 2019 is a unique example of city planning and execution. Moreover, dismantling the entire city within a few weeks to return the land to the river is nothing short of an engineering marvel. The shifting floodplains cover an area of around 610 hectares between the western banks of the Ganga and northern banks of the Yamuna. This land parcel is bound by the rivers on one side and Prayagraj city on the other, starting from the Prayagraj fort in the south to the Phaphamau Bridge in the north. This part of the city is the epicentre of all activities and is home to many commercial hubs (Civil Lines, Balson crossing, Vinayak City Centre, etc.).

Perhaps a few authors or historians have described the complexity of the task better than Rahul Mehrotra and Felipe Vera in their book,

Kumbh Mela: Mapping the Ephemeral Megacity. 'How can we start to manage the rapid, unprecedented process of urbanization that aims to assemble the city in a matter of weeks, on an area that is no longer than the span between the North End and Roxbury in Boston or the northernmost extreme of Manhattan Island in New York City? How are these practical issues such as the aggregation and displacement of millions of people towards the Sangam on major bathing days, managed by the administration?' they ask.

Their question finds resonance among others too. During the monsoon season, from July to late October, the Ganga and Yamuna expand dramatically, inundating the riverbanks completely. Only when the water recedes, exposing a large sandy surface, we find ground for the temporary megacity. The shifting river floodplains and large fluctuations in the number of people attending the Kumbh make it near impossible to create a permanent layout, but given the short time frame, it presents challenges in design, planning, construction and administration. Hence, the temporary city must have extremely elastic boundaries, calling for flexible planning, leaving enough margins for last-minute changes in design.

Creating an ephemeral city requires as much, if not more, attention to detail as any permanent city. Land identification and notification, land acquisition, planning for urban services, and physical infrastructure, including tents, vending areas, public gathering spaces, spaces for cultural and social events, all become an integral part of the planning process. Similarly, allocation of identified lands to different akharas or sects and others call for rigorous, meticulous, strategic and integrated planning by all stakeholders. These include the Prayagraj Mela Authority, the Prayagraj District Administration, Prayagraj Development Authority, Prayagraj Municipal Corporation, Health Department, the Public Works Department, Electricity Department (Hydel)—all working with a mission. The active participation of the police department is also imperative to ensure the safety of the followers and to maintain law and order in the mela area.

'Unlike a more permanent city where the construction of the physical environment happens as a simultaneous aggregation of relatively permanent parts that progressively materialize this space, the Kumbh Mela,' argue Mehrotra and Vera, 'takes the form like a choreographic process of temporal urbanization, happening in coordination with environmental dynamics.' The authors underline the five stages in the development of the temporal city: planning, construction, assembly, operation and disassembly and deconstruction. 'These stages,' they argue, 'are directly linked to the makeshift context and timing determined by the presence of monsoon.' Once the world's biggest religious gathering ends (early March), the progressive dismantling of the ephemeral city has to be completed in a few weeks without polluting the river. While some of the material is either kept aside for later use, the softer organic materials are either left on the ground or are allowed to be washed away by the coming monsoon.

The logistical challenge of construction and dismantling of a city in a compressed time frame presents its own set of disadvantages. During its 2,000 years of existence, the Kumbh Mela has grown to tremendous proportions, and the supporting infrastructure has had to keep pace. For the 2013 festival, a crew of 1,700 workers constructed 18 pontoon bridges to accommodate vast numbers of pedestrians needing to cross the river. Two of the largest bridges covered a distance of 725 metres. Hence, it was only natural that the scale and size of the Mela in 2019 would increase. Thus, materials and equipment had to be procured, lugged to the venue, stored and kept handy during the monsoon season before the infrastructure frenzy began. Like any permanent city, this too would require residential tents and community centres, roads and bridges, power stations and electricity, sanitation facilities and clinics, police and fire departments, transportation and telecommunications for the convenience of locals and visitors alike.

STARTING THE PROCESS

Making arrangements for Kumbh is not something new to the governments of the day. Of course, the same is being continuously done for thousands of years. Successive governments had taken efforts in this regard and improvised the arrangements leveraging the learnings of the past. However, with the increased population, the challenges also kept growing. The Kumbha Mela in 2013 saw some focused attention from the government of the day and received accolades also but was marred with the tragic incident of stampede at the railway station.

Preparatory work for the auspicious 2019 Kumbh Mela started at Prayagraj two years ago on 21 April 2017, with the first meeting chaired by Uttar Pradesh's Chief Minister, Yogi Adityanath. Titled *Divya Kumbh, Bhavya Kumbh,* its focus was divided equally between 'setting up permanent infrastructure for the city and its people and the development of the Mela area for all irrespective of their age, gender, physical ability, nationality, caste, social-economic status.' The successful execution of such a developmental plan was to be tested at a rehearsal at the Magh Mela of 2018. It was also decided that all the major infrastructure projects should be completed by October 2018 to iron out glitches in time.

The rallying cry among the organizers under the grand vision of *Divya Kumbh, Bhavya Kumbh* was to take a pledge to make the religious congregation not just clean but also open defecation free. There was going to be zero tolerance for open defecation for the first time in the mela's centuries-old history. With the sole aim of enhancing the pilgrims' experience, the vision document focused on five key pillars to make the world's largest gathering a success. It comprised inclusion of all sections of society, improved quality of services and new cultural/spiritual experiences, an aesthetically coherent and pleasing Mela, and finally, the creation of a worthwhile legacy for future Kumbh Melas. The last pillar led to the creation of a permanent Prayagraj Mela Authority, another landmark decision, which would become a nodal agency for all future Kumbhs and would provide an implementable model.

The Mela authorities also roped in global strategy consulting firm E&Y (formerly Ernst & Young) as consultants to 'support the religious festival through innovation, technology interventions, user experience planning, process documentation and bringing in international best practices.' They were also made responsible for documentation, data collation, facilitation of collaborations and knowledge management. The advisory firm was also asked to set up a full-time Project Implementation Office (PIO) at Prayagraj to work closely with the Prayagraj Mela Authority. And, for the first time, user experience-based planning or 'human-centred design' was used as a problem-solving technique. This method uses a deep understanding of what users need, what they value, their abilities, and their limitations through what is called 'persona mapping'. Persona mapping also allows for the creation of detailed journey maps for identified end-users to the Kumbh by attributing 'personas' to them and understanding their thought process while undertaking the journey. The government, therefore, sought to deliver a once-in-a-lifetime experience on the lines of a more 'inclusive', coherent and 'visually pleasing' Kumbh for all sections of the society, integrated with 'digital' interventions, thus ensuring a lasting 'legacy', contends the Kumbh Mela 2019 report.

The new developmental model called for the reimagining of the thought behind the management of the Kumbh Mela, as well as structural changes in the organization. It led to the creation of three major committees: an overall supervision and guidance team under the chairmanship of the Minister of Urban Development, a review and sanction committee under the supervision of the Chief Secretary and an execution and evaluation committee headed by the Vice Chairman of the Prayagraj Development Authority. Moreover, six key areas were identified for action. These were swachh Kumbh, safe and secure Kumbh, city development, comprehensive movement and accessibility planning, establishing the Kumbh city, aesthetic events, community engagement, and media outreach and social media.

Yet for the Mela authorities, the key was to provide an effective waste collection and transportation system with state-of-the-art equipment, scientific liquid waste management, and adequate toilet facilities to promote Kumbh as the festival of cleanliness. 'Sanitation and waste management,' as the Administrative Report of the Prayagraj

Kumbh Mela 2019 pointed out, 'was accorded top priority to Kumbh 2019 and numerous innovative measures were adopted to ensure an open defecation free and Swachha Kumbh.' Like the previous Kumbhs, the planning process started with the creation of a grid for the 20 sectors to act as a rough layout for the whole mela. The final layout would only fructify once the details of the total number of visitors, the status of the floodplains, the number of akharas and so on assumed certain clarity. It was followed by allocating space for different akharas and infrastructural projects like the pontoon or floating bridges, residential, commercial and cultural centres, temporary roads and permanent ghats.

Statistics provides a better measure to understand the magnitude of facilities made available to the faithful during those days. The 55-day pilgrimage extends over an area of over 3,200 hectares. It began on 15 January 2019 and was expected to last till 4 March 2019 but got extended till 15 March by popular demand. The Mela witnessed a total turnout of 240 million pilgrims and visitors, another record. And during Shahi Snan or the Royal Bathing Days like Mauni Amavayasya, which are considered astrologically auspicious, the crowd taking a dip in the holy Sangam had swelled to 50 million.

Managing the Kumbh is about managing this large floating population because it puts enormous pressure on the civic system. Kumbh Mela 2019 attracted nearly 18 per cent of the Indian population and was 40 times the size of the local population. This called for the installation of 100,000 tents, 90 public accommodation camps with a capacity of 222 beds per site, five conventional centres (including a major Ganga pandal or a conventional centre that could accommodate 10,000 people at one time). It became a focal point and landmark for VIP events and seminars during the event as it boasted a grand and illuminated stage, carpeted floors, theme-designed facades, drapes and decoration with high-quality furnishings. Moreover, 1,800 luxury tents were pitched for the well-off visitors descending on the venue from different parts of the world as well as those living in India.

The city's infrastructure and beautification drive, an integral part of the Kumbh Mela plan, included the construction of nine roads over bridges (ROBs), six roads under bridges (RUBs), widening of 140 roads, laying of 444 km of temporary roads inside the mela, redrawing of several parks and the placement of aesthetically designed murals on 60 traffic junctions. The upgradation of the public transport system such as railway stations, footbridges, skywalks, underpasses, development of a Prayagraj Civil Airport in less than a year by the Airports Authority of India played a major role in the success of this grand festival. Five hundred shuttle buses, 500 e-rickshaws, 1,000 CNG auto-rickshaws, 95 parking lots (including 18 lots developed as satellite towns with special parking zones) with a capacity for over 500,000 vehicles were also built to provide a robust transportation system and last-mile connectivity to visitors and locals. To ensure a pedestrian-friendly mela, the authorities minimized the walking distance between the strategic points and put traffic and crowd management at the top of the government's to-do agenda.

The task of developing seven ghats along the riverfront as part of conservation work was undertaken by the Irrigation Department with a budget of ₹47.61 crore. The Uttar Pradesh Power Corporation (UPPCL) also spent some ₹18 crore on upgrading and strengthening existing power infrastructure and electricity systems. The UP Jal Nigam, with a budget of ₹136.10 crore, augmented the water supply system and improved the drainage and sewerage system. Around 300 km of drinking water pipeline was laid to provide a round-the-clock water supply to all the 20 sectors of the Kumbh mela from 70 borewells.

Multinational companies, like Hindustan Unilever and LG, were roped for setting up water kiosks. Similarly, the Uttar Pradesh Health Department also contributed by building a brand new 100-bed central hospital and 20-bed smaller hospitals in 11 circles of the city. They also assembled a team of 72 quick medical response teams and 25 first-aid posts throughout the Kumbh area to attend to any kind of emergencies.

These initiatives, like the upgradation and modernization of existing facilities and construction of new infrastructure, became possible only because the Prayagraj Mela Authorities were not bound by any budget constraints. The authorities had a generous budget allocation of ₹4,091.95 crore, with ₹2,706.53 crores being explicitly allotted for the Mela works. Funds were made available directly to the executing departments and were given a time frame to complete their projects and meet laid down quality standards. The Prayagraj city, too, received a shot in the arm during Kumbh 2019 because 66 per cent of the overall expenditure was spent on creating permanent infrastructures for the city and its citizens. Another 12 per cent was spent on renewable items that could be reused in the next Magh or Kumbh or elsewhere in the state, such as pontoon bridges (floating bridges), checked plates, LEDs, etc. Only 22 per cent of the expenditure was revenue expenditure, which did not result in the creation of assets.

Transforming Prayagraj into an ultra-modern city under the Prayagraj Smart City Plan saw the establishment of an Integrated Command and Control Centre (ICCC). The ICCC was not only to assist in managing operations during Kumbh 2019 but, when fully functional, would provide technological solutions to various facets of the city's administration, including monitoring security, traffic and other utilities. Similarly, the newly-built Prayagraj Civil Airport would also help put the city on the global map.

A three-pronged security strategy was implemented for the safety and security of the devotees: river security was placed directly under Jal Police, fire security under the Fire Department, and surveillance under communication. Altogether 15,386 police personnel were deployed, a much higher number than in 2013. Further, 20 anti-mine teams, 20-member bomb detection and disposal squads teams, 20 companies of PACs and 54 companies of central paramilitary forces were put on high alert.

THE SANITATION CHALLENGE

The focus of Kumbh Mela 2019 was to strengthen the city's solid waste management system following the government's diktat of a 'zero-tolerance policy for open defecations'. A campaign to clean the chronic dirty hotspots was launched, and compactors were used to remove dirt and garbage efficiently; eight hook loaders, 253 special bin lifters, 33 port stations, 75 compactors, 1,180 dustbins and 370 tippers were used to clean the Mela area as well as the city. Apart from procuring and deploying 122,500 temporary toilets for the total duration of the gathering, over 120 permanent toilets were constructed in the city using state-of-the-art construction techniques, out of which five were dedicated to female users only and called 'Pink toilets'.

Two major types of toilets were built: septic tank toilets and soak-pit toilets. The first type was installed in areas along the riverbed to be cleaned regularly through the suction process, whereas the second type was set up at some distance from the riverbed. For the first time, it was decided that mobile toilets would be rented rather than built for a sum of ₹218 crore, jointly funded by the NMCG and the government of Uttar Pradesh.

The toilets were procured under 12 packages and saw participation by 30 vendors across the country. The vendors were mandated to set up the toilets, maintain and clean them throughout the period, and finally decommission them once the religious congregation ended. Kumbh 2019 provided an ideal platform for the authorities to use digital tools like setting up the ICCC for better security, surveillance and policing, besides ensuring river and fire safety, including the use of video analytics for crowd flow management.

To ensure an efficient sewage system, the city was divided into five zones, where each zone had to build its own sewer lines, sewage pumping stations and sewage treatment plants, including the upgradation and maintenance of STP and road reinstatement. Of the five zones, sewage work in Zone F, G and Jhunsi was carried out under the public-private partnership (PPP) model. The civic work also included Interception and Diversion (I&D) of drains to the nearest STP. In all, 575 sewer lines, 32,530 home connections and 13 sewage pumping stations were created at a cost of ₹2,400 crore.

Learning from past mistakes, a decision was taken for an odour-free Kumbh for 2019. Vendors were mandated to deploy clean technology for toilet sanitation and odour removal using a non-microbial, environment-friendly advanced oxidation process, as per the United States Environmental Protection Agency (USEPA) or equivalent guidelines. Such a process was to ensure speedy odour removal within 10–15 minutes and degradation of toilet waste within 24 hours. Kumbh 2019 also saw the introduction of environment-friendly, disabled-friendly and easy to maintain prefabricated steel toilets along with the traditional FRP mobile and Kanath toilets.

To monitor on-ground work progress by the vendors, a 'Swachhta Sena' was formed, comprising sanitation workers and 'Swachhagrahis'. Septage management was ensured through round-the-clock operations, and more than 250 cesspool vehicles were deployed to transfer the sludge to STPs for treatment and further use. Garbage bins (with messages about cleanliness) were installed every 25–50 metres at different points—in vending areas, inside camps, near ghats and in circulation areas of the Mela. These bins had a liner bag with strings built on the edge so that garbage collected could easily be transported to tipper vehicles, with minimum chance of a spillover.

The solid waste management plan was comprehensively designed with three layers of operation, beginning with the primary collection, secondary collection and finally, its transportation for disposal at the Baswar Solid Waste Plant, which is operated and maintained by Municipal Corporation, Prayagraj. For street sweeping and collection of waste from all camps, institutes and the mela area, 650 groups were deployed (12 sanitation workers per group) during the entire duration. A total of 120 tipper vehicles were circulated four to eight times a day along the Mela roads. The route of the tippers was dotted with garbage bins and liner bags to collect garbage from all the 20 sites. These tipper vehicles then transferred garbage bags to 40 compactors deployed in the Mela area.

A total of 34 transfer stations were developed to facilitate secondary collection and waste transportation. All the waste collected through the trash skimmers and during the ghat cleaning was then collected and transported to the Baswar plant for further processing and handling. The plastic waste collected during the mela and post-mela was also transported to Baswar plant for further processing.

A well-orchestrated sewer network of more than 800 km of unlined drains and more than 200 km of piped drains were laid to prevent contamination of the Ganga and the groundwater. More than 250 cesspool vehicles were hired to empty the septic tanks provided with toilets located within 200 feet of the river bed. Collected septage was treated at the existing STP in the city, and temporary bio-remediation plants were set up in the Mela area. During the Kumbh Mela, septage was collected through cesspool/suction vehicles. More than 2,000 toilets in Sector 1, 2 and 3 were connected directly to the sewerage line. All the sludge collected from various sectors were transported to STPs at Rajapur, Salori and Naini, operated and maintained by Ganga Pollution Control Unit (GPCU), Prayagraj.

THE BIOREMEDIATION DRIVE

Like many other pioneering achievements of the Kumbh 2019, the NMCG too launched a new initiative—the bioremediation treatment to clean the drains as part of its overall drive to clean the river. The process uses microbes like fungi, algae or plants to degrade contaminants like oil and organic matter in the flowing sewage, converting them into carbon dioxide and water, thereby reducing health hazards and environmental pollution. The NMCG sanctioned two projects (one for 23 drains and the other for 30 drains) which would treat or clean 238.61 MLD of untreated wastewater through bioremediation at a cost of ₹105.3 crore.

The UP state government also invested ₹479.48 lakh to clean 70 drains discharging 20 MLD of wastewater into the river. These projects were executed by the UP Jal Nigam and monitored on a regular basis by the Indian Institute of Toxicology, Lucknow. These projects were bid out to eight companies, like Maple Orgtech India for five drains (10.75 MLD discharge) at a cost of ₹2.48 crore, Greenway Technologies, Ghaziabad for 16 drains (40.35 MLD discharge) at ₹1.34 crore, which would use different types of bioremediations for wastewater treatment. The largest project worth ₹48.3 crore for three drains (42.96 MLD) has been awarded to Fvil Ingeo Contractor, costing the NMCG ₹37 crore initially. All these companies were expected to clean up all the floating garbage and organic materials in the sewage and maintain the stringent standards laid down by the NMCG for biological oxygen demand (BOD), chemical oxygen demand (COD), total suspended solids (TSS), the potential of hydrogen (pH) and faecal coliform, and also to regularly monitor the quality of drain water.

During the uninstallation phase, proper disposal of sludge from the septic tanks and soak pits was planned. The pits were treated with bleaching powder and malathion, an insecticide in the family of chemicals known as organophosphates, which neutralizes the chances of flee breeding and other epidemics. The contractual arrangement also ensured that the final payment would only be made to the vendor only after the proper uninstallation of toilets following the prescribed guidelines.

THE BEAUTIFICATION DRIVE

Under the beautification drive, 29 existing parks were provided with amenities like benches, lights, toilets, nurseries and gymnasiums. While the Prayagraj Development Authority spent more than ₹20 crore on the development of 12 parks, the Municipal Corporation spent over ₹4 crore for the development of the remaining 17 parks. The Indian Railways also contributed to the city's makeover by upgrading nine railway stations and developing new platforms at Chheoki Railway Station and Prayagraj Junction. Construction of footbridges, skywalks, widening of underpasses and development of various flyovers over railways added to the sheen of the city. The railways also set up permanent shelters with amenities such as food, water, ticket counters and infotainment for pilgrims within the station.

To ensure transparency in its dealings, the Kumbh Mela authorities awarded more than 100 tenders across all domains for projects with an estimated value of more than ₹10 lakh. Previously, work on specific tracks, such as advertising, vendor zones and food stalls, were largely unregulated; specific tenders were released this time. Advertising was regulated for mela area as well as the city area, and innovative e-tendering modules were developed; each department executed innovative e-tendering modules for publicity of bidding documents and submission of vendor proposals, thus streamlining the entire procurement process.

Finally, to provide visual relief, a campaign supported by NMCG, called 'Paint My City' was launched to beautify public spaces in Prayagraj with high-quality street art projects, which would capture and depict the rich culture, history and heritage of Prayagraj with specific emphasis on the themes surrounding the Kumbh—it's mythological, religious and historical background, its scientific and astrological connotations, etc. The year-long campaign that started in April 2018, involving over 500 artists from across India, transformed the whole city into a walk-through art gallery with 1,727,528.40 sq ft of street art. The campaign also captured the country's imagination on social media by becoming one of the top trending topics in India on Twitter.

To ensure an enhanced and inclusive pilgrim experience, the Kumbh Mela 2019 saw 90 units of prefabricated steel structure tin sheds with a total accommodation capacity of approximately 20,000 pilgrims. The main purpose of the public accommodation was to ensure a dignified, secure, comfortable, clean and easily-accessible stay for pilgrims in need for temporary accommodation. This proved beneficial not only from a safety and security perspective but also from a health perspective. Further, similar structures were previously provided for in Ujjain, Nashik, Haridwar and many other melas across the country.

In keeping with the social reality of the times, 20 selfie points were identified as well. Additionally, 63 roads were beautified with 115 high mast lights and 5,000 LED lights. Some important buildings situated on prominent roads were identified, and arrangements of facade lighting were made. Landscaping was also planned for Yamuna

Bank, MG Road and Jhunsi where over 5,000 flower pots with unique combinations of flowers and plants were used to beautify prominent locations for the Mela and even for the period after that.

THE DISMANTLING PROCESS

Equally important was a clear plan and strategy for the post-Kumbh sludge and garbage disposal. In most cases, it was made the responsibility of the vendor who had initially constructed the structure. A decentralized monitoring mechanism was put in place where uninstallation in each sector was monitored by respective sector magistrates and sector sanitation in charge, and a team was also deployed by the health department. For instance, biodegradable materials such as thatch and bamboo were left to reintegrate with the site to serve as valuable agricultural land for the rest of the seasons.

Items like metals and plastics that could be effectively recycled or repurposed were kept aside for the next festival. Efforts were also made to ensure that the vendors would clear all the leftover liquid or solid waste before their last payment was released. The health department sanitation workers were on a mission to clear all debris and transport the same to the Baswar plant for further processing.

ICT-based monitoring ensured that the entire operation ran efficiently. A mobile application, customized in Hindi, was loaded on mobile devices, and a QR code was fixed and assigned to each public toilet in the Public Toilet Complex (PTC). Swachhagrahis were trained to use the mobile application and mandated to give feedback twice a day. They visited PTCs, scanned the QR code and provided feedback on each of the eight parameters of maintenance. An automated message was thus generated, which would then be passed on to the supervisor and vendor for necessary action. ICT-based solutions were deployed to monitor sanitation activities such as cleaning toilets, cleaning garbage collection areas, tracking the movement of sanitation vehicles, and monitoring sanitation workers' attendance. Each zone undertook works including laying of sewer networks, sewage pumping station (SPS) upgradation, construction of STP and road reinstatement. The work also included incision and drainage (I & D) of drains. Moreover, for work in all these five zones, 575 sewer lines, 32,530 home connections and 13 sewage pumping stations were created at a cost of ₹2,400 crore.

PERMANENT SEWERAGE INFRASTRUCTURE FOR PRESENT AND FUTURE

The management of the ephemeral city can be both aided and complicated depending on how the eternal city of Prayagraj and its sanitation is managed. Inadequate sewerage systems and treatment capacities can make a permanent dent in preparations for Kumbha Mela, etc. Prayagraj was considered anyway as a hotspot for river pollution even during Ganga Action Plan days and continued under the World Bank programme of the NMCG. It is the first city that was looked into for its complete requirement, and the entire sewerage infrastructure was funded, including sewer networks. This was a model investment in the World Bank component. Like Rome was not developed in a single day, similarly, the success of Kumbh was the result of planning and innovative interventions taken under the mission starting from 2014.

Under the Namami Gange Programme, 10 projects have been sanctioned at an estimated cost of ₹2,915.78 crore to create a total capacity of 271 MLD, of which 191 MLD has been newly constructed and 82 MLD is being rehabilitated. Through these projects, a 776-km sewerage network will also be constructed. So far, eight projects have been completed, which led to creating a sewage treatment capacity of 119 MLD and laying 763 km of sewerage network is already done in the core city. Two projects pertaining to Sewerage District C and part of Sewerage District E for 177 km of sewerage network to carry sewage to STPs at Salori, Kodra and Ponghat were inaugurated by the Prime Minister on 16 December 2019.

Tran-Ganga/Yamuna areas (namely Naini, Phaphamau and Jhusi) currently do not have any sewage treatment facility and thereby pollutes the Ganga and Yamuna. Core Prayagraj town area has been provided with a comprehensive sewerage network and sewage treatment facilities. However, these are with different operators and without long-term sustainable mechanisms for O&M. Accordingly, two projects are under progress for sewage management in the trans-Ganga/Yamuna areas and O&M of existing sewerage assets. These projects will lead to the creation of an interception and diversion network and three STPs with a total capacity of 72 MLD (Naini-42 MLD, Phaphamau-14 MLD and Jhusi-16 MLD) and O&M of all the sewerage assets for 15 years. These two projects were tendered as a single package on the 'One City, One Operator' concept for implementation on hybrid annuity-based PPP mode for the sewerage management of the town in a sustainable and accountable manner and improve governance. These would lead to the creation of a new capacity of 72 MLD, rehabilitation of 80 MLD, O&M of existing STPs of 254 MLD capacity and 10 sewage pumping stations.

PRAYAGRAJ: ITS HISTORY AND RELIGIOUS IMPORTANCE

The location of the city gives it such an iconic and godly status. In his book, *Ganga Water Machine: Designing New India's Ancient River*, Anthony Acciavatti describes the city as dangling at the tip of the Ganga-Yamuna Doab, where the lower Ganga Canal system terminates; Prayagraj overlooks the confluence of the Ganga and Yamuna rivers. While the Yamuna to the south of the city runs deep and narrow, the Ganges, to the north and east of the city, runs shallow and wide. His modern depiction of Prayagraj is no different from how India's ancient texts and scriptures have described it. For instance, the *Matsaya Purana* argues, 'Those who bathe in the bright waters of the Ganga where they meet the dark waters of the Yamuna during the month of Magh will not be born, even in thousands of years.' Similarly, the *Padma Purana Uttara Khanda* says: 'If one bathes and sips water from the Ganga, Yamuna and Saraswati meet, he enjoys liberation, and of that, there is no doubt.'

Ancient texts relate the story of the gods who sought the nectar of immortality which could be found deep in the ocean of milk. They decided to churn the ocean to bring it forth. Lord Vishnu obliged and became a tortoise; his shell became the base on which the churn could be placed. The Himalayan Mount 'Mandara' became the churning stick and the serpent 'Vasuki' became the churning rope. Yet to gain that nectar, the gods needed the help of the anti-gods, the asuras, to pull one end of the churning rope while they pulled the other. And so, they exerted themselves, each side pulling mightily until the Kumbh, the 'pot' containing the amrit emerged from the ocean. It was immediately seized by the asuras. It seemed like all was lost until Lord Vishnu took the form of an enchanting maiden named Mohini, the deluder, and beguiled the asuras into letting her hold the Kumbh. She delivered it immediately to the gods who swept it away to heaven. As they sped off with the pot, four drops of amrit fell upon the earth. According to tradition, these drops landed in the four locations where the Kumbh is celebrated. These are Prayagraj, Haridwar, Ujjain and Nasik. Each site thus hosts a mela every 12 years, in an astrologically determined, cyclic sequence that enables the Kumbh Mela to occur at approximately three-year intervals.

Ancient religious and other texts are replete with anecdotes about the importance and significance of Prayagraj in the lives of Indians. The earliest mention of Prayaga and the associated pilgrims is found in *Rigveda Parisistha*, a supplement to *Rigveda* (1,200 to 1,000 BC); the Mahabharata (400 to 300 BC) mentions a bathing pilgrimage at Prayag as a 'means of atonement' (penance) for past mistakes and guilt.' In 'Tirthayatra Parva', before the great war, the epic states, 'the one who observes firm (ethical) vows having bathed in Prayaga during Magha, O best of Bharartas, becomes spotless and reaches heaven.' Many Puranic Sanskrit texts like *Prayaga Mahatmaya* describe Prayag as a place bustling with pilgrims, priests, vendors, beggars and local citizens busy along the confluence of the river (Sangam).

The city's spiritual aspects are intertwined with its history. Perhaps the first historical description of the great mela in this region was in 643 CE, written by the Chinese Buddhist monk Hsuan Tsang, who had travelled to India to find Buddhist sacred texts. Hsuan Tsang wrote of a gathering of pilgrims to an 'age-long festival in the month of

Magh' (January-February). He explained how King Harsha displayed his generosity by giving away goods to all classes of people until he himself possessed nothing and returned to his capital wearing only a single piece of cloth. The *Narasimha Purana*, dating back to the fifth or sixth century, also gives evidence that a month-long mela was held during the Gupta period.

Sages used to come from different orders, assembling from various parts of India during the winter month of Magh. It was during the time of the Mughal Emperor Akbar that Prayag was renamed Illahabad, which later became Allahabad, and then Prayagraj. The Emperor visited the city in 1582 and asked that a fort be built at this strategic location where the two waterways converged. The fort continues to stand tall till this day, a lofty sentinel at one end of the Kumbh Mela grounds.

Historically, Prayagraj was an important commercial city as it occupied the furthest point upriver where cargo boats could dock throughout the year. However, by the end of the nineteenth century, the railways and the Grand Trunk Road (NH2) had replaced barge transportation. Prayagraj has again become important because of the Golden Quadrilateral, the highway which links Mumbai, Delhi, Kolkata and Chennai and assures that the city will continue to be a site of major urban and infrastructural development. Today, the riverfront is primarily used for agriculture and hosting religious festivals. Ever since the waterway between Ganges and Haldia (West Bengal) was declared as National Waterway No. 1, there are soaring hopes that it might again reintroduce barge transportation, reclaiming its pride of place as a commercial hub.

THE RECIPE FOR SUCCESS

The theme, Swachh Kumbh of 2019, aimed at higher standards of cleanliness and better user experiences; it required greater teamwork and close inter-agency coordination among the various agencies implementing the ephemeral religious congregations. Taking note of the previous successes and failures by interacting with senior and experienced officers deployed at the earlier melas contributed towards better planning and implementation. For instance, roles and responsibilities (including outcomes) were clearly outlined for the vendors, along with regular review meetings and informal interactions within various departments.

It was also a result of the years of effort put under the Namami Gange to complete the sewerage infrastructure projects at a city scale and keep them ready for Kumbh and supplement wherever needed through new methods like bioremediation, phytoremediation and other in-situ treatments. The river water quality has been showing the improving trend.

Meetings, training programs, workshops and an extensive contact system became the driving spirit in team building. Swachhagrahis were trained to supervise and monitor the progress of implementation in each segment of Swachh Kumbh plan. External experts were not only used to oversee the process of implementation and the monitoring of programmes but also in drawing up the tender documents, identifying the right vendors, preparing performance parameters for the assessment and assisting the authorities to monitor the implementation.

Yet, it is difficult, if not impossible, to comprehend how a nation with such a poor track record of infrastructure development could pull off such a mammoth task, and that too in such a short time frame on the shifting floodplains. Creating the world's largest temporary city with continually running water and electricity, a coherent layout of avenues and roads for 20 sectors, plus 22 pontoon bridges, 120,000 toilets, and 444 km of temporary roads for 240 million devotees is an extraordinarily difficult and complex task and needs to be seen to be believed. It is also clear that if Indians put their heart and minds into something, they can achieve the impossible. After all, a great recurring religious, social and cultural extravaganza like the Kumbh Mela is a metaphor that defines Hindu philosophy—the eternal and unending cycle of life and death through which all human beings have to pass. Something that is born must die and then be born again to die again in this world.

For Mehrotra and Vera, the most valuable lesson from the Kumbh Mela is a sense of humility.

Festival participants would say that the Kumbh festival is 'about renunciation', an idea that is embodied in its physical manifestation; no building, no road, no garden is permanent, no matter how carefully planned, arduously constructed or lovingly tended, the act of creation must necessarily be followed, even complimented by the act of letting go. 'The ground claimed from the river is only on loan; from mud, it was created, and to mud, it must return', argue Mehrotra and Vera.

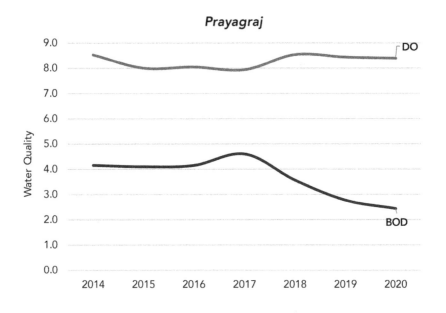

DO–Dissolved Oxygen, BOD–Biological Oxygen Demand. Improved levels of BOD and DO at Prayagraj with the continuous creation of sewage infrastructure.

8

Varanasi: The Eternal Existence with Ganga

'The Ganges front is the supreme showplace of Benares. Its tall bluffs
are solidly caked from water to summit, along a stretch of three
miles, with a splendid jumble of massive and picturesque masonry, a
bewildering and beautiful confusion of stone platforms, temples, stair-
flights, rich and stately palaces—nowhere a break, nowhere a glimpse
of the bluff itself, all the long face of it compactly walled from sight by
this crammed perspective of platforms, soaring stairways, sculptured
temples, majestic palaces, softening away into the distances; and there
is movement, motion, human life everywhere.'

—*Following the Equator* by Mark Twain

Kashi is the whole world, they say. Everything on earth that is
powerful and auspicious is here, in this microcosm. All of the sacred
places of India and all of her sacred waters are here. All the Gods
reside here, attracted by the brilliance of the City of Light (as Kashi
is known). All of the eight directions of the compass originated here,
receiving jurisdiction over the sectors of the universe. And all of
them say, for the lords of the heavenly bodies which govern time are
grounded in Kashi and have received their jurisdiction over the days
and months right here. Thus, all the organizing forces of space
and time begins here and are present here within the sacred
boundaries of Kashi.

—*Kashi Mahatmyas*, Puranas

Grasping at the significance of the most sacred and spiritual city of the Hindus is more than just trying to understand the historical evolution of a nation—its history, culture, commerce, traditions and even its deep-rooted beliefs, intellectual legacies and religious diversities. It is about experiencing the coming together of all these forces at one place to create its own unique identity. This is accomplished on the banks of India's holiest of the holy river, the Ganga. But more than her temples and ghats, silks and brocades, it is her cremation grounds (like the Manikarnika *ghat*) that hold pride of place among most Hindus.

Diana Eck, a Sanskrit scholar, biographer of the city and professor at Harvard University, argues in her book, *Banaras: the City of Light*, 'Death in Kashi is liberation—*Kashyam maranam muktih*. It is dying that unleashes the greatest holy power of Kashi, the power of bestowing liberation *moksha* or *mukti*. Death, which elsewhere is feared, here is welcomed as a long-expected guest.'

It is at these ancient temples, ghats and traditions that the famed author, Mark Twain, described, 'Varanasi is older than history, older than tradition, older even than legend, and looks twice as old as all of them put together.' Similarly, Eck, estimated that the city is older by more than 2,000 years than the metropolises founded by Muslim or British invaders—Delhi, Madras (Chennai), Bombay (Mumbai) and Calcutta (Kolkata)—and that its name survived an attempt by the Mughal emperor, Aurangzeb, to call it Muhammadabad. 'There are very few cities in the country that can rival the rich intellectual, cultural, social and ritual traditions of Varanasi,' she writes.

Varanasi is described as the 'spiritual capital of India' and the cradle of the Hindu renaissance. It was also a centre of worship for divinities and demons of the earth and the site of many lush forests and deep rivers. For over 2,500 years, it has attracted pilgrims and seekers from all over India. Sages such as Buddha, Mahavira and Shankara, had come here to preach; it has also attracted young men who came to study the Vedas with the city's great pundits. Over time, it also became an important pilgrimage site for Buddhist pilgrims.

Enduring images of a fast-flowing but serene Ganga are replete with scenes of people paying obeisance to four scores and more old temples lining its ghats, touching their steps; sadhus meditating, hundreds of people bathing, praying, chanting mantras to cleanse their bodies of its sins and to purify their souls, people scattering ashes of their near and dear ones in the river hoping that the deceased will finally achieve salvation. Then, there are the appalling sights of the destitute, widows and beggars, of untreated sewage being discharged into the river by hotels, guest houses, dilapidated buildings and temples. Moreover, discarded flowers, plastic bags, incense sticks, half-burnt wood and the occasional corpse floating down a highly-polluted river only add to the misery.

It is at Varanasi that we hear stories about the sixteenth century Mughal Emperor Akbar, who called Ganga's water 'the water of immortality' and insisted on serving it at his court. In 1615, Nicholas Withington, one of the earliest English travellers to India, wrote that water from the Ganges 'will never stink though kept never so long, neither will any worms or vernine breede theirin.' (The New Yorker 2016) Perhaps, it is this inherent belief in the self-purifying properties of holy Ganga—sometimes ascribed to the presence of sulphur springs high in the Himalayas, and the presence of bacteriophages, which can destroy bacteria in the river—that the river has been neglected for so long. But the river can never be impure, even if there is the unchecked flow of untreated sewage from households and toxic and other waste from industries; that was the belief of many Indians.

Thus, no image of Varanasi—sitting between the rivers Assi and the Varana—is complete without a picture of the majesty of the Ganga with the famous Kashi Vishwanath Temple, one of the 12 sacred centres of Shiva worship on its banks, or the Sankat Mochan Hanuman Temple, resting along with the Assi, or its various ghats with their daily aartis and numerous boats floating down the river. Hence, rejuvenating the river and saving its ecosystem requires saving the city itself, leading a clarion call to Central and state governments to take immediate action to bring alive a long-neglected river that been suffering from death pangs.

It has been a place for scholars since ancient times, such as

Mahamana Madan Mohan Malaviya's epic efforts to set up an institution like Banaras Hindu University (BHU) and his successful struggle to get an agreement with the British rulers to ensure the release of at least 1,000 cusecs of the flow of Ganga's waters at Haridwar. The academicians in the city articulated the need to rejuvenate the Ganga and return it to its pristine glory and called for immediate government intervention.

Varanasi has been blessed with academicians and professors like Veer Bhadra Mishra, a professor of hydraulic engineering and the former head of civil engineering in BHU, and a mahant of the Sankat Mochan temple. He founded the Sankat Mochan Foundation (SMF) towards cleaning Ganga, and his contribution is well recognized globally. He was also an expert member of the National Ganga River Basin Authority and raised several important issues at this apex forum for Ganga conservation. U.K. Chaudhary, a retired professor of civil engineering at BHU, is a prominent river scientist who wrote the book *The Living Similarity between the Ganga and the Human Body*. In the book, the constituents, organs, the effect of time and space on the Ganga and the human body is compared, and he says that the river should be understood as a living system. His expertise on sustainable sand mining, river morphology, medicinal properties of Ganga water and fundamental principles for the Ganga management has been relevant. Another senior expert actively working for Ganga for decades is B.D. Tripathi, a professor from BHU and who was also an expert member of the NGRBA. He is actively working on connecting people to the Ganga by training young minds as Ganga Mitras with the support of Namami Gange on the river's ethical, cultural, and ecological values. He has also campaigned for the cleaning of the river and the motivated Ganga Mitras are carrying forward this mission.

These academicians were shocked by the apathy and negligence towards India's holiest river and its tributaries, which had turned the once-healthy Assi into a nullah. They argued that unless the raw sewage flowing into the tributaries Assi and Varuna were treated first, Ganga could never be rejuvenated. Today, partnership is developing between several academics of BHU and NMCG in the complex and arduous task of cleaning the Ganga and research on 'river health' and also rejuvenation of Assi and Varuna.

However, it is in Varanasi that the 'clean Ganga' project ran into some of its roadblocks too. Even before the cleaning process could begin, ideological differences emerged. It had to be considered whether the nirmal (unpolluted flow) or the aviral (uninterrupted flow) approach would be adopted to ensure a cost-effective and efficient way of cleaning the river. The main objection to the nirmal way of cleaning the Ganga was that it was a costly, time-consuming and cumbersome process given the highly congested nature of the city. Therefore, creating a sewerage network connecting every household in the city and tapping open drains by diverting the flow of untreated waste to STP seemed like an unviable proposition. It was also argued that the 'aviral' approach—increasing the ecological flow of the river by removing all forms of barriers on its way—was a better bet. Dilution through increased water flow would reduce the damaging effects of the pollution, even though it would not eliminate the problem completely because the sewage and industrial waste had to be discharged somewhere. The biggest constraint of the 'aviral' approach is basically the need to find newer sources of water and remove all obstructions from its path.

The other big challenge was to come up with a way to carry the huge amount of sewage generated and find a dumping place so that it would not pollute the downstream stretch flowing next to the cities. Improving the natural flow of the river meant extracting less water from the river for irrigation and industrial use. Environmentalists have warned that the ecological flow would reduce in the coming years because of the adverse impacts of climate change, leading to longer dry spells and less rainfall and receding Himalayan glaciers. Moreover, it is impossible to raze the upstream dams and barrages constructed over time and were diverting the water from the river for irrigation and other purposes.

A way out of this problem, according to the BHU academicians, was to construct a big underground tunnel running under the city and the river to deposit the city's untreated waste, a few kilometres downstream into the river. They argued that the higher flow pressure would wash away the pollutants, but only a few takers were found. When the debate could not be resolved, the matter was raised at the Ganga Basin Authority meeting chaired by the then Prime Minister, Manmohan Singh. He referred the matter to a panel of experts, including professors of the IIT Delhi and asked them to prepare a feasibility report.

This expert group argued that an underground tunnel could prove to be an engineering nightmare. A thickly populated city like Varanasi, with crowded bazars, narrow lanes and by-lanes could turn out to be a major challenge and damage centuries-old temples and destroy many of the traditional but crumbling buildings of the city. Hence, that debate too was put to rest.

Another hurdle that came up while improving the ecological flow of the river (before it reaches Varanasi) was the presence of 12 dams and reservoirs like Bhimagoda barrage in Haridwar and the upstream Tehri Dam—one of the world's largest hydel dams— that were extracting huge amounts of water from the river. The Bhimagoda barrage diverts nearly 90 per cent of the leftover water from the Tehri Dam in the river to the Westerns and Eastern Ganga Canals. The last diversion of the river happens at Narora in Aligarh, where its water is used in the Narora Atomic Power Plant. Hence, after much debate, it was decided to adopt a combination of 'aviral' and 'nirmal' approach to rejuvenate the river. At Kanpur, the barrage is for abstracting water only for drinking purposes.

The concept of rejuvenation of the river defined by the IIT consortium study titled Ganga River Basin Management Plan meant restoring the wholesomeness of the river as it was years ago, when it housed not only aquatic life, various types of flora and fauna, but also carried rich alluvial soil as it descended from the mountains into the Indo-Gangetic plains. Hence, the concept of ecological and geological integrity too was incorporated in the definition of Ganga rejuvenation. While ecological integrity stood for maintaining a certain minimum flow of the river at all times, geological integrity meant maintaining the geo-morphology or the original shape of the river. A changed geo-morphology means heightened chances of flooding and a disturbance in the flow of the water. Excessive sand mining of the river had changed the river's course at many places and has been temporarily halted through various court orders.

The concept of a minimum flow was first advocated by Madan Mohan Malviya, founder of BHU, when he insisted that the British government should release at least 1,000 cusec water for Varanasi. After much deliberation, he finally managed to get his point across through an agreement in 1916. Using the agreement as a reference point, the NMCG has also ensured that little more than 1,000 cusecs of water is always available for the people of Varanasi. The government's stated policy is now to allow the unfettered flow of 1,000 cusecs, especially in three tributaries of the Ganga (Alaknanda, Bhagirathi and Mandakini) and in the main river.

Another theory propounded at a meeting of group of secretaries was the idea of vaporizing or incinerating the sewage of the city in huge burners. However, a detailed analysis of the costs and other associated construction needs failed the cost-benefit analysis test. The fuel cost alone turned out to be extremely high, not to mention the amount required to construct power plants to burn the sewage and the dangerous air pollution that it would cause. It was then decided to adopt the successfully-implemented path of building STPs and constructing a city's sewerage network.

To argue that the real rejuvenation of the river at a required scale began only in 2014—after Prime Minister Narendra Modi won a thumping majority from the Varanasi constituency—would not be wrong. It was only in November 2014, when the Prime Minister kicked off the campaign by personally wielding a broom at Assi Ghat that the mission's activities really took off. To sustain the fast pace of the cleanliness drive, both within the city and the river, the Prime Minister has been visiting the city regularly. He has also visited Kashi Vishwanath, the holiest of the holy temples, and has taken part in the Ganga aarati, blowing conch shells and chanting vedic hymns. After all, he has many electoral promises to keep, including the clean-up of the Ganga, especially in his very constituency, Varanasi.

Even before his electoral victory and becoming the Prime Minister of India, on 20 December 2013, Shri Narendra Modi had promised the assembled crowd that if the river Sabarmati could be cleaned, so could the Ganga. And if the Sabarmati could influence life in Gujarat, so could the Ganga across India. Similarly, at another election rally he said: 'After coming here, I felt neither the BJP has sent me nor I have come here on my own. I am here because Mother Ganga called me. I am like a small boy coming to my mother's lap.'

In fact, the city has always had pride of place in the minds and hearts of different prime ministers of India. The former Prime Minister Rajiv Gandhi had launched the first phase of the Ganga Action Plan (GAP) in 1986 from Varanasi on the banks of the Ganga by focusing mainly on the city's sewers and the tanneries —creating sewage management assets—but investment in ensuring its O&M got missed out. The action plan left it in the hands of state governments and local urban bodies, without ensuring adequate accountability. As Suresh Prabhu, who as union environment minister in 1998-99 had implemented phase-II of Ganga Action Plan and NRCP recalled: 'The plan was appropriately named GAP. There were so many gaps in the scheme, what's needed now is a comprehensive approach.' (Times 2014)

The failure of successive governments to accord priority to sewage treatment is evident from the rising mismatch between actual generation and its treatment capacity. While the city generates around 300 MLD of untreated waste—although many have reasons to believe that the number may be much higher—only 100 MLD was being treated. Before the Namami Gange mission was launched, the city had an old 80 MLD STP constructed under the GAP and another 20 MLD plants in different locations and many were lying underutilized. Officials of NMCG were shocked to discover that sanctioned projects, like a 140-MLD STP plant and upgradation of existing sewerage network by Japan International Cooperation Agency (JICA), a state-owned funding agency in 2009–10, had not been tendered out till 2013–14. While officials dithered, 200–250

MLD of untreated domestic and industrial waste was flowing freely into the river.

JICA had submitted a feasibility study on water quality management plan for the Ganga in 2002. There was approval from planning commission for the JICA assisted GAP-II project in the city. The project was discussed in the first EFC meeting held in December 2006 and more details from the state for the O&M recovery plan and institutional strengthening were sought. In 2007, Sankat Mochan Foundation (SMF) came into the picture when they proposed a river conservation plan at the PMO meeting to lay interceptor sewer at the ghats using costly trenchless/micro-tunnelling technology and an STP based on (advanced integrated wastewater pond systems) AIWPS technology. A technical committee was constituted to examine the proposal submitted by the SMF. Meanwhile, the Administrative Approval and Expenditure Sanction (AA&ES) was issued for the project, but the implementation of the deferred components was only to commence after the report from the technical committee arrived. Once the technical committee submitted their report, it was evident that the project was not feasible for the city of Varanasi. The committee stated the following observations: micro-tunnelling was not suitable for construction of interceptor sewer along the ghats due to serious limitations in conducting intermediate shafts along the ghats, possibility of construction of a 7-km-long interceptor sewer of 3 metres diameter either along the ghat or along the road behind the ghats on the left bank of the Ganga by tunnel boring machine may be explored but will require detailed surveys, investigations and impact analysis.

After the report, Prof. V.B. Mishra, President, SMF, expressed his willingness to undertake detailed survey investigations, preparation of feasibility report and DPR. In 2010, it was decided that a competitive bidding process would commence for the selection of a consultant/agency for this work where SMF would also be allowed to bid. Once the bidding process started, 10 firms were shortlisted, who would then be issued RFP and the PMC was appointed 23 months after the issue of AA&ES. After the work was awarded for the package 1, which was procurement and construction of relieving trunk sewer/ interceptor sewer, a request was received form the UP Jal Nigam to de-link the deferred components of JICA project from the SMF proposal.

Approval was granted by the MoEF to delink the project, as a decision on SMF proposal required the appointment of a consultant to undertake a feasibility study/DPR, which would have taken at least three years. No need for an interceptor sewer remained one of the possible outcomes of such study and even if required, the selection of agency and construction would have taken more time. So called 'Old Trunk Sewer', older than a century, is the backbone of the sewage system in Varanasi. JICA project due for completion in 2015 and other packages under implementation including a 140 MLD STP which requires conveyance of sewage from old trunk sewer got slowed down awaiting decision on SMF proposal.

The first set of projects were tendered out in 2015 by NMCG, but the major 140 MLD plant at Dinapur, Varanasi had to wait till 2016, because time was spent discussing and debating various clean-up approaches. Finally, the ₹235.5-crore project with an O&M contract of 10 years, was inaugurated by the Prime Minister Narendra Modi in November 2018. I remember my experience of meeting the Prime Minister in Varanasi when he visited the Namami Gange Pavilion. I explained the interventions under Namami Gange in the city through the Dinapur STP model. The STP, some 7 km away from the main city, is treating the sewage coming mainly from the old Kashi area, the most densely populated area of Varanasi.

This state-of-the-art Dinapur STP was designed and built by Chennai-based VA Tech Wabag, an Indian multinational that deals with the water treatment sector globally. It employs a sludge activation process, where bacteria are energized by oxygenating them through pipes, which then decomposes the organic waste in the sewage, leaving the water clean. Sewage from drains from Durgakund, Sigri and nearby areas are tapped—diverted to two sewage pumping stations in Kanaiya and the newly-inaugurated Chaukaghat—and brought to this plant for treatment. The Namami

Gange has also sanctioned ₹39.57 crore for the construction of three pumping stations in Chaukaghat, Phulwariya and Sanyal in Varanasi.

After going through various sequential steps, like primary and secondary screening, (discussed in detail in other chapter), bacterial treatment of sewage in chambers, allowing the clear water to settle in settlement tanks until the blackish water turns clear and transparent. The biochemical oxygen demand (BOD) is an index of the degree of organic pollution in water—the higher the number, the poorer is the quality of the water—and is nearly 140 mg/l when it enters the STP and is reduced to 15 mg/l when it leaves the plant. The plant, moreover, is powered by biogas, produced from the sewage sludge itself, which will significantly reduce the carbon footprint apart from lowering operational costs. The project is funded by JICA and is the first and the largest treatment plant implemented under the Namami Gange project. Fortunately, Dinapur has another 80 MLD STP plant, which takes the total sewage treatment capacity to 220 MLD, which is more than enough to meet the needs of the ghats and temples. Steps are also being taken to improve the old plant of 80 MLD at Dinapur.

There were many challenges faced during the construction of this 140 MLD Dinapur project, one of them being that the land for the STP was not procured earlier at Sathwa due to protest by the local farmers. The site was then changed due to non-availability of land at proposed location (Sathwa) and shifted to the existing campus of 80 MLD site at Dinapur leading to delays and resulting in modifications in the scheme and design of various sewerage components such as network re-routing, pipe sizes, pipe laying technology. Due to the limited land area available at the Dinapur STP, the treatment technology had to be revised to Activated Sludge Process from the UASB process, which resulted in re-design including re-routing of raw sewage pumping delivery system. The location change came with many other issues, such as the need to change the route as well. With re-routing, the number of railway crossing increased and subsequently, the cost on account of railway-leave charges also increased. For all these reasons, substantial implementation delays occurred at the start of this project.

The sewage from the old part of the city is being taken care of by the two STP plants at Dinapur. Cleaning up the newer areas of the city, the trans-Varuna area, is being handled by a 120 MLD STP plant in Goitha village on the Varanasi-Azamgarh highway. This fully automated STP plant, built by the infrastructure major, Larsen &Toubro (L&T), with its 149-km pipeline of sewage treatment network, is being connected to each and every household so that not a single drop of untreated waste enters the river. This STP was originally taken up under JNNURM scheme but NMCG has been reviewing and integrating it with overall plan for sewerage systems in Varanasi under Namami Gange.

The project, which was sanctioned for the rehabilitation of the old trunk sewer, is extremely challenging as the old trunk sewer runs through the core and congested areas of the Varanasi; on the route, there are many illegal habitations and many manholes are completely covered. Additionally, unauthorized direct connections in the old trunk sewer exist, breaking it indiscriminately at different locations, and a huge floating population and frequent religious events allow for limited working hours. According to reports of the 50,000 households of Varanasi, nearly half the households have now been connected to STPs, whose operation and maintenance will be taken care of by L&T. The drains discharging sewage into river Varuna has been capped. Thus, under the Namami Gange, an additional 260 MLD of STP has already been constructed with another 50 MLD STP under commissioning at Ramana. Along with the existing STPs, Varanasi now has a total capacity of 415 MLD—enough treatment facility to keep the Ganga clean till 2035.

However, it has not been smooth sailing all the way. After competitive bidding, the design and construction of a 50 MLD treatment plant in Ramana for the Assi was awarded to a consortium led by Essel Infra Project Limited. It was one of the first projects taken up under innovative HAM and foundation stone was laid by the Honourable Prime Minister. This project is an ideal subject to develop a management case study as this STP project was determined to prove Murphy's law correct. First the concessionaire M/S Essel Infra ran into several corporate level financial issues, not able to get support from its financer which happened to be YES Bank for this project. The NMCG team had to take it up with higher officials of the bank to see that the cash flow was continuous. Some special arrangements were made at the level of local engineers too. But, then the problem got compounded when YES Bank itself came under a cloud as one of its prominent partner Rana Kapoor got arrested. Later SBI came to the rescue of YES Bank. Fortunately the project is now completed with the NMCG team continuously finding ingenious ways of executing the project by going beyond usual call of duty. This achievement had a natural champion in Ashok Kumar Singh, Executive Director (Projects) who continued to display the same knack in many other projects. We were having more faith in 'Yphrum's law', the opposite of Murphy's law, 'Everything that can work, will work'. We would need to continue this to ensure and explain, if needed, options for O&M of STP for 15 years.

Even before bidding out the Ramana project, NMCG had approached INTACH, a non-governmental organization, for bio-remediation—bacterial treatment of the sludge— of the Assi to reduce the pollution load in the river. The idea was to start the process of the clean-up of the Ganga till a candidate was selected after the bidding process. However, the project never really took off because local authorities stopped the work, saying that the project had been sanctioned to a different company under its corporate social responsibility scheme. Today, INTACH is partnering with Namami Gange in the cultural mapping of all the districts along the Ganga, among other projects.

Statistics provide some understanding of the enormity of the task. Out of 23 drains, 20 have already been tapped and the remaining three, including those flowing into the Assi, will be tapped once the Ramana STP is completed in 2021. A total of 84 sacred ghats were entrusted to an agency for improving sanitation, cleaning and rehabilitation for three years at the cost of ₹5 crore. Repair work on 26 ghats have already been completed, including the repair of the steps leading to the river. This task is especially challenging because of the historical nature of these structures and lack of information about their foundations. Taking note of the sheer scale and the enormity of the task ahead, Namami Gange officials realized that it would be impossible for a single agency to carry out this massive task of keeping the riverfront clean and there is need for community involvement and ownership. Hence, it launched the Ganga Vihar Manch and roped in other local organizations to clean the ghats daily. Later several other community cadres such as Ganga Praharis, Ganga Mitras and NYK Ganga Doots also became active in Varanasi.

Rajesh Shukla, the leader of the Ganga Vichar Manch at Varanasi, has now become the face of Namami Gange because of his contribution to the 'Clean Ghat' mission. Even during the initial COVID-19 pandemic, he not only cleaned the ghats regularly, but also travelled from one ghat to another (on a boat) requesting people to maintain the sanctity of these places. Most of the ghats today are sporting a new look with well-known artists putting their skills to work on the walls.

Take the case of Brahma Ghat, where Lord Brahma rested after coming to Varanasi, according to mythological sources. Today, its walls are decorated with murals depicting the cultural and biological significance of the Ganga, painted by Kiran Maharajan and are titled 'Till Death'. Similarly, the walls of the Panchganga Ghat, where the saint poet Tulsidas composed the famous Vinay-Patrika, has a beautiful painting of a dolphin, titled 'Deflated' and is painted by NEVERCREW. The magnificent Alamgir Mosque, believed to be constructed by emperor Aurangzeb, showcases the rich artworks of ancient India and symbolizes unity in diversity.

To strengthen the river-temple connection, all encroachments along the way up to the Kashi Vishwanath temple have been removed so that believers can carry water from the Ganges directly to the temple, as was the practice decades ago.

Revitalizing water bodies or kunds is an important facet of Namami Gange's job profile. These kunds act as natural acquifers by storing excess water during the rainy seasons, restoring depleted groundwater levels, which can then be used during the dry seasons. The organization has already funded 10 such water bodies for rehabilitation, which will be implemented by INTACH. Incidentally, INTACH has also been tasked with the job of mapping the entire tangible and intangible heritage of Varanasi to keep alive its centuries-old traditions and legacies, where intangible heritage includes ancient artefacts, paintings, crafts and music of Varanasi lost over the years.

Other improvements along the ghats include setting up electric crematoria—an alternative to the traditional and less-efficient wood burning pyres. Then there are other smaller campaigns, such as raising public awareness about recycling flowers; directly or indirectly, tonnes of chemically-treated flowers were immersed into the Ganga every day, which are now being converted into incense sticks sold near the temple.

To increase awareness of the importance of a clean Ganga, a double-storeyed floating museum on a house boat has been set up, called Ganga Tarini. Through a film, it showcases the rich biodiversity of the river from Gangotri in Uttarakhand to Gangasagar in West Bengal. It is a pioneering initiative to inform people about the social, cultural, historical and economical aspects of the river. Ganga Tarini has been developed by the WWI in collaboration with NMCG. The house boat also has a panel that hosts messages about several threats to the river, for example, threat due to overuse and exploitation by humans, pollution from agriculture and industries, domestic sewage, and unsustainable extraction of water for irrigation. Then there is the Jalaj, a boat which moves along the ghats of Varanasi and the nearby villages, displaying and selling products prepared by the Ganga Praharis and local villagers to boost livelihood opportunities of the people living along the banks of the Ganga. Inside the boat are beauty parlours, where trained Ganga Praharis provide make-up to tourists. Trained Ganga Praharis also educate the locals and tourists about the river, its biodiversity and cleanliness. Now we have a very active wing of Ganga Task Force consisting of ex-servicemen and also Ganga Doots trained under Nehru Yuva Kendra activities under Namami Gange to reach out to youth in Ganga villages in addition to Varanasi. The District Ganga Committee at Varanasi is actively synergizing all the efforts.

As the Ganga at Varanasi tries to regain its original glory and splendour, hope floats among millions of Indians that the entire stretch of the river will be finally cleaned. After all, if the river can be rejuvenated in the most densely populated sections, other stretches too should be rejuvenated relatively easily. But its success will depend to a large extent on the support of the state governments propelled by the commitment and energy shown by the officials of the Namami Gange. Varanasi is growing fast and the city is expanding to include several rural areas.

We need to be agile and adapt to change, plan for future and continue this process. For Varanasi, the best is yet to come.

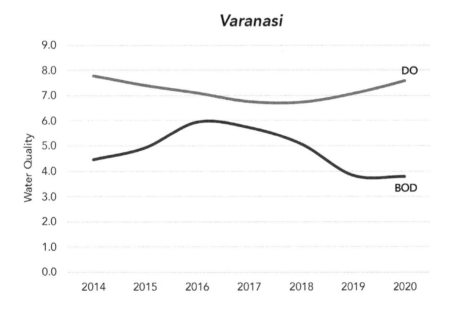

DO-Dissolved Oxygen, BOD-Biological Oxygen Demand. Significant reduction of pollution load in the Ganga at the Varanasi stretch.

9

Bihar's Ganga Redevelopment Plan: Refashioning the Citizen-River Connect

'In a land where it seldom rains, a river is as precious as gold. Water is potent; it trickles through human dreams, permeates lives, dictates agriculture, religion and warfare.'

Empires of the Indus: The Story of a River by Alice Albinia

While Alice Albinia's description of the significance of water underscores the historical description of Bihar, it misses out on another important aspect. The river system was one of the first economic transport corridors and it ushered in a bounty of nutrient-rich soil after seasonal floods. After all, 'it was the need and necessity of our times,' writes Fred Otto in *Occupying and Connecting: Thoughts on Territories and Spheres of Influence,* 'that led our ancient settlements around river systems over the ages, like most ancient civilizations of the world like Rome, Egypt and Mesopotamia.'

As the Ganga enters the floodplains of Bihar after meandering through several kilometres from Varanasi, its waters are enriched by more than two millennia-old history, culture, tradition, warfare, and also by a host of tributaries like Bagmati, Kali, Sone, etc. that add depth, volume and flow to the 400-km stretch. Such dilutions mean that the river appears cleaner than many of the other stretches of the Ganga; the sewage entering the river gets washed downstream because of the strong flow without any reduction in wastewater discharge. Such a natural phenomenon, however, has had a damaging impact on the overall ecology. The authorities in Bihar have never felt the need to stem the flow of raw sewage entering the river through domestic settlements and industrial complexes.

Personally, the Ganga stretch of Bihar is special, not just because I was born here, but also because I had my first glimpse of the majestic river in Bihar. My first sighting of the river in full spate was not really happy, because, within a couple of hours, the river had breached the embankments and flooded my house. Like in most Hindu families, I learned to revere and respect the river, but never in my wildest dreams had I expected that the responsibility to save the river would someday fall on my shoulders. It brought back childhood memories as I considered the enormity of the task at hand. But soon enough, I felt like I had returned to Ganga's folds, just like a little child.

GANGA'S JOURNEY

Although the river enters the state through the town of Chausa, it has to traverse through 20 towns and numerous districts before it can start watering the floodplains of Jharkhand, its next port of call. On its long journey through the state, it touches the shores of capital city Patna, the erstwhile famous Patliputra, cities and towns like Barh, Mokama, Begusarai, Munger, Katihar, Khagria, Bhagalpur, Kahalgoan, Pirapainti, each with its own identity, history, culture and traditions.

Mokama city, for instance, is sometimes referred to as the *tapobhumi* of Baba Chauharmal, a Dalit reformer, and Parshuram, the legendary fighter and saint. Others point to the contribution of Ramdhari Singh 'Dinkar', one of the country's foremost poets referred as Rastra Kavi, who spent his childhood near Mokama. The city is also referred to as a mini-Kolkata. But it is the town of Buxar that will always find a prominent place in the annals of Indian history because its plains are a witness to the two famous battles that changed the course of Indian history. The first was fought in 1539 AD between Sher Shah Suri and the Mughal emperor, Humayun, in nearby Chausa, and the second in 1764, when the combined forces Mir Kasim, the Nawab of Bengal, Shuja-ud-Daula, Nawab of Awadh and Shah Alam II, the Mughal emperor, took on the might of the British forces under Major Hector Munroe.

While the first battle saw the dramatic victory of Sher Shah Suri over the Mughal emperor, the second witnessed the strengthening of English forces in the country, with Major Munroe winning a stunning victory. The East India Company now secured the Diwani of Bengal, Bihar and Odisha, which not only gave them the power to collect taxes in these three provinces but also made them virtual rulers of these provinces. The Nawab of Awadh ceded Allahabad and Kora to the Mughal emperor, who began to reside at Allahabad under the protection of British troops. Those visiting Buxar can still walk through this battleground near Katkauli and see the stone memorial erected there.

Buxar also boasts of religious sites, including the famous Brameshwar Nath Temple, one amongst the few oldest shrines of Lord Shiva, and the Biharjui Temple, dedicated to Lord Krishna. Buxar is also home to the famous Ashram of Rishi Vishwamitra and Ramrekha Ghat where Lord Ram is believed to have crossed Ganga. It is also associated with Ustad Bismillah Khan, the eminent shehnai maestro, who was known for his music at the temple along with his father, Bachai Miyan in his childhood.

The town comes alive during the festival of the Chhath Puja (held twice in the months of March and November) when several activities are organized to celebrate the power of the Sun God. Then there is the famous Simaria Ghat, where Jayaprakash Narayan had spent time before launching the students' movement, which comes to life during the Kartika Mela, which has been recognized as a state fair of Bihar.

Similarly, Begusarai, once famous as the industrial capital of Bihar, was also known for being a communist stronghold (nicknamed the Leningrad of Bihar). It is also famous for being the birthplace of renowned historian, Ram Sharan Sharma. Sultanganj is a village in Bhagalpur district of Bihar, famous for two huge granite rocks in the river, one of which is crowned by a Shiva temple, the other by a mosque. People believe that it was the abode of the sage Jahnu.

MUNGER

Munger Fort is a historical site on the banks of the Ganges, which is known for its amazing architecture. With two hills, this fort is spread over an area of about 222 acres. There are many monuments as soon as you enter it, such as Shah Suja's palace, Shah's tomb, Chandisthan temple. The greenery spread here attracts the attention of the people.

The 'Bihar School of Yoga' is a prominent site in Munger on the banks of the river Ganges. It is an ideal place to learn life skills and yoga culture. Apart from the course of yoga here, physical and mental treatment is also done through yoga-kriyas. There is also a Kashtaharni Ghat in Munger on the banks of the Ganges.

It is mentioned in 'Valmiki Ramayana', according to which, Lord Rama stayed here for some time with his brother Lakshmana after killing the demonic Taraka. It is also said that when Rama was returning from Mithila to Ayodhya after marrying Sita, many of his companions went to take a bath at this Kashtaharni Ghat, literally meaning the one who removes all pain.

OF HISTORY AND ITS LEGACIES

Yet, like many other major state capitals of India, Patna or the erstwhile Patliputra, occupies pride of place in Bihar's socio-economic and political history, with a deep connection to the river. After all, it is the second-largest city in eastern India after Kolkata, with a population of 1.68 million (according to the 2011 census), with a population density of 15, 640 persons per square km and falls under the Patna Municipal Corporation (PMC) area. The city was the seat of government under successive kingdoms that dominated north-eastern India—and sometimes beyond the north between the sixth century BC and fourth century AD. It remains an important regional power today.

The name Patliputra finds a mention in the writings of Greek historian Megasthenes during the fourth century. Patna was, is and will always be a strategic riverine settlement, surrounded by the Ganges in the north, the Punpun in the south and the Son to the east, with the fourth river, the Gandak, just a little north of the city. This geography gave Patliputra an undeniable edge over rival cities, not only because it could be defended easily, but because it could control the waterway trade of the time.

It has also been the seat of learning and religion in ancient times. The first Indian university, Nalanda, was founded here, and Gautam Buddha achieved enlightenment in Bodhgaya, just a few kilometres away from Bihar's capital. The rulers of Patliputra—including the famous emperor Ashoka—actively extended their patronage to Buddhism, as well as to Jainism, another major world religion, which was born and flourished at the same time in these parts. The city's tryst with other religions was an important development during that period. Guru Gobind Singh, the tenth Sikh guru, was born in Patna in 1666 AD and endowed the capital with the Takht Harminnder Sahib, the Kangan Ghat Gurdwara as well as the Kangan Ghat situated on its bank. The city was also important for the Sufi sect, the Firdausi. Indeed, Patna today remains the gateway to major international religious centres and is a stopover for different communities of believers.

During the early medieval period, however, Patliputra began to lose its pre-eminence as political and economic power and the capital moved to Delhi because of its more strategic location. During the seventeenth century, Patna became an important trade centre. The Portuguese, Dutch, French, English and the Danes, all came to Patna due to the city's position along the major river waterways, and it became a major depot centre for Calico (cotton cloth), dye and food grains, as well as saltpetre, something which assumed great importance with the manufacturing of gunpowder. The British trader, Peter Mundy, writing in 1632, called Patna 'The greatest mart of the eastern region.' It was also a route for opium trade during the British era, a sanctuary for Gangetic dolphins and witnesses the congregation of lakhs of pilgrims at its ghats during the annual festival of Chhath (a major sun-worshipping festival in the region in early November). King Mahendra, son of Ashoka the Great, is said to have sailed to Sri Lanka to spread Buddhism from one of the ghats of the city, which is now called Mahendra or popularly Mahendru Ghat. Patna also has a locality called Mahendru Mohalla which came from Mahendrapur.

Patna fell into the hands of the East India Company after the Battle of Buxar in 1765, which marks the beginning of the British colonial period in Bihar. Patna remained an important regional trading centre as well as a gateway to Calcutta—now Kolkata—from the northwest and became the capital of Bihar Province, following the division of Bengal Province in 1911.

Since India's Independence in 1947, Patna has served as the state capital of Bihar and remains the most important city of the state. With the dwindling significance of river-borne trade and the rise of rail and road transport, Patna has now lost its importance in this respect. Its river banks, which were once teeming with activity, have become the neglected backyard of the city. Hence, a need was felt to prevent unregulated development and activity on the banks and to conserve historical landmarks, integrate the open spaces with the built areas of the city and enhance the quality of the riverine life.

THE NMCG INTERVENTION IN BIHAR

Unfortunately, little attention had been paid by the administration in the past, either for providing sewerage infrastructure in the city or for maintaining the numerous ghats or even to ensure the wholesomeness of the river as it glides past the various shores of the state. It was only with the establishment of the National Mission for Clean Ganga, under the Namami Gange project, that a gradual, holistic and continuous effort was made to improve basin management and governance of the mighty river. Under the Namami

Gange initiative, 54 projects for the development of the sewerage infrastructure, ghats and crematoria, biodiversity, afforestation was sanctioned at the cost of ₹6,245 crore, which today, are at different stages of implementation.

The need for such an intervention and for its speedy implementation was felt, keeping in mind the poor track record of the earlier initiatives like the Ganga Action Plan I and II (GAP I & II), NRCP and others. Against 700 MLD of sewage generation, only 122 MLD of treatment capacity had been created and only 64 MLD was functional even if not compliant to standards. It meant that a large part of the untreated wastewater was being released into the river leading to adverse ecological impacts. Under the Namami Gange Programme, a transformative change in the river clean-up process began with the sanctioning and construction of 30 new sewerage infrastructure projects with a treatment capacity of 632 MLD and construction of 1,753.56 km of the sewer network. These projects will increase the sewage treatment capacity of Bihar by almost 10 times. Several other important towns along the river like Buxar, Chhapra, Maner, Sonepur, Hajipur, Bakhtiyarpur, Barh, Mokama, Barahiya, Begusarai, Khagaria, Munger, Sultanganj, Bhagalpur, Naugachia and Kahalgaon have also benefitted immensely through the sanctioning and implementation of STPs.

THE BEGINNING OF THE CLEAN-UP PROCESS

Historically, the ghats have received attention from local municipalities and elected offices because of its religious importance. The attention was in the form of repairs, upgrades and the construction of a few new ghats undertaken by the tourism department and temporary setups for large-scale usage of ghats during the Chhath festival. In 2011, a joint initiative of the NGRBA, NMCG and Bihar Urban Infrastructure Development Corporation (BUIDCO), a state-owned government enterprise receiving funding from World Bank, was started. It provided a 'bureaucratic synergy' among municipal, state and Central governments, all seeking a larger vision for the riverfront on a pilot basis.

The plan also received a systematic stage-wise review by World Bank experts in its eventual implementation in 2014. The state government also brought in INTACH, Delhi, for heritage assessment and IIT Delhi for crowd-modelling simulations and a safety review of the implementation plans.

Under the NMCG platform, 34 ghats and seven crematoria were also sanctioned in Buxar, Munger, Jamalpur, Hajipur, Sonepur, Chhapra, Sultanganj, Danapur, Muzaffarpur and Gopalgaunj for ₹155 crore. Projects in Sonepur, Munger and Jamalpur have also been completed and those still in the works will be completed shortly. Additionally, several projects on afforestation, biodiversity, river surface cleaning, treatment of drains and rural sanitation (in 468 villages) for ₹338 crore have now been taken up in Bihar. A model toolkit for integrated management and rejuvenation of urban wetlands, in partnership with the School of Planning and Architecture, Delhi, (with a case study on Bhagalpur) has been developed. With help of the Ganga Prahari program, wetland conservation with community participation has also been taken up.

To address the issue of sewage pollution in Patna, a thorough assessment has been done with respect to the city profile, its master plan, the existing infrastructure and the wastewater treatment deficit. The assessment has indicated that the gap between the sewage generation versus the sewage treatment is significant and the sewerage infrastructure that was created earlier is not operational and poorly maintained.

Moreover, the rising population of Patna has significantly contributed to the rise in the flow of untreated sewage being discharged directly into the Ganga. The current sewage generation of Patna is about 230 MLD, which is projected to increase to 320 MLD by 2035. To tackle the pollution load in the Ganga from Patna, the NMCG with the state government prepared a comprehensive city-wide sewerage network scheme, which included creating new sewerage infrastructure and their O&M at a sanctioned cost of ₹3,237 crore to augment the existing facilities.

Earlier, the state capital had only four sewage treatment plants, maintained and operated by the state-owned Bihar Rajya Jal Parishad (BRJP). The total combined capacity was 109 MLD, with individual STPs contributing 45 MLD, 35 MLD, 25 MLD and 4 MLD, respectively, but these did not work to their full potential and some became defunct. The capacity available truly has been less than 60 MLD and old infrastructure needed rehabilitation and upgradation.

Under the Namami Gange mission, all six sewage zones in Patna have been covered with 11 sewerage schemes for providing a complete sewage treatment facility with 350 MLD STP along with a 1,140.3 km sewerage network to cater to the demands of the population by 2035. Two projects, Beur STP (43 MLD) and Karmalichak STP (37 MLD), were completed on 15 September 2020 and were inaugurated by Prime Minister Narendra Modi. These two projects will benefit approximately 800,000 people and will have a total sewage treatment capacity of 80 MLD.

Another new STP of 60 MLD capacity at Saidpur has also got completed and is under commissioning. For the first time, a HAM, an agreement based on a public-private partnership was launched in Bihar, which included performance-linked payments and a 15-year-long O&M contract for sewerage projects. Today, Bihar boasts of going for sewage treatment capacity of more than 10 times its earlier avatar—from 60 MLD to 620 MLD.

Under the concept of 'One City, One Operator' the development of new STPs with the existing treatment infrastructure in the city and town under HAM has been adopted. This is to improve accountability and governance with city-wide contracts, allow the integration of old and new assets for meeting better performance standards, and to produce a bigger project size attracting sound players from the market and ultimately better service.

Two large projects, Digha (100 MLD) and Kankarbagh (50 MLD), have been sanctioned under the HAM and are in progress. It is a case of an interesting evolution of developing a composite project procurement and contract document for both these projects together combining the EPC as well as HAM with sewerage networks being developed under EPC and STPs and associated assets under HAM. This is first of its kind model of project and contract management bringing the advantage of ensuring that different components get executed and completed without lag for ensuring realization of benefits at the earliest.

NMCG is also working on a model policy document for the re-use of treated wastewater for various purposes. NMCG is also working with the Ministry of Power for the reuse of wastewater in thermal power plants in accordance with the Tariff Policy 2016 of the Government of India. The Government of Bihar has already shifted its interest towards the water re-use policy and has adopted a policy that the treated water from STPs should be used for agricultural purposes.

As a part of the river surface cleaning project, a trash skimmer has been also deployed in Patna for the past four years to clean floating garbage from selected stretches of the river on a daily basis. Patna had nine open garbage dumps within a 1 km buffer of the Ganga, all of which have been closed or rehabilitated.

In addition, screens have been installed in 20 drains flowing from Patna and are regularly cleaned. The impact of the program is reflected in the improving trend of water quality, which is targeted to achieve the bathing standard. The important parameter of DO is more than 5mg/l throughout the 2,525-km-long river, including the stretch of Patna. There is also a significant improvement in the BOD standard. CPCB monitors the water quality of the Ganga through 97 manual water quality stations and 36 real-time water quality monitoring stations (RTWQMS), installed throughout the stretch of the river. Two such stations are installed in the upstream and downstream of Patna.

MAKEOVER AT THE RIVER'S EDGE

However, the NMCG team soon realized that for the long-term sustainability of the river would require more than just tapping the drains—directing the drainage waste to an STP—constructing more STPs or creating a state-wide sewerage network connecting all houses in the city. The real challenge was resurrecting the umbilical cord binding the river to its citizens. And to do that it needed to develop a state-of-the-art riverfront, which would address vital civic concerns like safety during festivals, public space, lack of facilities along with environmental awareness and work towards ecological restoration. It would also provide time and space for the visitors to learn about the sustenance and relevance of the river.

Thus, under the Patna Riverfront Urban initiative, a six-meter-wide promenade was constructed to allow citizens to walk along the shores without any obstruction, with a clear view of the majestic Ganga. Four community centres, education and recreational public buildings have also been added for the benefit of the citizens.

The importance of toilets, changing rooms, lifeguards, first-aid kits, food kiosks, way-finding and upgraded network of access streets too was not lost sight of. An article on Patna Riverfront Development by NilaA Architecture and Urban Design, which played an important role in its design, argues: 'The promenade offers the residents face time to the river and nurtures a collective civic mind towards it. It also offers respite from tight urban conditions and a renewed connection with the natural systems.' 'The Riverfront initiative,' writes Nishant Lall 'acts as a platform to preserve and mend fragmented spatial connections, enhance local potentials and create adequate open space standards for the city.'

With urban densities rising and coupled with a paucity of public places in Indian cities, the forgotten edge of the river had become a dumping ground and waste disposal zone. Hence, over the 7-km stretch of the 28 ghats, only a few like the Mahendru, Collectorate, Kali, Gandhi, Patna College, Anta and Adalat ghats are regularly used. The ghats, however, come alive during the Chhath festival every year, when more than 1 million people assemble at the riverfront to take a holy dip in the river.

The relevance and reverence for the river had also been lost because densely populated residential neighbourhoods have their back to the riverfront and use the river's edge as a dumping ground and garbage disposal zone. The riverfront comprises a thin strip of land varying from 30–50 metres (as per the local condition) and some ghats were also being used as boat jetties to transport passengers and vegetables from the larger riverine villages and plains. Throughout the project, it has been vital to preserve and augment these connections to the river—both from the city side and from the river to the city— via boats. To ease pedestrian movement during festivals, a network of loop roads and emergency access roads have been carved out of government properties.

Yet, the development of the riverfront did not come without its own set of challenges. Existing embankments, heritage structures and sewerage lines placed physical limitations on what could and could not be done in that area. Hence, a complete mapping of the area was done and those important structures were incorporated in the overall landscape design. The riverfront development was done keeping in mind the connectivity network and land availability for public parks. To enhance mobility, a smaller shuttle loop bus system has been integrated with the citywide public transit network. New programmes and facilities, such as awareness and ecology centres, viewing decks, terraces restaurants, café community centre and amenities, like seating, adequate lighting and seating arrangements, hawking zones and kiosks have all been added to make the river's edge functional and user-friendly. To make the riverfront a visual delight, artists and curators have installed public artworks all along the promenade, and a 50-seater audio-visual theatre and a small library have been constructed.

For the rejuvenation of river Ganga, conservation of its signature species, the Gangetic dolphin, is also important. Hence, the Central government announced 'Project Dolphin' (on the lines of 'Project Tiger'). This will go a long way in conserving this species with a more focused approach. The entire stretch of the Ganga, from Patna to Bhagalpur, is the habitat of dolphins and 'Project Dolphin' will involve major conservation measures in Bihar. The new-found importance for biodiversity conservation in general and dolphins in particular traces its origin in the rock edicts of Ashoka which mandates protection of dolphins with many others.

Bhagalpur, in particular, has the unique distinction of being the world's largest rescue and rehabilitation area for Garuda, which according to India mythology, is the vahana or carrier of lord Vishnu. In 2015, the Bihar government started supporting the conservation of Greater Adjutant Storks and a rescue and rehabilitation centre was set up in Bhagalpur. A temporary rescue centre has also been set up in the breeding zone where people can administer first aid to injured birds. When the birds recover, they are released into their natural habitat. Today, the endangered birds have not only staged a comeback but their number has increased from 78 to more than 500.

The state also boasts of a wetland area of international importance in Kabartal, in Begusarai district, which covers 2,620 hectares of the Indo-Gangetic plains in the northern Bihar. It is Asia's largest freshwater oxbow lake and one of the 18 wetlands within an extensive floodplain complex. It floods during the monsoon season to a depth of 1.5 metres and the absorption of floodwaters is a vital service in Bihar, a state so vulnerable to inundation. Its biodiversity includes 165 plant species and 394 animal species along with 221 species of birds. The wetland is an important stopover along the Central Asian Flyway, with 58 migratory waterbirds using it to rest and refuel. It is also a valuable site for fish biodiversity with over 50 species documented. In 2020, this wetland has been declared a Ramsar Site, first one in Bihar.

Similarly, a first-of-its-kind rehabilitation centre for freshwater turtles has been inaugurated in Bihar's Bhagalpur forest division in January 2020. The rehab centre, spread over half a hectare, will be able to shelter 500 turtles at a time. The need to build such a centre was felt after several turtles were found severely wounded and sick when rescued from smuggling operations.

In realizing that sustainable agriculture is key to ensuring both aviral (ecological flow) as well as nirmalta (purity) of Ganga, scaling up the programme for organic farming along the shores has become a part of the action plan of states and the Ministry of Agriculture and Farmers' Welfare. Organic farming will be done within 5 km on both sides of the Ganga within the district. It will be mainly done by Jeevika, a self-help group. An organic corridor is being developed under Namami Gange passing through 13 districts—from Buxar to Bhagalpur at ₹155 crore, which will assist in keeping the Ganga clean. All the self-help group members are female and carry out farming activities. Capacity-building training has been imparted to the members. The on-farm training (OTF) helps the members to take advantage of the nutrient and fertile soil of the Gangetic belts by farming strategically; they have experienced good vegetable production in the recent past. There are 234 farmers engaged on 128 acres of land who have planted 250,000 plants in the Ganga Grams as part of organic farming.

Moreover, the NMCG officials in partnership with INTACH is carrying out the cultural mapping of natural, built and intangible heritage along the main stem of the Ganga from origin to Ganga Sagar in West Bengal. Through this mapping, the cultural and built heritage of Patna and several other places along the Ganga is being documented.

An afforestation drive along the bank has also been launched based on the scientific plan prepared by the Forest Research Institute (FRI) keeping in mind the need to maintain the wholesomeness of the river. Under a massive plan, nearly 134,106 hectares have been identified for afforestation for conservation and rehabilitation of degraded forests and wastelands to increase the forest cover and also conserve wetlands that play an important role in ensuring water supply during the lean season. In Bihar, the total forestation drive spans across an area of 12,963 sq km, including four tributaries of Ghagra, Sone, Gandak and Kosi in 27 districts. Personnel from the forest department, District Ganga Committees, non-governmental organizations are participating in this massive drive.

For a state that had seen so little investment previously in terms of cleaning the Ganga, there is much to be appreciated about the holistic approach of the present. It is not just ticking the right boxes in the Ganga cleanliness drive by strengthening the STP and sewerage networks to connect with the maximum number of houses and drains but is also ensuring a river development plan that will hopefully bring back the citizen-river connection along with the urban renewal, an afforestation drive to rebuild degraded forests and fast-disappearing wetlands and a model to ensure that the need for an aviral and nirmal Ganga remains a reality even in the future. With this approach, the future of Ganga seems safe and secure.

10

Jharkhand: Small is Beautiful

We are reminded of the Prime Minister's review meeting of Namami Gange on 6 January 2015 during the early stages of the finalization of the Namami Gange Programme. While deliberating on various aspects, Jharkhand came up in the discussion and it was decided that a holistic development plan for the complete stretch of Ganga in Jharkhand may be taken up on priority. As the total length is lower compared to other states, it would be possible to fast-track the work to bring it out as a model for other states/stretches. Namami Gange was formally approved by the Union cabinet in May 2015.

In May 2016, the early days of the Namami Gange programme, Uma Bharti, Union Minister of Water Resources, River Development and Ganga Rejuvenation (now Ministry of Jal Shakti) travelled on a steamer to cross the Ganga and reach Sahibganj in Jharkhand. She, along with the chief minister of Jharkhand, was to initiate a basket of projects under Namami Gange. These projects ranged from sewage treatment plants to sewerage lines, redevelopment and construction of new ghats and making the villages open defecation free. For the first time, an entire stretch of the river had been considered for taking up projects in one go to rejuvenate Ganga. The idea was to make Jharkhand a model state in this mission. It did not matter if the stretch under consideration was only 83 km of the Sahibganj district.

It was doable and the state government was willing to go the extra mile to declare itself Ganga-compliant to say so. After all, 'small is beautiful.'

The decision to make Jharkhand a model in this programme was both an administrative and political necessity. While the Central government was sweating to make a tangible start of the Namami Gange on the ground, this was the only state under the ruling party at the Centre at that point in time. The choice was logical and also manageable keeping the limited stretch of Ganga in the state. NMCG looked forward to this as a pilot for its newly launched programme and the new methods it was coming up with.

COMING OUT OF OBLIVION

The Jharkhand connection of Ganga is not common knowledge and many of us still believe that Ganga enters West Bengal straight after leaving Bihar. Sahibganj is not so well known in Jharkhand as compared to certain other bigger places like Ranchi, Jamshedpur or Dhanbad. But Sahibganj and Rajmahal, touched by the Ganga, are of tremendous historical significance. The area has been indicated as inhabited since time immemorial by the early settlers of Rajmahal Hills, known as Malers (Mal Paharias), still residing in the hills and mentioned as Malli by Megasthenese in the third century BC. The Fort of Teliagarhi gets a mention in the travelogues of Hsuan Tsang in sixth century AD. (Jharkhand 2021)

From the thirteenth century onwards, history indicates the evolution of Teliagarhi as the main gateway for armies marching to and from Bengal. In 1538 AD Humayun and Shershah had a face-off near Teliagarhi and later in 1592, Rajmahal became the capital of Bengal under Man Singh, the trusted general of Akbar. It was only for a short while till 1608 when it was shifted to Dacca only to be regained in 1639 under Shah Shuja, the second son of Shah Jahan. As the story goes, it was at Rajmahal that the daughter of Shah Shuja was cured by Dr Gabriel Boughten, a British, earning them a farman to trade in Bengal and laying the foundations of British rule. After the Battle of Plassey in 1757, the fugitive Nawab Siraj-ud-Daula was captured at Rajmahal.

The region kept gaining prominence time and again during the British period as the site of their ongoing clashes with the Paharias and after the creation of Daman-i-Koh, meaning 'skirts of the hills' a territory directly managed by the British. This region was significant during the Santhal Rebellion led by four murmu brothers—Sidhu, Kanhu, Chand and Bhairav—from the Sahibganj district. Sahibganj was not immune from patriotic fervour and played its role in the country's struggle for freedom from 1921 onwards with Lambodar Mukherjee rousing the people with folktales and lanterns. Later the district played its role in the Salt Satyagraha and in the boycott of foreign liquor and clothes with Paharias reacting favourably to the former. The 1942 Quit India Movement also engulfed the entire Santhal Pargana division including Sahibganj.

STILL SIGNIFICANT

Both Sahibganj and Rajmahal are also subdivisions of the Sahibganj district. Apart from the villages along the course, these two are the major urban areas on the banks of the Ganges giving them the unique status of being labelled river towns. At one point, their economies had been heavily dependent on the river. The Ganges forming the northern boundary of the district enters at its north-western corner and journeys eastward up to Sakrigali where it takes a turn towards the south and forms the southern boundary of the district up to a little beyond Radhanagar in Rajmahal subdivision. The river has been a major part of the culture and economy of the town, giving it the status of a port town providing access to the water bodies in Bengal. There are ferry services across the river between Sahibganj ghat in the Sahibganj district on this side and Manihari ghat in the Katihar district on the other side and Rajmahal ghat in the Sahibganj district and Manikchak ghat in the Maldah district of West Bengal. Country boats also ply in the river.

Kanhaiyadham is a major temple for the devotees of Krishna,

now under management of ISKCON, and is a major attraction for tourists. It is believed that Bhagwan Chaitanya Mahaprabhu on his way back from Gaya after performing shraddha stayed at this place and had the darshan of baalroopa (Childform) of Bhagwan Krishna with his signature mormukut. It is also the place where Lord Krishna hid himself anguished with the gopis and was found by Radha herself. The temple has the imprints of the feet of both Radha and Krishna.

Deoghar, also known as Baidyanath Dham, is a very important pilgrimage site and is one of few places where the Jyotirlinga and the Shaktipeeth are together. This is an important site for a famous mela during shravan when seven to eight million pilgrim from all over country congregate, pick holy Ganga water from Sultangaj in Bihar, about 108 km away, carry it by way of Kaanwad Yatra and offer it to Lord Shiva at Deoghar.

The Ganga in this stretch is completely different from the one we see in relatively upper stretches. The width gained by the river after Varanasi keeps getting wider. The river flow is slightly sluggish but seeing the river in its full expanse just after rainfall is a unique experience. You might completely forget your being in the vast expanse of the water and its continuous flow, with the banks steeply cut and the huge open fields on both sides. The sunset and sunrise make for an inspiring sight capable of instilling hope and peace at the same time. Lieutenant Colonel Forrest, a British artist-traveller, has written of the water body when his fleet of boats comes upon it as 'an immense and grand expanse of water, rather resembling an island sea than a river. The opposite shore, being very low and flat, was scarcely to be distinguished; and looking up the stream, it had apparently no bounds'. (Forrest 1920)

The average width of the Ganges in this sector is about four and a half kilometres. The new bridge planned between Sahibganj and Manihari in Katihar with a projected length of 6.km will be the third longest in India after those on Brahmaputra and Dibang. The bridge will be a game changer connecting Jharkhand with the Northeast opening up new opportunities from access to the coal mines and southern part of India.

However the river poses challenges as well. It generally swells during the rainy season and inundates the lowlands lying east of the railway loop line. The meandering nature of the river is quite prominent here. The river has been drifting gradually to the north and the Sahibganj town, located on the banks, had been inching farther away from the river but after the 2021 floods the river started approaching closer to town. Being located just upstream of Farakka, the siltation in the river is a major challenge.

Moti Jharna is the most picturesque waterfall in Sahibganj district, at the head of a picturesque glen of the Rajmahal Hills where the water of a small hill stream tumbles over two ledges of rock, each 50 to 60 feet high. Not much known to the outside world as yet, it is a great place with enormous potential for tourism. A nice description of Moti Jharna has been given by Lieutenant Colonel Forrest, 'In a profound ravine of the thickly wooded mountains may be discerned from the river's bank, a beautiful cataract of water, which apparently bursting from a deep chasm, descends in a sheet of silver for some distance, and then breaking into showers od sparkling spray, has received the appropriate and beautiful appellation of "*Motee Girna*", or the "Fall of Pearls". (Mahajan 1984). It is a pity that such a beautiful spot is yet not so well known to people though they were documented so early. Namami Gange mission highlighted the spot this year in its episode of Rag Rag Mein Ganga travelogue which is likely to increase the tourism potential.

POWER OF THE MODEL

While the STP projects for both Sahibganj and Rajmahal towns had been under consideration for some time, now they were expedited. The major pollution challenge in the Ganga was addressed by approving the two STP plants of 5 and 7 MLD capacity with 53.15 km of sewerage line in Sahibganj and one STP plant of 3.5 MLD capacity with 34.21 km of sewerage line in Rajmahal. A comprehensive planning has inherent advantages, facilitating better project monitoring and more efficient resource allocation. In earlier times, many projects especially

STPs had languished because of non-availability of sewage feed in absence of sewerage lines. This was not likely to happen. Sahibganj wastewater project has been successfully completed and has been in operation since its inauguration by the Prime Minister in early 2019. Rajmahal STP project too is complete and presently under a trial run. The Sahibganj wastewater project had been delayed in the past due to uncertainty around connection for about 12,000 households and its funding. Ensuring that households are connected to sewerage systems is a prerequisite for proper functioning and capacity utilization of STPs. But, often it is not given due priority either at the level of sanction or execution at town level. The households are supposed to pay a small amount for taking such connection, which they are too happy to ignore. NMCG has been bringing the issue to focus and the state has started the house service connection work for both the projects. In Sahibganj, the connections have already been put in place and is in progress for Rajmahal.

NMCG had observed the ill effects of projects being taken up in piecemeal and hence considered many supporting projects to ensure success of major projects. To enable the State Pollution Control Board to take up pollution monitoring in an efficient manner, NMCG has supported them with a project grant of ₹9.35 crore. This will facilitate the construction of new laboratories as well as older ones and help with respect to cost of quality and manpower too. NMCG did not forget to deploy trash skimmers, the mechanized river cleaning machines, at Sahibganj too along with other cities from 2017 onwards. Sahibganj already has three manual water quality monitoring stations and two real-time stations are being set up under the programme. The data obtained so far indicates that the water quality meets the prescribed standard on both counts of BOD and DO. While the BOD ranges less than 3 mg/l the dissolved oxygen content is in excess at 5 mg/l in the entire stretch. Monitoring of faecal coliform will be the next target of the mission.

The game plan for successful river cleaning in Jharkhand is evident. It is to leverage the opportunity of comprehensive planning, effective project execution and ensuring actual utilization of the treatment capacity created. Often we miss at least one of these three aspects. At the same time, interaction of the people with the river needs to be enhanced for which the interface, i.e., ghats are to be upgraded and maintained.

But the highpoint of Namami Gange interventions in Jharkhand had been its Ganga Gram component, making all 78 villages along Ganga open defecation free improving the quality of life for 45,000 households in these villages and evolving model villages with liquid and solid waste management, afforestation and community involvement for upliftment. The initiative was further enriched under NMCG project with WII linking conservation with livelihood opportunities for the community workers trained as Ganga Praharis.

An intensive plantation drive along the river under a scientific afforestation project at a cost of ₹31.87 crore complements the rejuvenation efforts and makes it a truly comprehensive scheme. By now, more than 650,000 plantations have been completed in the district. This stretch is quite rich in biodiversity and a very good habitat for the Gangetic Dolphins, not very far from Bhagalpur, their main one. Ganga Praharis, under the project with WII, are sensitizing the local communities about their conservation. The project launched in 2016 with Jharkhand Forest Department has been quite effective with siting of dolphins, smooth coated otters and 15 species of waterbirds, four of which have been included in the endangered list of the International Union for Conservation of Nature. Central Inland Fisheries Research Institute is simultaneously working on native fishery conservation involving local fishermen. Jalaj, a boat,[16] is being used by the Ganga Praharis for livelihood support.

Jharkhand being a model state, NMCG has focused its attention on tributaries too after completing the projects for sewerage infrastructure along Ganga. A 15 MLD STP project been sanctioned

---

[16]Jalaj is a boat which moves along the Ghats of Varanasi and the nearby villages, displaying and selling products prepared by the Ganga Praharis and local villagers. It helps boost livelihood opportunities for people living along the banks of the Ganga. The trained Ganga Praharis also educate the local people and tourists regarding Ganga river, biodiversity and cleanliness.

at Phusro in Bokaro district on Damodar, a major tributary of Ganga. Similar projects at Ramgarh and Dhanbad are also being constructed.

REJUVENATING RIVER BANKS CONNECTING PEOPLE

River banks of Ganga have been connecting people with Ma Ganga since ancient times. Construction of eight ghats and one crematorium along the Sahibganj-Rajmahal stretch was sanctioned at a cost of ₹33.58 crore out of which seven ghats and one crematorium had been constructed. Development works of ghats at Bijli Ghat, Ferry Ghat and Munnilal crematoria have been completed at Sahibganj; ones at Singhi Dalan, Ferry Ghat and Madhusudan Crematoria have also been completed in Rajmahal. Further, a dedicated project for riverfront development at the famous Kanhaiyasthan, in addition to rehabilitation and development works at four older ghats and two crematoria, have also been completed.

RIVER OF THE PEOPLE

NMCG team is convinced about the need for public involvement in Ganga rejuvenation and accordingly supported the state in taking up many communication activities for the same. Much to their surprise, the initiatives of the state government and the public were far more than anticipated. The state unit not only ensured participation in the events like Ganga Utsav organized by NMCG, but also launched several other initiatives like regular cleaning of the ghats and a series of awareness activities for local communities and students including a documentary. The initiatives have been taken up not only in Sahibganj and Rajmahal but in Ramgarh, Dhanbad and Ranchi too. It was a pleasant surprise to see maximum participation from Jharkhand, with more than 100,000 people from all over the state taking part in a global online quiz, Ganga Quest, in 2021. The enthusiastic participation in Ganga Utsav from the state is also inspiring. In the most unprecedented and interesting development during Ganga Utsav 2020 from 2 to 4 November, parents named their daughters born during this period after various names of Ma Ganga and other rivers. Ganga may have its shortest stretch in Jharkhand, but its people have given it a larger space in their heart and mind. The public connect programme in Jharkhand has indeed made it a model state for all of us in other cities to come forward for Ganga's rejuvenation. The initiative might have been launched considering the government of the day, but the support received for the programme, even with change in political dimension, is phenomenal. That convinces us that Ganga as an idea is free from political changes and is truly supported by the people as a national objective. This also is a great binding force for the people. If people can join hands to achieve the ideal of a clean river in Jharkhand, why not elsewhere.

Sahibganj, literally means the land of the Sahibs, i.e., the masters, but people of Jharkhand have reacted contrary to their names; for them, Ganga is their only master. Is this the start of the culture of 'river cities'[17] that we long for?

---

[17]River Cities–Cities and civilizations grow on the banks of river but as cities grow, often rivers are lost and cities turn their bank on river. 'River Cities' need to grow together and contribute towards mutual well-being.

11

Future-proofing the West Bengal Stretch from its Enemies

Into the Ganges flow multitudes of great rivers from each side, which gives it matchless inland navigation. It receives in the course through the plains eleven rivers, some of which are equal to the size of Rhine and none lesser than the Thames; it maintains 30,000 boatmen, by their carriage of salt and food for ten million people in Bengal and its dependencies, which occasions a vast expenditure; add to this the exports and imports, the common interchange off diverse articles within its limits, its fisheries, and its travellers, which do all together occasion an expenditure of two million of money.

Thomas Pennant, *Volume II, Indian Zoology, 1798*

West Bengal's rise and fall as India's premier riverine trading hub and its changing fortune mirrors the ebb and flow of the continuously shifting and course-changing nature of the Ganga as it traverses some 2,525 km from its origin to the Bay of Bengal, dispensing its gratuitous bounty to some and wrecking devastation on others. Kolkata port's history is like the ebb and flow of Ganges, a pattern of rise and fall and perhaps, regrowth again.

The shipbuilding industry is witnessing a revolution in technology. Ships larger than the ones built in the twentieth century with greater and deeper draughts have started to dominate the maritime trade. The once all-powerful Kolkata Port has lost its preeminent position to newbies like Paradeep Port and others. Large sea-going vessels require a draft of more than eight metres to approach the inland port at Kolkata and to move up the Bhagirathi-Hugli estuary during the high tide, which the Kolkata Port cannot provide. Yet, the river remains and will continue to remain important, for every city, town, district village through which it passes and for the people fortunate enough to live on its banks.

The highly-populated state of West Bengal with as many as 40 towns on its banks is no different. Even today, Kolkata (earlier Calcutta) remains the main port not only for Bengal, for India's north-eastern states and also for the independent Himalayan nations of Nepal and Bhutan. And nobody can deny the historical, cultural, religious and academic importance that made it the jewel in the crown of the British Empire, the then capital of India.

Tagging a city with a name for its relative importance has always been the job of historians and writers. Hence, if the city of Kanpur is all about the industry and its polluting tanneries, Benaras is all about religion and the ceremonies of death. Calcutta, some 232 km from the sea, is all about trade and business. Its claim to fame as a top-notch trading hub even finds a mention in ancient texts, modern literature, travelogues and biographies.

Records show that even during the time of Lord Buddha in the fifth century BC, sea-going vessels were loaded with merchandise brought from Benaras, and later from Patliputra (now Patna) and Champa (now Bhagalpur), all three cities on the Ganges in Calcutta, which then travelled to the mouth of the river. Even the *Arthashastra*, a manual on statecraft of the Mauryan era, talks of a superintendent of ships responsible for ports and navigation and trade taxes.

A SHORT HISTORY OF THE PORT

Modern history traces the growth and importance of Bengal, and particularly that of the Kolkata Port, from the sixteenth century when

European merchants visited the city and made Satgaon, located on the eastern bank of Saraswati, a distributary of Bhagirathi-Hugli, the most important trading centre. During the sixteenth and seventeenth centuries, the river was the gateway and playground for many competing European nations: France, Portugal and Holland, till the British government stamped its authority on the city.

But it was no walk in the park, as the East India Company had to struggle and negotiate for years before the Mughal emperor Aurangzeb acceded to their demand. He granted a tax-free trading license to Job Charnock, an agent of East India Company, in 1690, which allowed British ships to travel all the way up to the River Hooghly, one of the biggest tributaries of the Ganga. (Britannica, Job Charnock 2021)

However, it was the victory of the British forces under Lord Clive over the combined forces of the Nawab of Bengal Siraj Ud-Daulah and the French troops at the Battle of Plassey on 23 June 1757 that ensured the complete British domination over the Bengal Presidency. (Britannica, Battle of Plassey Indian history [1757] 2021)

The Kolkata Port provided a large and protected anchorage where scores of ships could shelter simultaneously or load and unload cargo. In fact, from 1750 onwards, about half of India's sea-borne trade—boosted by the export of tea and jute in the early nineteenth century—passed through Kolkata and its hinterland, which extended across North India as far as Punjab in the West.

As the march of the industrial revolution picked up pace in Britain so did the importance of the Kolkata Port and the face of Bengal. The factories and mills for jute, paper, leather and engineering products developed along both the banks of the river Hugli. The riverfront reflected how the agrarian world changed into an industrial landscape.

The hinterlands of the port at Kolkata kept growing to a size larger than the combined geographical area of England and France. Soon, Kolkata became the capital and the great port of British India, serving not only the immediate hinterland—the fertile delta region of Bengal—but the whole of the part of the northern area of the subcontinent through which the Ganga flows and deposits its silt.

Moreover, Kolkata became a crucial part of the British and its allies during the two World Wars. According to reports, in World War I (1914-18), no fewer than one million Indians fought with the British and 70,000 died.

There is more to West Bengal than just the Kolkata Port. It is a land of many rivers, which covers an area of about 88,752 sq km and is home to more than 90 million (as per the census of 2011). The Ganga divides the state into two unequal hubs: the north and south, which is then divided into 20 districts with seven districts in north Bengal and the remaining 13 districts in south Bengal.

West Bengal is the only state in India that extends from the Himalayas in the north to the Bay of Bengal in the south. It offers wide topographic diversity and an intricate drainage network of 29 basins. Moreover, the rivers of West Bengal have been divided into five groups: the rivers of North Bengal, the Ganga-Padma system, the Bhagirathi- Jalangi-Churni system, the western tributaries to Bhagirathi and the tidal creeks of Sundarbans.

LAMENTING THE DEATH OF RIVERS, TRIBUTARIES AND WATER BODIES

Unfortunately, many experts lament the death of many rivers, tributaries and water bodies in the past 100 years. Anup Halder, a researcher on the rivers and other water bodies of Bengal is quoted in the newspaper *The Telegraph* of 22 June 2019, saying: 'But in the past 100 years, nearly 700 rivers have died in the delta of the Ganges (in Bengal), and the Padma and the Meghna (in Bangladesh). In Bengal, we have lost many tributaries and distributaries flowing eastwards of the Hooghly. Even those that are alive are on the verge of death because of human intervention.'

Reckless extraction of water damages the aquifers (an underground layer of water-bearing permeable rock), mobilizes minerals deposited deep inside the earth and leads to contamination of drinking water with arsenic, fluorides, chlorides and other harmful chemicals. Rivers on their deathbed include Icchamati, Churni, Jamuna, Lavanyamati,

Suvaramati, Kodalia, Samara, etc., and those declared dead are Morali, Hanger Bachko, Kanaganga, Saraswati, Kunti and Nunia, among many others.

The Ganga is obviously the most significant river in the state. It enters West Bengal along the Rajmahal hill of Jharkhand and flows about 80 km down to Farakka where a mighty barrage tames the river. The barrage was dedicated to the nation in 1975 to resuscitate the navigational status of the port of Kolkata by inducing 40,000 cusecs of water into the Bhagirathi-Hugli River. The Ganga flows about 102 km between Farakka and Jalangi and delineates the Indo-Bangladesh border. However, the perpetually changing course of the river between Rajmahal and Jalangi has led to undesirable conflicts between Jharkhand and West Bengal.

Apart from the 2.64-km-long Farakka Barrage, other major interventions include construction of the flood control embankments, bank revetment with boulders, construction of spurs to deflect raging currents and others. But most of these bank protection works have not yielded results. Hence, the mighty Ganga devastates its banks and causes innumerable damages to human settlements.

THE POLLUTION CHALLENGE

The Hooghly or Kati-Ganga flows south for about 260 km into the Bay of Bengal through a heavily industrialized area with more than half of West Bengal's population. West Bengal treats only 49 per cent of the wastewater before dumping its waste into the Ganga, says a recent assessment report on the pollution in the river prepared by the CPCB.

The current dismal state of the river, lacking in depth and flow because of the damming of the main river in the upper reaches of the Ganga, is no reflection of its illustrious past. As Dr Robert Ivermee, who teaches at SOAS University of London and the Catholic University of Paris, writes in *Hooghly: The Global History of a River*, 'There was a time, however, when the Hooghly was a waterway of truly global significance, attracting merchants, missionaries, statesmen, soldiers, labourers, and others from Asia, Europe and elsewhere.' In fact, as a major artery between lower and upper Bengal, it facilitated travel and communication between the coast and inland areas, and with its tributaries and distributaries, connected the Mughal heartland of Hindustan, linking northern and eastern India with territories across the Indian Ocean and beyond.

From the sixteenth to the twentieth century, the Hooghly attracted the attention of the Portuguese, Mughal, Dutch, British, French and Danish governments and the river was integrated into networks of encounter and exchange, spanning different cultures and regions, institutions and ideas of these different players. Its incorporation into the global networks meant that it witnessed improvements in navigation that facilitated travel between Europe and India, practices of European trading companies through which Bengal was integrated into the global economy; from the military revolution that underpinned European expansion, to the intellectual currents that sustained colonial rule, it was witness to great change.

That golden era of global importance is long gone; today that same poor river is fighting for its life. The pollution control board study has thrown some light on the inefficiency of STPs in West Bengal, which generates 1,311 MLD of wastewater. While the thirty-four STPs in the state have a total installed capacity of 457 MLD, their actual utilization is only 214 MLD, which means that 51 per cent of the total untreated waste goes directly into the river. Of 1,311 MLD of wastewater, 47 per cent is generated by Kolkata alone.

There are 351 polluted stretches identified by the CPCB in the country, four alone are from Ganga main stem. A total of 351 polluted stretches of rivers in the country, as selected by CPCB based upon BOD data from 2016-17, were prioritized in 2018 in category I to V—category I being most polluted or critical and V, least polluted. The stretch from Tribeni to Diamond Harbour is one such stretch that now comes under Category V, but was in priority III in 2018.

Yet, the BOD—the amount of oxygen required by the bacteria and other microorganisms to break down organic matter and make the water pure—along the stretch in the state is higher than the standard criteria, even though it is decreasing, signifying an improvement in the health of the river on that stretch. However, since the pollution load of the river was less due to higher flow from the tributaries, it does not imply that all is well within the state. Hence, a lot more work needs to be done to rejuvenate the river in the future. Moreover, it is important to realize the critical role of a clean Ganga and of maintaining the minimum ecological flow in saving the Sundarbans.

SOLUTIONS IN EACH TOWN

Cleaning the Ganga along the West Bengal stretch is challenging because of the presence of many towns or urbanized areas along its banks—settlements that deposit both toxic industrial pollution and domestic waste into the river. Several of these are quite in contiguity of each other, making it even more difficult as the river does not get much space to recover from one town to the other. A study by the NMCG predicts that the total domestic waste output, which was nearly 1,432 MLD in 2016, will increase to around 1,638.1 MLD by 2035. Thus, there is a need to design a comprehensive plan for West Bengal to reduce municipal, industrial and agricultural waste from being dumped into the river.

Hence, the NMCG has set an ambitious target for the West Bengal stretch of the Ganga. It plans to set up 22 projects worth ₹3,789.71 crore and create 864.67 MLD of STPs. Its agenda includes the renovation of 24 old projects worth ₹204.39 crore and the construction of four new projects at ₹16.77 crore comprising nine ghats and three crematoria. Moreover, under the Clean Ganga Fund, a project worth ₹7 crore has been sanctioned for cleaning up seven ghats.

There is also a plan for a bioremediation project of ₹3.11 crore and three afforestation programmes totalling ₹29.73 crore. In fact, as of 10 February 2021, the total number of projects was increased to 23 for ₹3,811.63 crore.

TAKING THE CLUSTER APPROACH

While sanctioning the projects, the need, urgency and future demand of various towns along the banks of the Hooghly was kept in mind. One of the biggest projects is the construction of a 165 MLD STP plant by the Chennai-based global water major, VA Tech Wabag. It includes interception and diversions of existing drains and construction of new STPs. The project, awarded under the HAM will take care of the sewage disposal needs of the four adjoining towns of Howrah, Bally, Baranagar and Kamarbati, part of the most polluted stretch of the Hooghly. The concession agreement was signed for ₹596 crore and later financial closure for the project was also achieved in 2021.

According to NMCG, Howrah alone produced nearly 135.7 MLD of untreated sewage, followed by Kamarhati with 39.7 MLD, Bally with 33.7 MLD and Baranagar with 28.9 MLD in 2016 leading to a total domestic sewage discharge of 238 MLD. That number is likely to touch 276.1 MLD by 2035, with Howrah alone contributing a whopping 160.1 MLD, just 5 MLD less than what Wabag plans to build for the four towns.

The massive wastewater discharge from Howrah should not have come as a surprise. Located on the western bank of the Hooghly, it was and still is an important transportation hub and the gateway to Kolkata. Howrah is the second-largest city in West Bengal, both in terms of its size and population. Hemmed in between the Hooghly in the east, and the Rupnarayan on the west, and intersected by the river Damodar, the city is famous for its textiles, iron and steel and jute industries.

The existing industrial units were mainly ancillaries belonging to the iron and steel industry engaged in the manufacture of ships, rail, locomotive, industrial furnaces, etc. A host of factors like militant trade unions, political unrest and the migration of industries to other states have led to its decline. A far cry from what Venetian explorer, Cesare Federici, who travelled in India during 1565–79, mentioned. He wrote about a place called Butter in his journal in 1578. As per his description, this was a location enabling the travel of large ships (presumably through the Hooghly) and he mentions the presence of a commercial port. Even the description of Howrah by the hymn writer Bishop Reginald Heber, who served as a Bishop of Calcutta till his death in 1942, mentions Howrah as 'chiefly inhabited by shipbuilders'. It was once considered one of the most industrialized districts of West Bengal with a large concentration of die casting, forging, electric installations, steel fabrication; it retains only a pale shadow today.

BARRACKPORE

Similarly, the ancient town of Barrackpore has been sanctioned a 24-MLD STP, which has also been constructed by infrastructure major L&T, keeping in mind the future needs of the city. The house service connections to sewer lines are in progress for ensuring proper utilization of STP capacity. By 2035, the total sewage from the town is expected to touch 20.1 MLD, increasing from the 17.4 MLD of 2016. Hence, arrangements have already been made to keep the town and the river clean beyond 2035.

Barrackpore's history not only boasted of a thriving jute, engineering, textiles, paper, chemicals and aluminium industries but also served as a chief trading and marketing centre. Since all the jute mills were clustered on the banks of the Hooghly, this gave a fillip to agro-based industries. Floriculture, pisciculture or fish farming and horticulture also flourished in the town, with the establishment of the Central Inland Fisheries Research Institute in Barrackpore to promote fisheries in ponds and rivers. A well-developed irrigation system has now been constructed in the subdivision to promote agriculture.

Historically, the town was a military and administrative centre under British rule. History books remember the town with pride as its soil gave birth to two revolts: the first one was the 1824 insurgency led by Sepoy Bindee Tiwary, and the second was the Sepoy Mutiny, led by Mangal Pandey. The town is thus linked to India's freedom movement. Barrackpore also saw the launch of Bengal Chemicals, founded by P.C. Roy, where Satish Chandra Dasgupta worked as a chemist. Dasgupta later founded the Sodepur Khadi Pratisthan for promotion of cottage and village industries inspired by Mahatma Gandhi and is also known as Gandhi of Bengal.

NORTH 24 PARGANAS

This district in south West Bengal has a strong industrial base and is trying to give a boost to the service sector too. According to a report by the MSME-Development Institute, Kolkata, about 180 large/medium scale units have been set up in the district, in addition to 63 electronic units in the Salt Lake Electronic Complex. Most of the large-scale units, like the jute mills, engineering units, textile mills, etc. had come up during British rule and would procure a huge quantity of their requirements from small-scale units. Hence, the area is also a breeding ground for small-scale industries. The district is most famous because it is the birthplace of Bankim Chandra Chattopadhyay, the famous writer, novelist and creator of Vande Mataram, the national song of India.

The district of North 24 Parganas also includes an international border with Bangladesh in the east, spreading to about 230 km. This is an area of 4,094 sq km and has a population of 10,009,781 (as per the 2011 census) thus having the highest density per sq km among all the districts of the state. It has several rivers like Ichhamati, Kalindi, Raimangal, Dansa, Benti, etc. and the river Hooghly lies between Hooghly town and North 24 Parganas district. Besides, the Sunderban delta is also responsible for the flow of the many rivers because of the high tidal waters entering the Bay of Bengal.

The North 24 Parganas district will see the modernization and upkeep of its existing STPs, many of which have either been lying unused or have been working at reduced capacity. These include the treatment plants of Naihati, Garulia, Titagarh, Panihati and Khardah municipality.

HALISHAHAR

Another district that has the attention of Namami Gange is the district of Halishahar, sometimes referred to as the Haveli Shahar or the city of palaces. The district has been rewarded with a ₹275.29 crore 16 MLD STP, whose wastewater discharge of 15.5 MLD in 2016, is likely to increase to 17 MLD by 2035. Fortunately, this district had found favour under the Ganga Action Plan (GAP) programme in 1990. Pollution abatement measures were designed as per the guidelines framed by GAP and NRCP and the execution of schemes were planned under two phases. However, no work was completed under GAP-I.

Works completed under GAP-II include an I&D scheme which was executed in the town with the view to diverting the contaminated flows of city drain to an STP. But there was no comprehensive sewerage project under the NGRBA. According to a detailed project report titled 'For Development of Sewerage System in Halisahar Municipality under NRGBA ESAMP' by IPE Global, an international consulting firm, nearly 15 to 20 per cent of the population, particularly from slums defecate in the open and even on the banks of the Hooghly. 'The city is deprived of door-to-door sewerage and residents depend on septic tanks or bore-hole type latrines, while sullage is passed to open drains. In the absence of comprehensive sewerage coverage of the town, the dry weather foul liquid wastes from the town continues to find its way to the river and particularly from large slums in the town.' The NMCG intervention has not come a day earlier.

NABADWIP

According to Narchari, a renowned author of Vaishnav literature, Nabadwip is surrounded by nine islands that are separated from each other but called one village. The district is covered under Presidency Division and occupies the eleventh position in the state with respect to its size with an area of 3,927 sq km. It lies in the heart of the Bengal Delta, held within the arms of Ganga and Bhagirathi on the west and Mathabhanga on the north. The whole district is a network of rivers and streams. The principal rivers of the districts are Bhagirathi, Jalangi and Mathahbhanga. Nadia is not as well developed as other industrialized districts of West Bengal. The small district of Nabadwip too has not escaped the attention of the NMCG officials. It is using the I&D process and construction of a 20 MLD STP to clean up the domestic sewage of this 'island'. It has sanctioned ₹58.32 crore to Sri Ram Constructions not only to construct a 20-MLD STP but also to renovate an existing 10.50 MLD STP. After all, Nabadwip's wastewater discharge, which was 14.2 MLD in 2016, is likely to increase to 16.6 MLD by 2035.

Other sewerage infrastructure projects sanctioned by NMCG include a 9.3 MLD STP at Budge Budge at ₹190.06 crore; ₹48.77 crore for the construction of I&D and an 18 MLD sewage plant at Kanchrapara, etc. As of today, six STPs with a cumulative capacity of 80.23 MLD capacity in Bhatpara, Kalyani and Halishahar towns have been built in the past three years. Work is also underway for STP construction and the rehabilitation of 37 STPs with a capacity of 579.44 MLD.

KOLKATA'S UNIQUE CHARACTERISTICS

Despite generating a huge quantity of domestic sewerage of 750 MLD, the highest in West Bengal, Kolkata's problems seem easier to tackle than many other states. And that is because the state is blessed with unique characteristics. For instance, the East Kolkata Wetlands (EKW), spread over 12,500 hectares, comprising nearly 254 sewage-fed fisheries, distributed across the districts of South and North 24 Parganas, forms one of the largest assemblages of sewage-fed fishponds.

It also nurtures the world's largest waste water-fed-aquaculture system. Sewerage sent to the wetlands is subjected to solar purification, followed by natural oxidation through which the water becomes conducive for algal and plankton growth, which then becomes the primary feed of fishes. The goods and services provided by the EKW include, in addition to fisheries, a very cheap, efficient and eco-friendly system of solid waste and sewer treatment system for the city of Kolkata, habitat for waterfowl, and is home for a large number of flora and fauna. Its importance has even been recognized by the international community when it included the EKW into the Ramsar list of 'Wetlands of International Importance' on August 19, 2002.

Kolkata's wastewater is converted into food and used in fisheries and agricultural systems across the sprawling 12,500 hectares of wetland area through a unique process. The wastewater from the city is led by underground sewers to pumping stations in the eastern limit of the city and then pumped into open channels. This sewage is then drawn by the local fishery owners into the fish ponds or bheris directly from the tributary wastewater canals. Bheris are a unique feature of the Kolkata wetlands and are shallow fishponds fed by naturally treated wastewater rich in algae, which allows for low-cost fish cultivation.

Once the organic waste is loaded in the bheris at the rate of 20 to 70 kg per hectare per day, it is allowed to stay in the sun and these sewage-filled fishery ponds act as solar reactors. The heat generated by the sun is adequate for photosynthesis to take place and helps in the growth of a dense plankton population in the bheri, which in turn grows on the organic matter in the wastewater. This fast-growing plankton serves as food for the fish population, which thrives on this nutrient-rich plankton. The fish play a twofold role—they maintain the balance of the plankton population in the pond and convert the available nutrients in the wastewater into readily consumable form (fish) for humans.

The whole process reduces the organic pollution in the wastewater by 80 per cent and that of coliform bacteria by 99.9 per cent in these ponds. Channels drain out the effluents and slurry from the treated wastewater, which is then used to grow rice and vegetables. Around a quarter of the city's fish and vegetables are grown from the bheris. Not only do the wetlands help in providing cheap food and vegetables for the city, but also support the livelihoods of about 118,000 people.

This ecological and sustainable solution for sewage management is successfully working in Kolkata, making West Bengal the only state in the Ganga basin which is using a natural system to help reduce the pollution load in the river. West Bengal, therefore, provides an opportunity to other basin states to work on such ecological solutions which are sustainable, of low cost and natural. It also makes the case for conservation and rejuvenation of wetlands and other water bodies that much more important—a most natural solution to conserve the Indian river from pollution load or from flowing dry in the lean season.

Unfortunately, because of the increasing pressure of urbanization, change in the quality and quantity of solid waste and sewers as well as human neglect, this site is under threat from various directions. The challenge for every well-meaning official is to ensure that this sustainable, low-cost and natural solution, is not only not lost because of neglect or oversight, but implemented in other states as well.

West Bengal also has a very enlightened set of Ganga Praharis, some of them university students as well working for conserving aquatic life and making the community aware. Several species including dolphins have been rescued and the Gangetic Shark from Hooghly has been located by them. Ganga Doots mobilised by NYK are also connecting community. The culturally rich community has come up with innovative and creative participation in various activities. A special project with help of CIFRI has been taken up with encouraging results for improving population of hilsa and facilitate its migration upstream of Farakka as was the case originally. There is an air of optimism and enthusiasm even though there is a long way to go.

12

Sundarbans: In the Crosshairs of an Impending Calamity

'But here in the tide, transformation is the rule of life: rivers stray from week to week, and islands are made and unmade in days. In other places forests take centuries, even millennia, to regenerate, but mangroves can recolonize denuded island in 10-15 years,' writes Amitav Ghosh in *The Hungry Tide*. He adds: 'They number in thousands, these islands, some are immense and some are no larger than sandbars; some have lasted through recorded history while others were washed into being just a year or two ago. These are the rivers' restitution, the offerings through which they return to the earth what they have taken from it. The rivers' channels are spread across the land like a fine mesh net, creating a terrain, where the boundaries between land and water are always mutating, always unpredictable.'

Ghosh describes, in the most picturesque fashion, the ever-shifting, course-changing and unpredictable nature of the world's largest and only surviving mangrove forest. Patches of tidal estuaries, mud banks and backwaters not only house some of the poorest tribal populations in the world, but it is also home to some of the most exotic and endangered species of animals—not found anywhere else in the world. This seemingly infinite and shifting series of these beautiful mud islands with dense forests constitute the coastal belt of Bengal.

While the beauty of this extraordinary ecosystem, located in the interface of land and sea, has been the subject of interest of a host of Indian and foreign authors, none have been able to capture it better than Godfrey Charles Mundy, a British writer and historian: 'Nothing can exceed the luxuriant richness of the Sundarbans vegetation ... Whilst the eye is feasted by the infinite variety of tints in the foliage of groves and banks, the scent is regaled, almost to surfeiting, with spicy breezes which float through the atmosphere, loaded with sweets from the surrounding forests,' he writes.

THE EXISTENTIAL THREAT

Sadly, the Sunderbans is facing an existential crisis today. The inevitable threat grows and the Sunderbans may be subject to drowning because of several factors. Some of these threats are homegrown, as the steady encroachments by people into the forests for livelihood resources like timber, honey and agricultural land, coastal tourism, etc.; other factors are more global in nature, such as the challenges of climate change represented by global warming, which results in rising temperatures of the sea. While a larger habitation in this fragile ecosystem creates its own pressure on the island's limited resources and its varied roles, higher sea temperatures pose a grave threat by stirring up cyclones, high tides and storms in the sea, raising the level of water and inundating the low-lying areas of the forests.

People in the ecologically-fragile Sundarbans face a daily battle against high tides and regular cyclones. Every cyclone throws up new challenges to the forest and its inhabitants—something the people had never before imagined, and a situation policymakers are not prepared for. Over the past three years, the Sundarbans, which is home to close to five million people, has been battered by four tropical cyclones—Fani (May 2019), Bulbul (November 2019), Amphan (May 2020) and Yaas (May 2021). On each occasion, the region has suffered damages because of gale winds and breached embankments, leading to the entry of seawater into the island, destroying its fertility.

In fact, the trees that nourish and shelter myriad wildlife have not only learnt to tolerate different levels of salinity in different seasons—the changing mix of salt and seawater—but have also developed their own uniqueness to survive these harsh conditions. In their evolutionary journey, the trees have learnt to trap oxygen from the air through roots that protrude out from the soil. The forest that grows up here, the trees and the grasses, fixes the new land that the rivers create during the monsoons in months, which would otherwise take years.

For naturalists, the Sunderbans, are important in their own right as 'biodiversity hotspots' of extraordinary richness: 250 species of fish, 44 crabs, 20 prawns and scores of birds as well as dolphins, crocodiles and rare marine turtles. A few of the globally endangered species include the Royal Bengal Tiger, Ganges and Irawadi dolphins, estuarine crocodiles and the critically endangered endemic river terrapin (Batagur Baska). It is the only mangrove habitat in the world for the Panthera tigris species.

The danger to the very survival of the Sunderbans is not just an empty warning; the looming threat is right here and now. From being a dense forest that covered some 17,000 sq km in 2011, the forest cover has shrunk to 10,000 sq km in a span of just five to six years. A study by G. Gopinath and P. Seralatham, both from the Department of Marine Geology and Geophysics, Cochin University of Science and Technology, titled *Rapid Erosion of the coast of Sagar Island, West Bengal, India*, underscores this threat rather well. Their study shows that between 1967 and 1994, about 29.8 sq km of the island had been eroded, and the accreted area is only 6.03 sq km. 'Since mudflats, salt marshes and mangroves are primarily built by silt and clay, they can be easily eroded by waves, tides and cyclonic activities than a sandy coast,' the authors argue.

THE THREAT OF CLIMATE CHANGE

The threat due to climate change is even more daunting. In the past three decades, the sea level has been rising at a rate that is almost double the global average, according to many experts. The intensity of cyclones and high tidal waves and irregular monsoons too has been increasing. It is observed that the severe cyclonic storms over the Bay of Bengal have increased by 26 per cent over the last 120 years, according to a 2012 report by the New Delhi-based Centre for Science and Environment (CSE). It appears paradoxical that while the Ganga-Brahmaputra-Meghna annually carries more than one billion tonnes of suspended load and about 15 per cent of that is discharged into the sea. The riverine tracts of West Bengal is being eroded at the speed of 4.20 sq km/year leading to encroachment of the sea. (Goodberg and Kuehl 1999)

For those who are more statistically minded, here are some of the important numbers. The mangrove forests cover an area of more than 9,630 sq km and are delineated by Dampier and Hodges line in the north, Ichhamati-Hariabhanga in the east, Baratala estuary in the west and the Bay of Bengal in the south. The western part of the Sundarbans had been completely deforested since 1784 and the area caters to a population of more than 4.5 million people. Some 4,266 sq km with numerous tidal creeks, intricate interlacing drainage, dense mangrove forest has marked it as a distinctive geographical region within the Ganga-Brahmaputra delta. (Rudra 2016)

The area includes 1,330 sq km of Sundarban National Park, 362 km of Sajnekhali Wildlife Sanctuary, 38 sq km of Lothian Island wildlife sanctuary and 6 km of Halliday Island Bird Sanctuary. Out of the 13 creeks flowing through Indo-Bangladesh Sundarban, six flows through the Indian territory. These are Saptamukhi, Jamira, Matla, Bangaduni, Gosaba and Baratala. The large part of the Sundarbans is only three metres above mean sea level and tidal fluctuation is more than five metres. Thus, an extensive area goes underwater during high tide.

THE BEGINNING:

The British government in the second half of the eighteenth century started premature land reclamations in the Sundarbans with dangerous consequences. Extensive areas were deforested and creeks and rivers were embanked to restrict the spillover of saline water into the floodplain without much success. This impaired the 'delicate hydro-geomorphology balance of the delta'. Since the spillover into the floodplain was now restricted, uninterrupted sedimentation on the creeks and rivers led to the gradual decay of the drainage system. As a consequence, the human settlement finds itself challenged by challenges of drainage congestion and waterlogging.

Moreover, most experts argue that coastal forests help fight global warming by removing carbon dioxide from the atmosphere. When mangrove tree roots, branches and leaves die, they are usually covered by soil, which is then submerged under tidal water, slowing the breakdown of materials and boosting carbon storage. There are other benefits of saving mangrove forests. A study by the Economics of Ecosystems and Biodiversity (TEEB) shows that planting and protecting nearly 12,000 hectares of mangroves in Vietnam cost just over $1 million but saved annual expenditure on dyke maintenance of well over $7 million (World Disaster Report, 2002).

The demise of the Sundarbans, however slowly, does not bode well for the future of either Bangladesh or India, two countries that are hemmed in by these nutrient-rich mangrove forests that provide nourishment and life to a host of aquatic life. Since 40 per cent of the total Sundarbans falls in the West Bengal state, the former capital of India assumes significance and priority for the conservation of the Sundarbans. After all, a journalist and author Victor Mallet writes in *River of Life, River of Death*: 'Many species of commercially important fish found in the Indian Ocean depend on the mangroves, which act as a nursery for 90 per cent of the aquatic species on India's east coast and sustain the sea and estuarine fisheries of Bangladesh as well.' The delta flooded by the rivers of Padma (Ganga), Jamuna and Meghna is not only one of the most productive agricultural land, but is the confluence of the Ganga and Brahmaputra and has a rich cultural and economic significance. For instance, at Ganga's endpoint—where the Hooghly, the main tributary of the Ganga, meets the Bay of Bengal at Gangasagar—every year on Makar Sankranti (14 January) thousands of pilgrims take a holy dip in this sacred meeting point as part of the Gangasagar Mela. It is followed by devotees offering prayers at the Kapil Muni temple. Many devotees believe that taking a holy dip at this confluence once is more important than going to any other holy place for a dip every year. On Makar Sankranti, when the sun makes a transition to Capricorn from Sagittarius, it is said that the bath becomes a holy source of salvation.

A 2013 study of mangroves in Florida estimated that a mangrove forest could reduce the effects of a storm and its intensity. Mangroves are also more effective when the storm is more violent. A series of studies in the early 2000s discovered that mangroves with an average height of 6-10 metres could shorten a cyclone's waves by 60 per cent. Their roots form a complex interweave just above the soil. Together with the trees' trunks, they work like speed-breakers to slow the tides. Preserving what mangrove tract we already have can dramatically reduce the damage to our coasts due to tropical storms.

The 6,000 sq km of the Bangladesh Sundarbans are only a remnant of the mangrove forests that once ringed the Bay of Bengal from Thailand to the coast of India. Yet, many experts worry that the very existence of Bangladesh could be threatened if the water rises above a certain level. Climate models—based on current and projected temperature increases worldwide, along with melting ice and expanding oceans—indicate that global warming will continue. In the past decade, both the IPCC and the World Bank have established estimates that higher seal levels of a metre or more will affect low-lying countries like Bangladesh by the end of this century. Other sources have predicted an even faster rising. 'A one-meter rise in sea level could completely engulf the Sundarbans. Thermal expansion would account for about half the increase in sea levels because warm water takes up more space than cold water, and ocean temperatures are rising. Melting glaciers will do the rest,' argues Cheryl Colopy in her book *Dirty, Sacred Rivers: Confronting South Asia's Water Crisis*.

SAVING THE MANGROVE FOREST

While saving the Sundarbans calls for immediate emergency measures from both India and Bangladesh, it is no easy task. Limiting the adverse consequences of global warming will call for worldwide cooperation and action, and hence, it is beyond the scope of any one country. One of the best ways to keep these forests alive is to rejuvenate Ganga's waters and maintain their purity. In the monsoons, when the rivers are in full spate they keep the saline waters of the Bay of Bengal at arms length by pushing them deeper into the sea. This prevents the saline water from entering the mangrove forests. However, when the water level recedes during the lean season, the saltwater pushes into the mangrove forest and even further into the farmlands, thereby destroying not just the crops but the soil for future cultivation. Hence, it is extremely important to have a minimum environmental flow in the river at all times to prevent the sea from degrading the soil, making the groundwater unfit for drinking and irrigation.

As Colopy explains in her book: 'A sufficient quantity of fresh water flowing down the rivers would counteract the minimal encroachment of seawater into the mangrove forests from the Bay of Bengal. But, the further the saline water pushes inland regularly, the greater the likelihood that groundwater will become more saline, making it useless for drinking and irrigation.' The water could also seep into the soil and make it too saline for agriculture. In fact, the water flowing into the Bay of Bengal is actually not wastewater, as proven by a recent theory. It actually flushes the coastal region, keeping the land fresh and the Sundarbans from becoming saline. And as the land becomes more and more saline and unfit for cultivation, it will give way to shrimp cultivation, as it is already being witnessed in parts of West Bengal and Bangladesh. Even more, water would be needed to offset the effects of rising temperatures on thirsty land and crops; increased withdrawals upstream would mean less water downstream and increasing salinity near the coast.

As researchers generate more data about how climate change

is affecting specific locations, global warming is increasingly being understood as a multitude of local crises instead of a single looming catastrophe. 'Hence, politicians must include the realities of climate change in all aspects of governance as they plan for the future,' argues Colopy. The forest is not just a protection against frequent cyclones and shelter for the wild animals that once inhabited the entire coastal region. Today, it has been realized that the many pressures on the potential of the Sundarbans—from the surrounding human population and increase in salinity—will continue to erode the ecosystem. A prime example of this is Sundari, as the tree which gives Sundarban its name is already showing serious signs of stress. The top branches of the tall Sundari tree die while the rest of the tree continues to stand. So, in the absence of freshwater, either the trees will die or have to be made to adapt.

To take care of the challenges of climate change, a worldwide effort of unimaginable proportions would be required. Even if developed and developing countries finally agree to steep emission cuts, warming will continue for a long time before the trend might reverse. 'Reversing the trend of mangrove loss and the growing vulnerability of coastal people,' argues a UNESCO report titled 'Securing the Future of Mangroves', 'will require a real commitment by governments to develop and implement robust high-level policies.' The report also points out that mangrove management should be integrated into a broader spatial framework of coastal zone management. These efforts should also cross all sectors and involve all stakeholders. However, as Mallet prophesies in his book: 'Seas may have to rise, and salinity increases before the sea fall again. Till that time, the survival of the world's largest mangrove forests hangs on a delicate balance. In this regard, India can learn from the mechanisms successfully deployed in Bangladesh in recent decades, such as an effective early warning system, extensive community awareness campaigns, cyclone shelters, coastal embankments, extensive mangrove reforestation, and a decentralized yet connected disaster response system.

This balance is required among the different components of the fragile ecosystem but mainly in its interactions with human beings.

This can be done effectively by learning from its past and the local traditions, notable among them is that of 'Bonbibi Pujo'. Bidisha Banerjee in her book *Superhuman River: Stories of the Ganga* shares her experience of spending some time on the island with local people and Annu Jalais, an expert on Sundarbans. Annu mentions in her own book that forest fisher people narrate the story of Bonbibi in order to address 'equitable sharing of food and resources between humans and tigers'. Annu explains that the highlight of the story or the learning is about the agreement between non-humans and humans that permits them both to depend on the forest and yet respect others' needs. Is there learning here for us in our dealing with the Ganga? Can we also have an agreement with the river to depend on her and also respect her needs, in terms of controlled exploitations and e-flows? That will immediately solve many of the challenges this book narrates.

13

Rejuvenating Tributaries: Healing Ganga's Intricate Water Web

'I have never yet seen a river that I could not love. Moving water, even in a pipeline or a flume, has a fascinating vitality. It has the power and grace, and associations. It has a thousand colours and thousand shapes, yet it follows laws so definite that the tiniest streamlet is an exact replica of a great river.'

—Roderick Haig-Brown

Haig-Brown may well have been describing the holy Ganges in its pristine form in its upper reaches, where untouched by human hands and unencumbered by the march of civilizations and urbanization, it flows along merrily, unhindered by man-made obstacles like dams and barrages. Today, it is a pale shadow of its original self after years of destructive human interventions and neglect. The sacred river is now crying out for rejuvenation. Yet, returning the holy Ganges to its virgin state, as officials of the NMCG, realized soon enough, was an extraordinarily difficult and a complex task that called for cooperation and activism from all stakeholders on a mission mode, a perfect example of tackling the so-called 'wicked problem'.

Their job not only entailed saving the dazzling varieties of fish and wildlife and trees and plants that are an integral part of the river but also saving the 1,000-odd tributaries and innumerable water bodies that add volume and ecological flow to the river as it hurtles through deep gorges and meanders through three countries, 11 states in the basin with five on its main stem. It directly passes through 97 cities/towns (47 with a population of more than 100,000, 19 with population between 50,000 and 100,000 and 31 towns with population less than 50,000). Ganga basin is not just a lifeline, but it also defines and determines the fortunes of three countries.

The river basin impacts the lives and livelihoods of about 655 million inhabitants that rely on its waters for everything. It presents great opportunities and challenges, providing water for drinking, agriculture, hydropower generation, navigation and ecosystem, and it spans more than one million square kilometres of the river basin. But the river can be destructive as well—devastating floods and periodic droughts are routine affairs—causing immense hardships to the people and undermining the country's economic development. Hence, the NMCG has decided to adopt a more holistic GRBMP, in line with the strategic roadmap drawn up by the consortium of seven IITs, selected as advisors for this gigantic and complex clean-up. A radically different and all-encompassing approach, markedly different from the earlier piecemeal and uncoordinated strategy of different successive governments.

The rejuvenation of tributaries has been an integral component of the Namami Gange programme in tune with its vision to rejuvenate the entire Ganga Basin. The approach was very clearly explained by the Honourable Prime Minister on the occasion of dedicating to the nation several Namami Gange projects in Uttarakhand.

'The government is working with a four-pronged strategy simultaneously. First, we have started laying a network of sewage treatment plants to prevent the polluted water from flowing into the Ganga. Secondly, building such sewage treatment plants that can meet the needs of the next 10–15 years; thirdly, to make 100 big cities/towns and 5,000 villages situated on the banks of the Ganga free from open defecation, and fourth using all means to stop the pollution of Ganga ji's tributaries.'

Shri. Narendra Modi, Prime Minister of India

THE NEED FOR REGIONAL COOPERATION

A report published by the World Bank South Asia Regional Report titled 'Ganges: Strategic Basin Assessment: A Discussion of Regional Opportunities and Risks' underlines the importance of a consultative and coordinated river basin development plan for riparian countries like Nepal, Bangladesh and India, whose landmass is a part of this strategic basin. Hence, a knowledge-based partnership among countries becomes crucial to tap into its numerous benefits—from potential hydropower development and agricultural modernization to an effective flood and drought management systems—to protect the lives and livelihoods of the people in these three countries.

International cooperation, argues the report, is critical 'to sustain the river ecosystem, capture its potential benefits, and mitigate its mounting costs—requires enhanced regional knowledge and cooperation. The basin is so large—more than one million square kilometres—and so complex, with thousands of tributaries fed by glaciers and snowmelt, monsoon rains, and groundwater base flows, that it is impossible to be managed by a single country. Hence, the report suggests four areas of cooperation to enhance the productivity and sustainability of the river systems and to help manage water-related hazards like floods through better groundwater management, reduction in sedimentation and by building the right kind of infrastructure in both the upper and lower reaches of the Ganga basin. These are the development of cooperative nationwide information systems and institutions, flood management using both hard and soft techniques, hydropower trade and development and groundwater development for irrigation. The vision of the multilateral agency for these countries is 'about a cooperative and knowledge-based partnership of states fairly managing and developing the Himalayan river system to bring economic prosperity, peace, social harmony and environmental sustainability from the source to the sea.'

Similarly, in a 2014 paper titled 'Water for Growth and Development in the Ganges, Brahmaputra and Meghna Basins: An Economic Perspective,' researcher Golam Rasul points out that the economic structure of the region is highly water-dependent since a vast majority of the people are dependent on agriculture, livestock, forestry and fishery for their livelihoods. 'Agriculture contributes about one-third of the gross domestic product (GDP) and provides employment for about two-thirds of the rural labour force,' claims the paper. Besides irrigation, the Ganga riverine system supports fisheries, navigation, transportation and energy production. 'Thus the quality of life, livelihoods, and economic prosperity of the people in the region depend on sustainable management of water resources. Rational, efficient and equitable water management can act as an engine for socio-economic development and meet the growing demand for the burgeoning population for food, water and energy in the face of climatic and other socio-economic changes,' contends Rasul.

The World Bank report breaks new ground by suggesting that infrastructures like dams and embankments, seen as saviours, are unlikely to be effective in preventing floods because of the high variability of the monsoon and a river driven by thousands of tributaries. The reason is that the storage potential of these dams is approximately 25 to 30 per cent of the average annual river flows, too small to regulate the full river system. Even the Kosi High Dam could not completely control floods during peak flows because the dam, which would provide only 9.5 billion cubic metres (BCM) of live storage, would be built on a river with an average annual flow of 55 BCM, which can see rising volumes in different years.

While dams may not be able to effectively control floods, their benefits lie in ability to store it during the wet season and release water during the dry season to augment low flows for ecosystems, agriculture and other uses across the basin, especially in the dry months. 'The effects of increased low flows may make important contributions in the Ganges delta areas to better manage saline intrusion, enhance the Sundarbans ecosystem, and maintain navigational services. Although underground aquifers, lakes, glaciers, snow ice and even soils are all forms of natural water storage,' argues the World Bank report.

A FLOOD CONTROL STRATEGY

The World Bank suggests a shift from 'flood control' to 'flood management,' a combination of structural and non-structural interventions marked by a greater emphasis on regional forecasting and warning systems, embankment asset management and drainage. It will also call for more localized 'soft' responses, including disaster preparedness, land-use zoning, safe havens, flood insurance and training and communication campaigns, which entail local and transboundary solutions. The same is equally true for the sedimentation load of the basin. Given the high terrain and the sediment source region, the nature of the sediment and its flow and the ongoing tectonic process in the Himalayas, it is highly unlikely that a single country can find a solution to this recurring problem.

In fact, floods already take a significant toll on the lives and livelihoods in the Nepal lowlands known as Terai, as well as Bangladesh and in some states of India. Floods account for 90 per cent of the economic cost of natural disasters in Nepal. States such as Assam, West Bengal, Uttar Pradesh and especially Bihar are highly flood-prone. According to the Government of Bihar and the World Bank's Kosi Post Disaster Needs Assessment report of 2010, the estimated damage is ₹593.5 crore (US$ 134.9 million). The river Kosi, one of the tributaries of the Ganga, is known as 'the river of sorrow' in Bihar. In 2008, flooding in the Kosi basin affected about 2.8 million people in India and Nepal and caused huge economic losses. In India, more than 22 million people are affected by floods every year. (Bihar and World Bank 2010) The worst affected districts of Bihar are Muzaffarpur, Sitamarhi, Saharsa, East Champaran, Darbhanga, Patna, Supaul, Bhagalpur, West Champaran, Katihar, Madhubani, Samastipur, Sheohar and Nalanda. Multiple breaches at 32 points (in many rivers) have caused major havoc across the state.

Country-wide cooperation is required as well because the source of many Ganga tributaries lie outside India. The Ganges originates in the Gangotri Glacier about 4,000 metres above sea level in Uttarakhand and flows nearly 2,525 km to its final destination in Bangladesh and the Bay of Bengal. Its major tributaries include the Himalayan tributary rivers of Yamuna, Mahakali or Kali, Gandak, Kosi and Mahananda rivers from the North. These northern Himalayan tributaries have their source primarily in Nepal and India, with some portion of Kosi and to a lesser extent, Karnali, rising in China. From the south, the tributaries of the Yamuna (the Chambal, Sindh, Betwa and Ken rivers) and rivers Tons and Son flow north into the main stem of the Ganga. The biggest flow contributor to the Ganga basin is the Yamuna, Kali, Karnali, Ghagra and the Kosi.

IMPORTANCE OF TRIBUTARIES

The importance of the tributaries is best understood from a detailed analysis of the country's precipitation and by comparing it with the anatomy of a human body. Tributaries are like the smaller arteries and veins that run throughout the body, helping to maintain blood pressure (not just during the good times but also in difficult times, when the main arteries may be partially blocked and unable to function properly). Managing the health of these smaller arteries and veins, the tributaries, are as important as that of the main arteries, or the Ganga. Moreover, every year the basin records an average of 1,200 billion cubic metres (BCM) of rainfall, mostly from the southwest monsoons. Of this, about 500 BCM flows into the river system and becomes the Ganges river flow. The rest, 700 BCM of water, is captured by the landscape, recharging groundwater or is returned to the atmosphere through evaporation and transpiration. The monsoon delivers about 80 per cent of the annual rainfall in just three months of the year (mid-June through mid-September) with the river's flow peaking from July to October while registering relatively low flows for the rest of the year. April and May witnessed the lowest flows with little or no rainfall to augment the water supply.

Since many tributaries are glacier-fed, they continue to feed and augment the mainstream even during the non-monsoon months and serve as important habitats that carry various sediments, chemicals, organic matter and volumes of water and contribute to the unique ecosystem of the river, the home of various flora and fauna and their interactions. Hence, under the Namami Gange, a large number of smaller tributaries have been mapped along with their catchment area, watershed and water bodies. The rejuvenation of these tributaries is one of the objectives of the programme as these tributaries impact the flows, quality and quantity of the Ganga. But like the main river, encroachments, siltation, degradation of their watershed, the proliferation of point and distributed sources of pollution, solid waste dumping, and negligence reduce these tributaries to a trickle and they often struggle to survive.

Experts term the confluence of Ganga with its tributaries as 'biochemical hotspots', which create 'spatial discontinuities in habitat, species diversity; and biological productivity in rivers.' The water and sediment delivery from the tributaries add ecological complexity to the main stem of the river by augmenting its flow, leading to a proliferation in the biodiversity of the main river and this changes the prey-predator numbers and transforms the water quality by increasing the effluent, sewage, metals and chemical discharge into the main river. As tributaries merge with the main stem of the river, they introduce both vital ecological components and dangerous contaminants into it. Hence, their health is crucial for Ganga.

The river Ganga and its tributaries are indispensable to the thinking of Indian consciousness and have deep roots in our culture and several practices. Several ancient temples across our country depict the statue of our river as goddess, especially that of Ganga, Yamuna and also Saraswati. The deep connection of these rivers can be seen from the following quote from Professor Sudipta Sen's book, *Ganges: The Many Pasts of an Indian River.*

> 'The river Ganga and her two sisters, Yamuna and Saraswati, are identified, for example, with the three subtle conduits (nādīs) of the life force in Yogic conceptions of the human body. The solar pingalā is the Yamuna, the lunar iḍā is the Ganga and the medial, fiery suṣumna is the hidden Saraswati. When yogis perform breath control (prānāyāma), they are supposed to inflate and clear the two peripheral channels so that the third is filled with the subtle breath of life, forcing it upward through the body, leading them towards blissful liberation. As David Gordon White points out, the identification of the body with the triad of the sacred Indian rivers is fundamental to the learning and practice of traditional yoga.'

YAMUNA (UTTARAKHAND, HP, HARYANA, DELHI AND UP)

A case in point is the Yamuna, the second-largest tributary river in terms of flow. It is the longest tributary in India. It also has great cultural and religious value and is considered holy, just like the Ganga. If Ganga symbolizes salvation, Yamuna denotes limitless love and affection. It traverses a distance of 1,376 km with a drainage system that spans 366,223 sq km or 40.2 per cent of the entire Ganga basin. It merges with the Ganga at Triveni Sangam, Prayagraj, which is a site of the Kumbh Mela, a major Hindu festival held every 12 years. But over the years, its depiction in the ancient texts, as a natural paradise of lilies, turtles and fish and as the playground of flute-playing Lord Krishna and all his adoring gopis, has changed for the worst. Instead, it has become a toxic mixture of domestic sewage and industrial waste in the 22-km stretch flowing through Delhi between Wazirabad and Okhla barrage, especially during the lean season as it flows between Delhi to Agra.

Yamuna's tragedy is that it passes through some of the most densely populated cities, many of them also boast of numerous industries in Haryana, Uttar Pradesh, Delhi and Uttarakhand, whose civic authorities have failed to keep pace with the pressing challenges of rapid urbanization. Moreover, at the Hathni Kund Barrage, most of its waters are diverted into two large canals: Western Yamuna Canal flowing towards Haryana and the Eastern Yamuna Canal towards Uttar Pradesh. Beyond that point, the Yamuna is joined only by the Somb, a seasonal rivulet from Haryana, and by the highly-polluted river Hindon near Noida. Flowing to this point, it has already become a trickling sewage-bearing drain before it is given a fresh lease of life from the inflow of river Chambal at Pachnada in the Etawah district of Uttar Pradesh.

In fact, the Yamuna water is of 'reasonably good quality' throughout its journey from Yamunotri in the Himalayas to Wazirabad barrage in Delhi, about 375 km, but its onward journey becomes toxic and severely polluted as wastewater discharge of 15 drains between Wazirabad and Okhla barrages enter its waters. However, Yamuna can expect some respite in the coming years from Namami Gange's newly-designed programme for integrated rejuvenation and conservation of the National River Ganga and its tributaries. The NMCG has sanctioned ₹4,283.50 crore (1 crore is 10 million) for the construction of 1,840 MLD of STPs through 21 projects in the 11 towns of Delhi, Panipat, Sonepat, Agra, Mathura, Vrindavan, Baghpat, Firozabad, Etawah, Paonta Sahib and Kairana. The plan in Delhi is being executed by the Delhi Jal Board.

Additionally, to ensure that the Yamuna remains squeaky clean till 2035, the NMCG has created a futuristic demand-supply model for the river. Under this model, the organization has predicted that the total population of 30 major cities along the banks of the Yamuna, like Vikasnagar, Paonta Sahib, Yamunanagar, Karnal, Panipat, Auraiya, Noida, etc. is likely to touch 12,741,980 and generate nearly 1,448.92 MLD of domestic and other wastes. By sanctioning 1,840 MLD of STP at a total cost of ₹4,283.50 crore, it has put in place projects to take care of the health of the Yamuna for at least the next 14 years.

Despite all its trials and tribulations, the Yamuna continues to play a critical role in creating the highly fertile alluvial soil at the Yamuna-

Ganga Doab region in the Indo-Gangetic plain. This nurtures nearly 57 million people and accounts for 70 per cent of the capital's water supply. It has an annual flow of 97 BCM, and 4 BCM are consumed every year, of which irrigation accounts for nearly 96 per cent of the water consumed.

The challenge of rejuvenating this important tributary essentially lies in improving the flow and creating and ensuring the utilization of sewerage infrastructure and enforcement of industrial effluent standards. After successful determination and implementation of the e-flow regime for Ganga, the NMCG has now set up a study by experts for scientific assessment of minimum e-flow for the entire stretch of Yamuna through a project entrusted to the National Institute of Hydrology. The report has been finalized and consensus of stakeholders is being tried out. It has not been easy as the Haryana government has raised concern about reducing the water allocation for agriculture to maintain this e-flow. Hopefully, this process and the support from the orders of NGT will help hasten this process. Steps have also been initiated for protecting and rejuvenating the wetlands and also towards piloting some storage in floodplains in Delhi to recharge groundwater harvesting. The organizations like 'Yamuna Jiye Abhiyan' has been raising their concerns at NGT and helps in protecting the floodplains and taking other conservation measures.

Protecting the floodplains of the Yamuna in Delhi is critical. Development of an eco-friendly riverfront without concrete, improving natural and constructed wetlands and biodiversity parks have been taken up by the Delhi Development Authority (DDA). The DDA is also developing similar infrastructure on other banks of the Yamuna (falling in UP area under an agreement with the government of UP) to improve ecology, aesthetics and a people-river connection. A review of all these has been mandated by NGT and by the principal committee headed by the Ministry of Jal Shakti. This committee includes reputed experts, such as Prof. C.R. Babu who has done wonders by regenerating wastelands and developing biodiversity parks and conserving wetlands.

The NMCG has also visited the ghats of the Yamuna and has taken up cleaning drives with staff and other organizations and NGOs. There have been good results in making this clean-up a weekend activity with some NGOs such as Tree Craze Foundation, Leher Foundation, Lakshya and many others. Several local initiatives on the Yamuna, such as Ragas for the Yamuna, are also a welcome sign to connect people for helping in the clean-up process.

The Delhi 2021 Master plan attempted to address Delhi's complexities through a zoning plan for different areas. But these master plans have not been successful in providing a strategic vision to address the complexities of Delhi, or its exponential urban growth and endangered ecology. We are leveraging our collaborative project with the National Institute of Urban Affairs (NIUA) to position Yamuna as a central idea and bring it to the mainstream as the new master plan 2041 for Delhi is being finalized now. This would provide a much-needed long-term perspective for both Delhi and Yamuna to happily coexist.

The importance of Mathura-Vrindavan on the banks of Yamuna is well known. Many local saints have shown concern for the Yamuna similar to Ganga. The Namami Gange mission has been conscious of this. As far as pollution abatement is concerned, sewerage infrastructure has been sanctioned for both these places. It is now completed in Vrindavan. At Mathura, it is at an advanced stage and will soon be creating a model for the reuse of treated wastewater in the industry through its 'one city, one operator' approach on HAM. I had the occasion to interact with saints and activists from that area and also explore options for improving the flow and work towards effective enforcement measures with respect to industries.

Along with these measures, improving the flow is needed. The Mathura project is designed to reuse 20 MLD of treated wastewater from the Mathura refinery, which will save a quantity of fresh water from the Yamuna. Delhi sewerage infrastructure is also in progress and will help in improving the incoming quality of water. It is also proposed that the treated wastewater from Okhla STP of 560 MLD capacity—the largest in India—be released into the river directly to help with better quality flow. An e-flow regime and the examination of the release of more freshwater from the irrigation system of the Ganga-Yamuna canal is also being explored with the provision of the extra release of water from the Tehri reservoir storage.

Agra is another major city of importance on Yamuna's banks. It fares relatively poor in terms of its drains and sewerage system. A comprehensive project has been sanctioned at a cost of ₹842.25 crore under Namami Gange for citywide integration of all existing STPs, their rehabilitation, upgradation (as needed), creation of new capacity and ensuring operation and maintenance for 15 years. The project will create a capacity of 177.60 MLD. Once completed, it will provide relief from pollution. Wetland conservation has also been given importance. Further, closer to Agra, the Keetham Lake (Sur Sagar) has recently been included in the list of Ramsar Sites.

A nearby town, Firozabad, a well-known centre for bangles and glasswork, is significant for treating the pollution in the Yamuna. The city has an STP of 63 MLD, but was grossly underutilized, treating less than 3 MLD. Namami Gange mission is constructing the required sewer lines to intercept drains and divert them to the STP and 50 to 51 MLD is now being treated after preventing the flow from all major drains. STP is still left with enough capacity to meet future demand as well.

Are we neglecting the holy Yamuna by focusing on Ganga? The answer is no, as can be seen from several of these interventions. The main stem of the Ganga was given priority in the initial years of Namami Gange but work on the Yamuna also got going. Yamuna is also very badly impacted by Hindon, a highly polluted tributary containing toxic industrial effluents and untreated sewage flow. Despite all this, even in Delhi and its surroundings, the much-condemned Yamuna regains its magic in the monsoon. It receives most of its flow during the monsoon and it is critical that the Yamuna is allowed to broaden into its full monsoonal floodplains to recharge its groundwater, remove silt and stagnant water algae and improve its soil fertility.

CHAMBAL (MADHYA PRADESH, RAJASTHAN, UTTAR PRADESH)

A mighty river, originating in Mau in Madhya Pradesh (MP), traversing through and forming the boundary between MP and Rajasthan and later MP and Uttar Pradesh before joining the Yamuna at the confluence of five rivers—the Pachnad—of Yamuna, Chambal, Kuwari, Sindhu and Pahuj (near Etawah).

A sewerage project under Namami Gange is likely to be completed soon at Etawah for improving old STPs of 23 MLD and constructing a new STP of 21 MLD capacity apart from sewer lines of 75-km for interception and diversion. District administration along with an active group 'The Society for Conservation of Nature' has launched a 'Namo Kalindi' campaign to initiate cleaning drives on Yamuna banks, protection of wetlands, biodiversity and public awareness.

Chambal is an example of a free-flowing river largely still retaining its natural condition, very rich in biodiversity and forests with no large city on its bank, except Kota. A project for developing the required sewerage infrastructure has already been taken up under Namami Gange for creating a capacity of 36 MLD. It is said that the Chambal was cursed by Draupadi for being a silent witness to her humiliation, and the belief spread that whoever drinks its waters will thirst for revenge. From known badlands, with stories of dacoits in its past, the place is turning into a paradise for eco-tourism with a lion safari, rich biodiversity with sightings of Gangetic dolphins, crocodiles etc. It has not seen much larger habitations and is largely forested and natural, retaining good flow, which is then able to give life to the Yamuna from the Etawah area onwards.

Is the curse to Chambal a boon for the Yamuna and hence for the Ganga? It is natural to wonder this. What is the lesson for human society? From Chambal, we receive a message to respect nature and to let it develop sustainably. Should we not care for auspicious rivers like the Ganga and the Yamuna or is our behaviour only guided by fear of curses or more recently the pandemic enforced lockdown!

TRIBUTARIES IN UTTARAKHAND AND UP

Ramganga

The story of another tributary, Ramganga, is no less painful. It originates as a pristine river in the southern slopes of Dudhatoli Hill in the Chamoli district of Uttarakhand and is also the first major tributary joining the Ganga. The 596-km-long river passes through mountainous terrain in great turbulence before it enters the plains at Kalagarh near the border of the Garhwal district, the site of the famous Ramganga dam. Beyond Kalagarh, the river flows in a south-easterly direction and finally joins the Ganga on its left bank, near Kannauj in UP. The river flows entirely in the states of Uttarakhand and UP.

The river flows by the Corbett National Park, near Ramnagar of Nainital district, from where it descends upon the plains. As it passes through the densely-populated cities of Moradabad, Bareilly, Badaun, Shahjahanpur and Hardoi cities of UP situated on its banks, it is inundated by domestic sewage and industrial pollutants. As the 2011 CPCB report points out that while Moradabad may not be a particularly large city by Indian standards, the absence of sewage treatment plants in a city with scores of paper mills, sugar plants, brass foundries and plastic factories that spew waste into the Ramganga and its tributaries, is a recipe for environmental disaster. Moreover, a lot of water is channelled for irrigation and hydroelectric generation, thereby reducing the flow of the river. The important tributaries that join the Ramganga are the Ban, Khoh, Gangan, Gagas, Aril, Kosi, Haldgadi Rao and Deoha.

To help the Ramganga retain some of its pristine qualities, the NMCG has sanctioned three STP projects for two towns—Bareilly and Moradabad—to create a treatment capacity of 146 MLD at a cost of ₹669.99 crore.

The first sewerage project, at a cost of ₹279.91 crore, has been put forward for the creation of an STP of 58 MLD capacity and a 264.25-km sewer network at Moradabad. After a long tale of horror stories during its execution as several problems kept cropping up, finally it could get completed. During this period, another project for 25 MLD capacity in the remaining parts of the city was taken up in 2019 on HAM at ₹118.69 crore. For the sake of feasibility, it was decided to tender out this project along with STPs proposed at Bareilly with a total capacity of 63 MLD in one package under HAM in March 2019. But the land parcels required for Bareilly ran into severe roadblocks and hence, Moradabad and Bareilly were delinked later in the tendering process so that at least the Moradabad project was kept moving. Moradabad was tendered separately and work was awarded in April 2020.

It is a pity that an important commercial and cultural centre like Bareilly (where several developments including an airport have been planned) did not have any capacity to treat its domestic sewage. The land constraint was once again making this attempt to clean up impossible. As DG, I visited Bareilly in March 2020 and after a detailed discussion with the divisional commissioner, the district magistrate and concerned departments took certain policy decisions to change the location of land from environmentally-sensitive river land to an alternate location, which was earlier allotted to the police department. Getting land back from the police department is next to impossible. A telephonic discussion with a close friend and batchmate working at the level of Additional Chief Secretary in Chief Minister's Office was a great help in convincing the district officials to send an alternate proposal. It was done and ultimately got approved by the state cabinet. Bareilly was tendered in October 2020 and evoked an excellent response from the market. The work got awarded in July 2021. One sanctioned project is being built on the tributary of the Ramganga, the Kosi River. The other ₹55.06 crore sanctioned project will create a treatment capacity of 8.5 MLD in the Ramnagar town.

E-flow assessment for Ramganga has been taken up with the multi-agency collaboration of WWF, C-Ganga and GIZ. A pilot for Ramganga basin management planning cycle is being taken under India-EU water partnership and assistance from GIZ with community level extension work being done in association with WWF and state/district agencies.

River Kali (East)

Another infamous tributary of the Ganga with a huge pollution load is the Kali East (named after the Hindu Goddess, Kali) flowing through eight districts of UP before merging with the mother river, near Kannauj. The river has over 1,200 villages situated on its bank and is highly populated by a predominantly rural population which is entirely dependent on the Kali for domestic, agricultural and industrial use; its untreated groundwater is the primary source of drinking water as well. Some villagers use the water for animal rearing too.

The river begins its journey from the Anthawada village, situated in the north of Daurala block of Jansath tehsil of Muzaffarnagar district, and travels nearly 300 km while passing through overcrowded and industrial cities of Muzaffarnagar, Meerut, Ghaziabad, Bulandshahar, Aligarh, Etah, Farrukhabad and Kannauj before merging with the main river near Kannuaj. This river never flows straight, moving in a zigzag manner and is also called Nagin; in the area near Kannauj, it is known as Kalindi.

However, over the past two decades, the river has been used as a dumping ground of substantial quantities of contaminants and untreated effluents from numerous sources along its course. The major factors are industrial untreated effluents, domestic sewage, agricultural run-off, indiscriminate use of polythene, etc. Once known as the resting spot for numerous species of migratory birds, particularly during the winter months, it has now been transformed into a soulless body just carrying industrial waste. And three major cities—Meerut, Hapur and Bulandshahr—and several industries drain their untreated sewage and effluent into the Kali. There are 31 industries within the Meerut district alone, which includes sugar mills, paper mills, textile and distilleries, along with villages and slaughterhouses that discharge their effluent into the river.

The biggest culprit is Meerut city, which contributes more than

60 per cent of the pollution load in the stretch, according to a study by the CPCB. It recorded three major drains—Abu Nallah-1, Abu Nallah-2 and the slaughterhouse drain—carrying 378 MLD of industrial and domestic wastewater of Meerut city. NMCG, under its tributary clean-up efforts , has decided to set up sewage treatment plants at Kasganj and Meerut to save Ganga and the tributary. While Kasganj will have a 15 MLD treatment capacity and 2.8 km sewer network worth ₹76.73 crore, Meerut will have a much larger treatment capacity of 220 MLD through several STPs for ₹690.1 crore. Thankfully, the river will not have to carry its infamy once these STPs are up and running.

It is heartening to see people joining the efforts to rejuvenate this polluted river. A group that has consistently been mobilizing locals for the rejuvenation of Kali in association with the NEER Foundation. They started working from Antawada village, the origin points of Kali and helped in its revival by recharging the lake and the riverbed with the help of locals and the administration. WWF has also chipped in, helping in conducting a study on the deterioration of the river water and groundwater quality. NMCG has been encouraging these efforts, roping in district officials and has also made a technical committee to guide them. NEER foundation's work has been widely recognized and Raman Kant Tyagi of the NEER Foundation has emerged as East Kali Waterkeeper. River Neem, which is one of the tributaries of the Kali East, was on the verge of drying but is now being rejuvenated by the foundation. There is a positive trend developing with local organizations taking lead and training administrative efforts.

Hindon-Kali West and River Krishni: Major Threat to the Yamuna

The Hindon, historically known as river Harnandi, is a major source of water to the highly-populated and predominantly rural population of Western UP province. The Hindon originates in the lower Himalayas at Purka Tanka village in the upper east area of the Saharanpur district. The river flows for 260 km through six districts (Saharanpur, Muzaffarnagar, Meerut, Baghpat, Ghaziabad and Gautam Budh Nagar) until its confluence with the Yamuna near Tilwara village,

Gautam Budh Nagar district, downstream of Delhi.

Hindon has two main tributaries, river Krishni which originates at Kairi village and joins the Hindon at Barnawa village, and the Kali (West) which originates at Dhanakpur village and joins the Hindon at Pithlokar. The river was once considered to be so clean that its waters were believed to cure the kaali khansi (bad cough). A river that once flowed with clean and clear waters of the Himalayas, is now black, odorous and largely devoid of life.

Hindon has historical as well as religious significance. Sardhana, a town on Hindon, has an ancient Mahadev Temple that belongs to the era of the Mahabharata and it is believed that the Pandavas prayed here before starting their journey to the Lakshagrih, the abode of lac created by Duryodhana. This temple exists at Barnava, the confluence point of Kali (West) and Hindon. An Indus Valley Civilization site, Alamgirpur is located 28 kilometres from Delhi along Hindon.

Low flows in the headwaters of the river are exacerbated by over-abstraction of surface water and groundwater. The Hindon is utilized by a wide range of industrial uses along its length. Indeed, the Hindon and its two main tributaries, together have 60 industrial manufacturing units. These industries abstract large volumes of water from the river for their manufacturing processes, and also discharge their industrial effluents without proper treatment directly to the river. This leads to the presence of toxic contaminants, which is very harmful for the biodiversity and ecology. Dissolved oxygen levels are very low throughout the river.

Around 1,215.43 MLD of sewage produced from Saharanpur, Muzaffarnagar, Budhana, Baghpat, Meerut, Ghaziabad and Noida are transported through 68 drains. About 450 MLD of this sewage is treated in different city systems but the rest, 765.43 MLD, remains untreated due to lack of proper STPs. All of this ends up in the Hindon and its tributaries.

Due to the polluted waters of the Hindon and its tributaries, the underground water of villages on the banks of these rivers are polluted and waterborne diseases have been witnessed in several villages. Use of this water for irrigation by some of the farmers in absence of an alternative is also harmful, especially due to the presence of banned persistent organic pollutants in the field soil and crops.

Two Namami Gange projects are under construction under HAM for Budhana and Muzaffarnagar to create a treatment capacity of 97 MLD at ₹282.79 crore. STP projects are also under execution at Baghpat and are being sanctioned for Saharanpur. In the case of Ghaziabad and Noida, STPs exist and NMCG is focusing on ensuring their proper operation, capacity utilization and compliance to standards. Similar to the Ganga, the grossly polluting industries are now being monitored closely with annual inspection by independent expert agencies.

Several NGOs and local associations are coming forward to rejuvenate this river, and campaigns like Hindon Kali and Krishna Bachao Abhiyan are held by locals. NGOs, youngsters and students are working to make the populace aware and to remove solid non-biodegradable wastes like plastic from the river. NEER Foundation too is working on the rejuvenation of Hindon. With the help of hundreds of volunteers, a journey started in 2017 to explore the origin of the Hindon. My Hindon—My Initiative, Nirmal Hindon Initiatives have brought villages, volunteers and activists together for the restoration of the Hindon.

A multi-donor trust fund 2030 Water Resources Group (WRG) is also supporting a participatory process, developing a multi-stakeholder platform of government, civil society, industry and academia to rejuvenate the Hindon. As a starting point, 2030 WRG and India Water Partnership (IWP) have documented 20 good practices by local authorities, NGOs, communities, industries, research institutes and others to clean the river. The vision for Hindon was prepared in consultation with local stakeholders across the basin and technical experts. It aims at reducing industrial, urban and agricultural pollution loads into the river and increasing (ground) water levels by 2030.

River Gomti (Uttar Pradesh)

ग्रहणेकाशी, मकरेप्रयाग। चैत्रनवमी अयोध्या, दशहराधोपाप

As a famous saying in Avadh, it is believed that bathing at 'Dhopap' in Lambhua tehsil of Sultanpur district, especially on Dussehra, cleanses all sins.

The other tributary of the Ganga, the Gomati or Gomti, too has cultural and religious sanctity attached to it. According to Hindu beliefs, the river is the daughter of Rishi Vashist and bathing in the Gomti on Ekadashi (the 11th day of the two lunar phases of the Hindu calendar month) can wash away one's sins. It is a monsoon-and-groundwater-fed river that originates from the Gomat Taal (formally known as Fulhaar Jheel) near Madho Tanda, Pilibhit. It travels 960 kilometres through UP and meets the Ganges near Saidpur, Kaithi, some 27 km from the Varanasi district. River Sai is its major tributary, with a drainage area of 12,900 sq km, approximately 43 per cent of the total catchment area of the Gomti basin. Sitapur, Lucknow, Sultanpur and Jaunpur are the four major urban settlements on the banks of the river.

Deterioration in the water quality of Gomti's waters has been a result of unchecked wastewater discharge from both households and industries from the municipal areas of Sitapur, Hardoi, Barabanki, Sultanpur, Lucknow, Jaunpur and Kerakat (Jaunpur). Its most polluted stretch has some 865 MLD of sewage and industrial effluent flowing through 68 drains and 30 MLD of direct industrial discharge from 30 industries. What is worse, of the 865 MLD of effluents flowing into the river from 68 drains, only 443 MLD of sewage is treated and the rest flows unhindered into the river. The stretch of the river from Sitapur to Rajwari, Varanasi (Gomti before meeting to Ganga), has been identified as a polluted stretch even by the CPCB.

However, there does seem to be light at the end of the tunnel with sewage treatment capacity being created under Namami Gange through three STP projects of 129 MLD in the towns of Sultanpur, Jaunpur and Lucknow for ₹490.14 crore. While Sultanpur will have a

17-MLD STP plant for ₹70 crore, Jaunpur will see the creation of a brand new 30-MLD STP plant for ₹206.05 crore. For Lucknow, it will be a mix of rehabilitation of an old 42 MLD plant and the creation of a new 40-MLD STP plant for ₹213.91 crore.

TRIBUTARIES IN UTTAR PRADESH AND BIHAR

River Ghaghara

Before entering the state capital, Patna, the Ganga is joined by the Ghaghara, also called Karnali. This is a perennial transboundary river originating in the Tibetan Plateau near Lake Manasarovar. It cuts through the Himalayas in Nepal and joins the river Sharda at Brahmaghat in India. Together they form the Ghaghara, a major left-bank tributary of the Ganges. With a length of 507 kilometres, it is the longest river in Nepal. The total length of the Ghaghara up to its meeting point with the Ganga at Revelganj in Bihar is 1,080 km. It is the largest tributary of the Ganges by volume and its second-longest tributary by length after the Yamuna. Its major tributaries include the Kuwana, the Rapti, and the Little Gandak rivers—all of which flow into the Ghaghara from the mountains to the north.

The Karnali basin is also the home of the Gangetic river dolphin, the largest freshwater mammal found on the Indian subcontinent. They are considered an endangered species, particularly vulnerable to threats from habitat deprivation.

Like many other rivers, Ghaghara in full spate can be extremely difficult to manage. Regular heavy flooding by the river during the monsoon months and a simultaneously increased glacier melting leads to large-scale destruction of life and property; the river has been nicknamed the 'Sorrow of Uttar Pradesh,' threatening many of the towns built on its banks. These towns include Akabarpur, Bahraich, Ayodhya, Faizabad, Gorakhpur, Barabanki, Dohrighat, Basti, Deoria, Gonda, Khaililabad, Siddharthnagar, Sitapur, Saint Kabirnagar, Deoria and Tanda in Uttar Pradesh and Chapra (Saran district) and Siwan in Bihar.

While the river may not be as toxic as the Yamuna or the Kali, 14 MLD of mostly domestic sewage through nine open drains constitute a threat to the long-term sustainability and purity of the river. A sewerage project is under construction at Chhapra (Saran district). Gorakhpur, Mau and Deoria city are located in the catchment area of the river. The sewage and other effluent generated from Gorakhpur city contribute to the organic load of the river. Technical assessment is in progress for sanctioning infrastructure for sewage and industrial effluent treatment for Gorakhpur.

River Gandak

Gandak is another tributary of the Ganga and one of the major rivers in Nepal and India. It is also known as the Kali Gandaki and Narayani after the confluence with Trisuli in Nepal. It originates in Tibet at a height of 7,620 metres near the Nepal border and overlooks the Dhaulagiri peak. Its distinguishing feature is that it passes through a deep gorge and provides water for a large hydroelectric project in Nepal. Its water also sustains a major irrigation-cum-hydroelectric power facility at the Indo-Nepal border at Valmiki Nagar. The river has a total catchment area of 46,300 sq km out of which 7,620 sq km is located in India.

The river enters India at the Indo–Nepal border and flows southeast 300 kilometres across the Gangetic plain of Bihar through West Champaran, Gopalganj, Saran and Muzaffarpur districts. The Gandak passes through the three towns of Bagaha, Gopalganj and Lalganj of Bihar. Sewerage projects are under construction at Sonepur under Namami Gange. A riverfront development project has also been constructed. State agencies are also investigating interventions for other towns. A beautiful riverfront has been developed at Narayani Ghat in Gopalganj under Namami Gange that has triggered renewed interest of visitors from this region, Aaratis and an NRI from this area has come forward to contribute for its maintenance.

The river joins the Ganges near Patna just downstream of Hajipur at Sonpur (also known as Harihar Kshetra). Its drainage area in India is 7,620 sq km. At its exit from the outermost Siwaliks foothills to the

Ganges, the Gandak builds up an immense megafan (a large mass of sediment deposited by a moving river) comprising Eastern Uttar Pradesh and North Western Bihar in the middle Gangetic Plains. The megafan consists of sediments eroded from the rapidly uplifting Himalayas. The river's course over this structure is constantly shifting.

The river, like many of its peers, finds a mention in the ancient Sanskrit epic Mahabharata. It is said that Valmiki Rishi wrote the great epic, Ramayana, here. It is also believed to be the birthplace of Luv and Kush, the two sons of Lord Ram and his wife Sita. The hermitage also has landmarks of Sita's 'Falahar' or eating place, and is the meditation site of the great Sage Valmiki.

The Chitwan National Park, Nepal and Valmiki National Park, India are located in proximity along this river in Valmikinagar near Gandak Barrage. Valmiki Nagar Sanctuary is the eighteenth tiger reserve and fourth-largest in terms of tiger density. For the first time, detailed profiling of the aquatic life along Gandak has been taken up under WII-NMCG project.

River Sone (MP, Chhattisgarh, UP, Jharkhand, Bihar)

Sone in central India is the second-largest of the Ganga's southern tributaries, after the Yamuna. It originates near Amarkantak in Madhya Pradesh, just east of the headwater of the Narmada River, and flows north-northwest through Madhya Pradesh state before turning sharply eastward where it encounters the southwest-northeast-Kaimur Range. The Sone parallels the Kaimur hills, flowing east-northeast through Uttar Pradesh, Jharkhand and Bihar to join the Ganga just west of Patna. Geologically, the lower valley of the Sone is an extension of the Narmada Valley, and the Kaimur Range is an extension of the Vindhya Range. Dehri-on-Sone and Sonbhadra are the major cities on its banks.

The 784-km Sone is one of the largest rivers of India, with Rihand (Chhattisgarh) and North Koel (Jharkhand) as the main tributaries. Sone has a steep gradient with quick run-off, and it turns into a roaring river with the rainwaters in the catchment area, while turning quickly into a steady stream in the non-monsoon months. The Sone, being wide and shallow, leaves disconnected pools of water in the remaining part of the year. The channel of the Sone is very wide (about 5 km at Dehri-on-Sone) but the floodplain is narrow, only 3 to 5 km wide. In the past, the Sone has been notorious for changing course, but that tendency has been checked with a barrage constructed 8 km upstream of Anicut (one of the oldest irrigation systems) at Dehri, and now more on the Indrapuri Barrage. In November 2021, three STPs with a total capacity of 21 MLD has been sanctioned for Dehri at a cost of ₹64 crore under Namami Gange. Arrah , near the confluence of Son and Ganga, is another historically important city and is also the place of Babu Kunwar Singh, the legendary freedom fighter. It is held that the area was heavily forested in ancient times and Lord Ram killed demon Taraka in this area. Proposal for STP at Arrah is under preparation by state and has been agreed in principle for support by NMCG.

After passing through the steep escarpments of the Kaimur Range, it flows straight across the plain to the Ganges. There is a vast expanse of sand in dry weather there. The hot west winds pile up the sand on the east bank, making natural embankments. But after heavy rain in the hills, even this wide bed is unable to carry the waters of the Sone and disastrous floods in Shahabad, Gaya and Patna are not uncommon. In fact, floods already take a significant toll on the lives and livelihoods in the Nepal lowlands known as the Terai, as well as Bangladesh and Bihar and eastern UP. Floods account for 90 per cent of the economic cost of natural disasters in Nepal. States such as Assam, West Bengal, UP and especially Bihar are highly flood-prone. In Bihar alone, the annual average economic damage is 45.8 crore.

The Sone, which flows past through 12 towns like Sidhi, Churhat, Rampur Naikin in Madhya Pradesh, Dehri, Koilwar, in Bihar and Chopan in UP with a total population of 824,659 in 2016 discharges 89 MLD of sewage into the river. This number is expected to rise to 125 MLD by 2035 when the population is expected to touch 1,157,000.

River Kosi

Koshi or Kosi drains the northern slopes of the Himalayas in the Tibet region and the southern slopes in Nepal. From a major confluence of tributaries north of the Chatra Gorge onwards, the Koshi River is also known as Saptakoshi for its seven upper tributaries. These include the Tamur Koshi originating from the Kanchenjunga area in the east, River Arun from Tibet and Sun Koshi from the Gosainthan area further west. The Sun Koshi's tributaries from east to west are Dudh Koshi, Bhote Koshi, Tamba Koshi and Indravati Koshi. The Saptakoshi crosses into northern Bihar, where it branches into distributaries before joining the Ganges near Kursela in the Katihar district. Kosi has several ancient and spiritual stories associated. It is mentioned in Mahabharat as Kausiki and is lifeline of Mithila region.

Several studies of past trends and 28 historical maps indicate that the river has a strong tendency of shifting its course over large distances in a random and oscillating manner. Its unstable nature has been attributed to the heavy silt it carries during the monsoon season. It leads to flooding in India and has an extreme effect on the populace and ecosystem.

Below the Siwaliks, the river has built up a megafan some 15,000 km^2 (5,800 sq m), breaking into more than 12 distinct channels, all with shifting courses due to flooding. The Kosi alluvial fan is one of the largest in the world, covering northeast Bihar and eastern Mithila to the Ganges. Kamalā, Bāgmati and Budhi Gandak are major tributaries of Kosi in India, besides minor tributaries such as Bhutahi Balān. Fishing is an important enterprise on the river but fishing resources are depleting.

River Damodar (Jharkhand, West Bengal)

The Damodar rises in the Palamau hills of Chota Nagpur at an elevation of about 609.75 metres It flows in a south-easterly direction, entering the deltaic plains below Raniganj. Near Burdwan, the river abruptly changes its course to a southerly direction and joins Hooghly about 48.27 km below Calcutta. The total length of the river is nearly 547 km. The upper catchment is rough, comprising hilly areas denuded with forest and vegetal cover and is subject to erosion while the lower catchment is silt covered and fertile. There are no irrigation facilities in the upper catchment and the cultivation depends on the monsoon season. However, the lower portion has irrigation facilities from the Anderson Weir situated at Rhondia on the Damodar nearly 19 km below the Durgapur Barrage.

Damodar basin lies in the states of Jharkhand and West Bengal and is highly industrial. The present water demand for industries is 663 million cubic metres (MCM)/year, which is about 15.36 per cent of the utilizable water potential of the basin. This demand is likely to increase to about 884 MCM/year by 2021 due to new thermal power plants, brickfields, rice mills and cold storages, etc.

The tributaries and sub-tributaries of the Damodar include Konar, Barakar, Haharo, Bokaro, Ghari, Jamunia, Khadia, Guaia and Bhera. The biggest tributary of the Damodar river is the Barakar, joining Damodar after travelling for about 241 km. The source of Barakar is located in the vicinity of the Padma in Hazaribagh district. Subsequently, the river runs through Jharkhand prior to joining the Damodar close to Dishergarh in West Bengal.

In the past, the Damodar has caused frequent and immense flood damages, so much so that the river came to be associated with sorrow and suffering. To overcome this, the decision to build a series of dams on the pattern of the USA's Tennessee Valley led to five dams in the Damodar Valley, namely Maithon, Panchet, Konar, Tilaiya and Tenughat and a barrage at Durgapur. Damodar Valley Corporation (DVC) was established in 1948 for the management of the Damodar Valley water resources and its dams serve multiple purposes: domestic and industrial water supply, flood control, irrigation and hydropower generation.

Damodar got polluted due to various industries that have mushroomed on its riverbanks which provide minerals. There are a number of coal-oriented industries that are scattered over this basin. A majority of them are government-owned coke oven plants, coal washeries, important iron and steel plants in India, glass, zinc and cement plants and thermal power plants. The contamination is a result of excessive excavation, oil, fly ash, poisonous metals as well as coal dust. Namami Gange mission has sanctioned projects in Durgapur, Asansol, Bardhaman in West Bengal, Phusro in Jharkhand to create a treatment capacity of 240 MLD at ₹968.30 crore.

Similarly, to prevent widespread floods in Bihar, a Burhi Gandhak Noon Baya Ganga link canal project has been conceptualized to divert partial flood water of River Burhi Gandak to Ganga with the help of the canal. It is assumed that not only 70 per cent of the average annual flood damages occurring in the districts will be reduced, but it will also irrigate 0.125 million hectares in the districts of Begusarai, Samastipur and Khagaria at a cost of ₹4,314 crore. The National Water Development Agency (NWDA) has prepared the detailed project report.

Even NMCG officials believe that despite their best efforts, the task of conservation and rejuvenation of the tributaries is only half done. Forty projects have already been sanctioned for 28 towns to create 2,675.85 MLD of STPs at a cost of ₹7,750 crore. The tributaries are priority now in Namami Gange having achieved major success in completing projects on the main stem of Ganga. Many tributaries continue to spew untreated domestic wastes and harmful toxic effluents to pollute the Ganga. Unlike the main stem of the river, cleaning these small rivers has different and varied challenges and suitable strategies need to be deployed. First, the focus of authorities is always on the main river, and not on the tributaries, which clouds their judgement. Believing that the river is an entire ecosystem and needs comprehensive planning is a point strongly propounded by the NMCG officials, but it has yet to find takers among many state authorities. That leads to reduced funding and less resource deployment for the 'not-so-important' tributaries. Ecologically all are important in the long run.

Additionally, the lack of proper governance and weak institutional structures makes proper planning and execution of the projects that much more difficult. Since every major river has a number of tributaries, it involves more and more local bodies, which make the structure extremely complex and difficult to manage. We are now extending the district level institution of District Ganga Committees to tributaries too and in 2021 almost 50 such DGCs have been constituted on tributaries. Since the challenge of one river is different from the other due to different ecosystems, local and boundary conditions, it becomes even more difficult to manage a river that passes through different towns because of the involvement of different administrations and local ecologies.

Different tributaries have different characteristics, unique local conditions, and differing social and economic conditions, which makes each river different and therefore entails a different management plan, which further complicates the issue. Finally, lack of data and information on these tributaries makes planning and execution of projects difficult and they are then based on intuition and a gut feeling rather than hard evidence.

While the crusade to clean the tributaries may be in its initial stages after its launch by the NMCG, it will only be successful if state authorities and common citizenry realize that when they save any river, they save an ecosystem, which in turn will save them and save their dependencies—physical, economic, spiritual—on the water and its community of life. In fact, if attention is given, resources for the rejuvenation of small rivers and streams may be formed at the district level by dovetailing funds from Mahatma Gandhi National Rural Employment Guarantee Act (MGNREGA), urban missions and other schemes. Along with all these streams, we need to protect and conserve their ecosystem—wetlands, floodplains and forests too. The Ganga is not just a single river and its tributaries are crucial for its sustenance.

In a river song from Bhagalpur (ancient Champa), the Ganga is personified as a lovely woman called Gango. Kamla is another stream, whose presence means a good harvest, while the sparkling adornments are the river's many tributaries. Tirhut is the upland region giving rise to two of these—the Gandak and the Koshi:

> 'East of Kamla and west of the Koshi
> There is no woman like Gango.

Where have you bathed, O Gango,
Where did you comb your hair?
Where did you find your sparkling adornments?
In the Ganga I bathed
In Tirhut I combed my hair.
Why did you bathe, O Gange?
Why did you comb your hair?
For grace, I bathed.
For the endless flowing of my braid,
I combed my hair
And set in it these bright adornments'[18]

[18]Assa Doron, Richard Barz and Barbara Nelson, *An Anthology of Writings on the Ganga: Goddess and River in History, Culture, and Society,* Oxford University Press, 2014, p. 222–223

14

People-River Connect

We met Swami Sanand in late 2013. The previous year, and even before that, Swamiji had gone on a fast unto death to bring attention to Ganga cleaning and to expedite the processes. He was beyond 80, but looked relatively agile; his energy was amply reflected during discussions on the Ganga. He had multiple credentials as a professor of civil engineering at IIT Kanpur, Member Secretary of CPCB and then a renunciate and a Ganga Bhakt. His fast unto death in 2012 had precipitated the third meeting of the NGRBA with the Prime Minister in chair. At first, he refused to entertain us, on the simple ground that mid-level government functionaries did not matter. We were taken aback but could appreciate his dejection and waited for some time. Our patience finally caught his attention and he started to open up.

His questions were asked with a child-like simplicity but they contained serious substance. 'Before we move any further, who, in your opinion is the owner of Ganga?' he asked and without waiting for a response kept on, 'Is it the government? Then which government, Centre, state or local? Of course, none of us can say for sure, that is what brings Ganga to this state, you don't even know whom to engage with and it is so easy for anyone to pass the buck.'

We tried to lead, 'But isn't the public custodian of all environmental assets including rivers?' He looked unimpressed but nodded in affirmative, 'Yes, but how to make them realize and who will do that?'

Yes, this was easier said than done. After discussing multiple issues, we left with more questions than answers. The connection between the people and the river is natural and organic. We need rivers for our sustenance, to hold life, to enjoy, to grow economically and spiritually. But is it the connection between people and the river which exalts the river from a geographical entity to a socio-religious one and even a deity? Rivers have been the hallmarks of our history, geography, sociology and psychology. Victor R. Shinde and others have noted in a famous article in Journal of Governance, January 2020 that 'the natural rhythms of the rivers were mirrored in the lifecycles of riverine citizens influencing local cultural and religious practices. From Indus Valley civilization in India to Nile for Egyptians, Tigris and Euphrates for Mesopotamians, Yangtze for Chinese rivers have been the focal point stemming not only sustenance but ready means of communication, a channel for civilizations to come together.' Only in the case of the Ganga and Indians has this become accentuated, the connection has seeped into the mind, the psyche and a particular religion to the extent that proximity to the river (or even for those outside of India) builds on the ultimate desire to be immersed in it.

In such a scenario, why does the nation have to worry about cleaning the Ganga? Why is Swami Sanand trying to figure out the real owner? Something has definitely gone wrong somewhere. We all know that civilizations and great cities have all grown on the banks of rivers drawing their sustenance from it, but unbridled growth of cities and aspirations have gone to such an extent that rivers are lost in cities and people have turned their back on the rivers. This leads to a degradation of rivers, particularly in urban stretches, causing their transformation, as often termed 'river to sewer'. It is not uncommon, even the notorious Najafgarh drain in Delhi, a major source of untreated water in Yamuna, used to be River Sahibi at one point of time.

With the clarion call of the Prime Minister in 2014 from the banks of Ganga at Varanasi, a new fervour was instilled in the otherwise maligned and suspected Ganga cleaning project. The official website of Prime Minister of India mentions that 'never in the world such a complex programme has been implemented and will require participation across sectors and each and every citizen of the country. There are various ways in which each one of us can contribute to the cause of cleaning river Ganga.'

During an earlier review meeting on Ganga, his direction to the NMCG had been even clearer. Namami Gange had to be made into a Jan Andolan and an economic success. Right in the first meeting on Ganga in August 2014, he talked about involving people especially ex-servicemen from areas along the Ganga. In his second meeting on 6 January 2015, I remember him asking a question about how many districts lay along the Ganga and what the district magistrates do for the river. Until then, Ganga cleaning programme was mainly oriented to cities, rather selected cities, held responsible for the pollution. Rural areas, district administrations, etc. were not focused upon. We could provide some estimate of the number of districts but were further told that we needed to engage with the DMs for better coordination and for reaching out to people at large. This later led to constitution of District Ganga Committees as an important institutional structure.

While some murmurs regarding peoples' involvement had been mentioned earlier, it had never gathered mass consensus. This time, the mandate was clear and the message was backed by strong political will. Under Namami Gange programme, 'Peoples Participation' came as a dedicated component with distinct budget allocation for it. The die had been cast, only nobody seemed to know how to go about the task.

NMCG, abiding by its methodology of agile implementation, though ignorantly, decided to move in a calibrated manner. The seeds of public participation had been sown during the formulation of the Namami Gange Programme itself. In July 2014, NMCG organized the first ever national dialogue on Ganga cleaning aptly titled as Ganga Manthan. This was a bold step and a major departure from the usual non-controversial approach followed by governments. NMCG invited religious leaders for the day-long summit at Vigyan

Bhawan. In four distinct groups, spiritual leaders (cutting across religions), environmentalists, academicians, civil servants, people's representatives and NGOs deliberated on different aspects and set forth on the long list of issues of national priority.

An issue raised in deliberations with spiritual leaders was about the popular belief regarding both Ganga and Yamuna vanishing by the end of Kaliyuga. If so, was there any need or the wherewithal to reverse this otherwise certain process? The answer was even more interesting. Swami Vishwesh Tirth (Pejavar Swami), the seer of Udupi, quoted from scriptures that a King possesses powers to reverse dictates for the sake of dharma. And in Kaliyuga, the people will be the king and hence, they will have the power to hold on to Ganga. This was indeed enlightening.

NMCG needed to know how to communicate to the people about Ganga cleaning, but it had to be a professional and scientific exercise. John Hopkins University-Bloomberg School of Communications had earlier taken up a study under the World Bank programme in which they tried to identify the communication needs through a direct survey of people in the Ganga Basin. The study recommended a Surround-Engage-Encourage model, starting with an inspirational multichannel campaign to make them participate in Ganga cleaning, followed by engagement of administrative agencies and public through well-designed activities culminating into encouragement of individual heroes and organizations working for a clean Ganga. The study found out that people were aware of the state of Ganga and wanted to participate in its clean up but felt inadequate to take any action and did not know where to start. Public looked to the government to build an action plan for them. It underlined the need for a sustained action plan from the government. Interestingly, the study also indicated that a significant population still believed that the Ganga had come to earth to clean the sins of humans and as such, it was unbelievable for them that the river itself was under threat. That partly explains the reluctance among citizens.

To make rain possible, you need to start with dust. To start a mission, you need an anchor. With the Prime Minister himself championing the cause, the anchor was there. But a rope was needed to bind the people to work for the Ganga. In the mission, we wondered and felt the need for a theme song. We had no idea where to start. This could not have been a typical sarkari tender work, the run-of-the-mill government messages, which most of us switch off physically and mentally even before they start. Almost like a miracle, through some reference, the Trichur Brothers joined the mission one fine morning. Their name was familiar, but most of us had not been initiated in formal classical music and did not understand the real worth. Srikrishna Mohan and Ram Kumar Mohan, the famous brothers, are celebrated Karnatic singers and children of Trichur R. Mohan, a famous mridangam player. They were christened as Trichur Brothers by none other than H.H. Jayendra Saraswati of Kanchi Mutt. They longed to create a song for the Ganga for some time. They already had a dedicated lyric scripted, a great mix of verses from the great Shankaracharya and Hindi verses specially written for the same. The sample paragraph itself once rendered left us spellbound. They needed an appropriate video to accompany the song and were then exploring whether this could become the theme song for Namami Gange programme, especially as the word 'Namami Gange' was a part of the lyric. Most of us who had been working in this project have had their own moments of realizing the divine presence in the work; this appeared to be one.

We were convinced but did not know where to start. Of course, this was not our regular work and though we had enough technical expertise, art was a bit too much to ask for. The bureaucratic processes gradually started taking their toll as time passed, and the patience of the Trichur Brothers started to run out. They were ready to work pro bono and just needed funding to finance the video without compromising the quality. But the government machinery had no means to appreciate that. The bottlenecks were many, some of us just did not understand, some were unimpressed and others were more interested in getting their own name and video included in the same. Finally, both brothers lost their cool and clearly told us that they may opt out. We felt dismayed when such a great thing seemed to slip out of our hands. Sometimes the best ideas come only in times of distress, and suddenly, it dawned on us that even if government funding was not possible, nothing stopped us from seeking funds through Corporate Social Responsibility (CSR) etc., for this project. A few phone calls and some persuasion later, the brothers landed up beaming as State Bank of India agreed to fund them.

The work moved fast thereafter and we appreciated their zeal to deliver a masterpiece. They travelled from Gangotri to Ganga Sagar, shooting and fine-tuning the song. Finally, the Namami Gange song saw the light of the day. We remember the first time we heard it. We had somehow arranged quality speakers and had called some of the team members for a preview. After the song was played, there was perfect silence, almost a sign of disapproval. But immediately, there was a burst, claps and some cries too, people were touched to the bone. On a trial basis, we played the first and truncated version of the song to the public at Pravasi Bharatiya Divas at Ahmedabad in January 2015, and many started gathering, asking for an encore. Not everybody understood the song, but all were connected. The Namami Gange anthem today does not need an introduction, it is the signature of the programme, played in every event of the NMCG and it feels good to be part of its creation. In the future, we will be able to tell our grandchildren about being able to see the masterpiece before it took this shape.

'Paani Jo Tera Khara
Tere Aansu Ki Dhara
Kaise Main Dekhu Santan Hun
Mana Hai Tujhe Maa
Ye Dharam Hai Mera
Main Tujhe Tera Vo Samman Dun'

—Namami Gange anthem

The last few lines of the song convey our commitment to the river in an even better way.

The polluted water of yours
Is nothing but your tears
How can I tolerate,
being your child;
You are my mother,
And it is my duty
To bring you back
Your glory.

The NMCG later came up with another inspirational song in 2018, titled 'Kartavya Gange', which was a call-to-action song. It is a beautiful piece written by Prasoon Joshi and composed and sung by Shankar Mahadevan. This exhorts the people to take up the cause of Ganga and work for the same, and to not rest till we have actually cleaned it up ('*Nahin rukenge, hum swachh karenge*'). Both the songs have now become a part of every household and can easily be identified with the programme.

The ball had started rolling but the main target of bringing people together lacked a clear-cut action plan. In subsequent discussions, it became clear that people needed to be drawn to the riverbanks for reasons beyond religion. The visible filth and solid waste on the riverbanks and in the main stream (including the ritual waste) was the main deterrent. We were convinced that it needed to be tackled first if we wanted people to face our divine river. We tried to take up a few projects, but immediately stumbled. This did not fit the design of the ongoing NGRBA programme since it did not address the water quality of the Ganga in a tangible manner. Learning from it, we brought in a new component in the Namami Gange Programme as a part of the main projects, called 'Entry Level Activities'. We listed activities such as riverbank clean up, construction or improvements to the riverfronts and crematoria as the first-stage activities while building large-scale STPs aimed at enhancing public confidence.

Inspired by the experience with Sabarmati, the NMCG deployed trash skimmers to collect the visible solid waste from the Ganga river in a mechanized manner at 11 places including Haridwar,

Garhmukteshwar, Kanpur, Allahabad, Varanasi, Patna, Sahebganj, Howrah, Nabadweep and later, at Mathura-Vrindawan and Delhi too. To improve public interest, dedicated ghat clean-up projects were undertaken at 84 ghats of Varanasi and later at 94 ghats of Bithoor-Kanpur, Prayagraj and Mathura-Vrindawan together with 72 ghats at Haridwar, Uttarakhand. These projects ensure cleaning of ghats through professional agencies for three years as a start. The effects are visible, ghats are cleaner and footfall has increased. This has also inspired many NGOs and community-based organizations to take up voluntary clean-up drives on the ghats at smaller scales at numerous places. The ripple effect has been noticed.

Temsutula Imsong, a girl from Nagaland, became a pioneer when she initiated an unsupported and voluntary clean-up drive at Prabhu Ghat, Varanasi, and made it spic and span in less than a month. This was noticed by the Prime Minister himself and she was included in his Mann ki Baat. Similar attempts are being encouraged and supported by NMCG at multiple places along the Ganga and Yamuna. Members of several organizations like Ganga Vichar Manch, Ganga Praharis, Ganga Mitras, Ganga Doots participate in ghat cleaning at different sites regularly. District Ganga Committees too coordinate and organize larger drives along ghats.

But the real challenge lay in moving the people to join the initiatives and in realizing the role of community-based organizations. NMCG started identifying larger groups of youth and citizens to engage them. Today, there are specific arrangements with National Cadet Corps, Nehru Yuva Kendra and National Service Schemes. These included dedicated programmes for ghat-based actions and awareness activities being undertaken by these groups.

Ganga Vichar Manch is a voluntary platform put in place by NMCG at district levels to engage individual citizens who are not part of any other group. The Vichar Manch has been taking up concentrated action on ghats on all festive occasions, like Ganga Dussehra, and encouraging citizens to participate. Several others are also able to effectively contribute in District Ganga Committees.

Ganga Prahari is a dedicated cadre organized and trained by the

WII that undertakes community-people engagement activities while working at a scientific level for biodiversity and river conservation along with livelihood creation in the process. After developing a well-trained cadre of Ganga Praharis along the Ganga, in the second phase we are trying to develop cadres along the tributaries as well. These cadets have been gaining confidence and one of the Ganga Praharis from Devprayag has recently been elected as a sarpanch of his village.

A new initiative has been made at Benaras Hindu University, Varanasi, to impart training in ecological skills among students and citizens as Ganga Mitras. The science clubs under the Vigyan Prasar initiative of Ministry of Science and Technology have been roped in to increase awareness. A lecture is arranged by experts on the last Tuesday of every month. But the most unique initiative among all is the creation of a uniformed Ganga Task Force by drawing the ex-servicemen as a part of the Territorial Army. Today, one of its battalions have already been raised and stationed at Prayagraj, Kanpur and Varanasi from where its sections are continuously being deployed wherever needed in large gatherings like Kumbh and Magh Mela. These soldiers are fully trained and are engaged in pollution checking, monitoring, afforestation, surveillance for biodiversity conservation, etc. These initiatives have built trust, commitment and discipline among the youth. They have also reached out to schools, interacting and motivating students and providing leadership to several other volunteer groups. They have taken up rejuvenation of historic McPherson Lake, once the pride of Prayagraj.

These arrangements are catalysts of public awakening and have become the nucleus of a much larger process creating a new generation conscious of its rights and responsibilities, capable and willing to consider themselves the owners of Ganga and to fight for its sustenance. A river-based Jan Andolan, a new awakening, is not far behind.

The challenge in creating these large masses of interested volunteers is to keep them engaged and to keep their energies channelled, failing which these masses have the propensity to be misled or become further disinterested and demotivated. To this effect, NMCG has launched a series of activities. Innovative ways to reach out to the people, especially students and youth in large numbers. The idea for a digital initiative for engagement through online quizzes on the Ganga came from Bhawna Badola, CEO, TREE Craze Foundation, a not-for-profit organization with activities related to environmental education and conservation. She had been part of the initial team of the NMCG. The initiative was launched in 2019 as Ganga Quest with some CSR support. This is a digital competitive knowledge enhancement programme in which all school children, students and others are encouraged to compete in an online quiz on Ganga and its ecosystem. The experiment was successful. We also got a chance to interact with students and teachers and to share their joys and anxieties, which helped us polish our programme. The initiative received extremely encouraging response from the Union Minister for Jal Shakti Gajendra Sigh Shekhawat himself, who also guided us to work on a platform for continued activity in an engaging manner. In its second season (in 2020), the Ganga Quest received an overwhelming response with participation of more than 1.15 million people in spite of the unprecedented lockdown. More than 20,000 schools and others participated and we heard a response from each and every corner of country. This year (2021) the Quest saw participation by more than a million from over 50,000 schools and has become a truly global quiz with participants from 113 countries. This has emerged as the largest-ever school contact programme across the world. Now the quest is linked with a continuous learning and activity portal (CLAP) to keep them engaged and to track them in their journey to emerge as environmentally responsible citizens. The vision shared by the minister is taking shape.

It is always said we become what we learn and observe. It is really important that we tap into the intellects of the future generation to make the interventions sustainable, and making them sensitive towards rivers or water system as a whole is one of the visions we hold at the NMCG. Young minds often have the unique ability for blue-sky thinking, which will be necessary to address the complex phenomenon of river rejuvenation. We have initiated many dialouges with universities to introduce river-sensitive design and planning. NMCG in co-ordination with NIUA organized 'Re-Imagining Urban Rivers', a national level thesis competition in September 2020, under a joint project to promulgate river-sensitive development in our cities. This is a first of its kind initiative to engage young minds to conduct research and envisage solutions for urban river issues. Its idea too came from Jyoti Verma, a young consultant, who also anchored it and is now expanding it with Victor Shinde of NIUA and their team. A new genre of young thinkers, a new set of expertise is emerging, a welcome spin-off from the programme.

Tapping into the intellect and creativity of students to arrive at innovative solutions for re-imagining the outlook and management of rivers that flow through cities was one of the core objectives of this initiative.

Ganga Utsav is an annual event organized by the NMCG in October every year to celebrate the Ganga. A series of events are organized as fun activity (with live quizzes, music and dance programmes). It started in 2017 with a one-night cultural event named as 'Ek Sham Ganga Ke Naam'. Then in 2018, the 'Ganga Bal Mela' (with corporate partners HCL, GIZ, NMCG) at Noida was organized as a half-day affair where school children were involved in the initiative and also a plantation programme was conducted. In 2019, Ganga Utsav was organized at the National Stadium, New Delhi as a day-long festival and exhibition. It also included Ganga Bal Mela, Live Ganga Quiz, storytelling, cultural programs, etc. Again in 2020, Ganga Utsav was organized as a three-day online event with activities in more than 50 districts and even in some areas outside the basin. This became the foundation for developing Nadi Utsav and restoring Nadi Sanskriti.

The success of Ganga Quest and Ganga Utsav was not easy to achieve. While Gaga Quest was first of its kind and heavily technology oriented, Ganga Utsav required organizational abilities normally not available in smaller entities like NMCG. We have been consistent witness to solutions emerging from nowhere on several trying occasions and this was no different. Rozy Agrawal, Executive Director (Finance) in NMCG, came forward and took the lead in making both the initiatives possible. His relentless follow-ups and discovering solutions to ever-springing technical and organizational challenges took all by surprise. He continues to lead the development of CLAP and strengthening of Ganga Quest.

We also had a chance to explore public outreach through adventure sports and have organized marathons, Ganga runs, rafting and boating experiences. In 2018, a rafting expedition led by Bachendri Pal in association with Tata from Haridwar to Patna, evoked good response from youth and students. Ganga Aamantran Abhiyan, more than a month-long rafting and boating expedition, was taken up in October-November 2019 by NMCG, covering the entire stretch of Ganga from Uttarakhand to Bengal, participating in several programmes with a special focus on the youth. I joined the Jal Shakti Minister in a rafting expedition from Devprayag to Rishikesh and it was a great journey down the memory lane. The Great Ganga Run, a running event, received an unexpected response from the citizens and celebrities in Delhi with more than 20,000 turning up. Many reached the stadium in the night from distant places and stayed there to run for Ganga in the morning. In Varanasi, a run exclusively for women had more than 8,000 women participants. Cleanathons are regular exercises of ghat cleaning conducted not only locally but nationally (taken up at hundreds of places over a single day). G. Asok Kumar, the then Executive Director (Projects) went beyond his core responsibility in conceptualizing and operationalizing these initiatives. Kalindi Kunj, an otherwise neglected ghat on Yamuna in Delhi was adopted by NMCG and its staff and cleaning was conducted there on a regular basis. Here, officials and ministers also participated. The cleaning is still being continued as 'Meri Yamuna Mere Ghat' campaign by TREE Craze Foundation and other NGOs.

Attracted by the cause, a number of citizens have also taken up voluntary clean-ups on ghats and that too in many innovative ways. Wing Commander Paramvir Singh, an officer of Indian Air Force, took up a swimming expedition from Haridwar to Kolkata, which was supported by NMCG. Further inspired, he joined NMCG later and anchored their major expeditions.

'Rag Rag Mein Ganga' is a unique 21-episode travelogue anchored by celebrated actor Rajiv Khandelwal and was telecast on DD National. The programme became a super hit in no time, indicating the immense interest of the public in the Ganga and the Namami Gange Programme. Through this travelogue, we have reached millions of lives and also an IMDB rating of 9.5. Currently its second season is in the running.

The ever-increasing number of such initiatives both under the aegis of NMCG as also by the public themselves and the number of participants in each of them indicates that the idea of a clean Ganga has caught the public imagination and gathered the necessary mass to keep it going. This still leaves aside a much larger group who otherwise cannot participate in such activities for many limitations and still want to contribute. We could ill-afford to ignore them.

CLEAN GANGA FUND

The Clean Ganga Fund (CGF) came up in 2014 immediately after the announcement of Namami Gange Programme to channel the tremendous support committed by citizens and NRIs together for the cause of the Ganga. It provided a platform for the people to pledge funds and donate seamlessly for innovative projects. CGF is registered as a trust with the Finance Minister at the helm. The Prime Minister made a point to announce its constitution at his famous Madison Square address and he has been leading this by donating the prize money, souvenirs/gifts and auction proceeds to the CGF. The fund has collected more than ₹400 crore as contributions from public, NRIs and under the CSR, which it later became eligible for. Many important projects have been taken up in CGF and through a direct CSR; 'Har ki Paudi' renovation, ghats at Gangotri, Badrinath, Mirjapur, etc. are some examples.

Public participation and enthusiasm can sometimes be baffling, especially when it is unexpected and one is not prepared for it. Immediately after the launch of Namami Gange Programme, NMCG received more than 3,000 responses through the office of the Prime

Minister. Flooded, most of us did not know how to utilize them meaningfully considering their wide-ranging nature and at times, their impracticality. But this enthusiasm was infectious for the team and we made sure that that every reference was taken into account and was responded to individually.

This was also a humbling experience. After the launch, CGF received unique messages from the donors. We cannot forget the soldier who contributed from his retirement gratuity and those who donate every month from their savings. This leaves us speechless. Even today, when pride takes us aback, these experiences immediately brings us back to reality. We are just privileged folks who had the opportunity to work for the Ganga at the cost of the taxpayers. Many others are ready to work and sacrifice their lives without anticipating any returns. NMCG has indeed achieved the first landmark, making people again look up to the holy river. But the test will be in seeing to what extent this enthusiasm is sustained over long periods of time and whether it will be confined to symbolic activities or if it will be factored into the real governance processes.

The seeds of such participation have been laid in the District Ganga Committees, which are joint bodies of government and public at local levels. They are supposed to identify the priority projects, work out local resources, find alternate sources of funding and make recommendations for viable and locally relevant projects. They are also expected to be the custodians, at least at the local level and to engage citizens towards producing a clean Ganga. However, the public representatives are still nominated members and the challenge lies in making them truly representative and still apolitical. Keeping the elected representatives as ex-officio members can meet this requirement to some extent. Another alternative can be to create local trusts for the rivers where every citizen is free to become a member and the trusts send representatives to the District Ganga Committees. Such trusts have done very well in the United Kingdom, where each river, small and big, have independent trusts constituted, managed and funded by citizens themselves and the government has only recognized them. When that happens, these forums will be really useful and bring in a more bottoms-up planning process. The public would then indeed become a partner of the government.

Six years after our cited meeting with Swami Sanand and more than two years after his death in another of his fasts in 2018 for the cause of Ganga, the answer to his question has started emerging. The people are indeed the owners of Ganga and it does exist for them. People have started realizing this and proving it correct is the responsibility of NMCG, to which we are committed. When this difficult, if not utopian dream, will be fully achieved, no one can say for sure but if the present is any indicator, it should not be far off. Till then and thereafter too, we will continue to remember Swami Sanand.

A quote from our Prime Minister is extremely relevant which he stated during 81st edition of Mann Ki Baat on 26 Sep 2021: हम नदियों की सफाई और उन्हें प्रदूषण से मुक्त करने का काम सबके प्रयास और सबके सहयोग से कर सकते हैं। 'नमामि गंगे मिशन' भी आज आगे बढ़ रहा है तो इसमें सभी के प्रयास, एक प्रकार से जन-जागृति, जन-आंदोलन, उसकी बहुत बड़ी भूमिका है।

On the occasion of Kumbh last year, the devotees expressed satisfaction over the cleanliness of the Ganga. This sense of appreciation in the country and abroad stems from the contribution of public in keeping the river clean. This is a national mission that is now going global. We all revere mother Ganga. We all have been taking so much from her. Now, all of us need to come together and join this movement and do our duty and give back so that river can sustain us!

'Hum tujhse lete aayen hain; Par ab teri puja karni hai
Karni hai nirmal lahar lahar, teri sachchi puja karni hai
Tujhe sish jhukana hai humko; Kartaya nibhana hai humko
Jai Jai Gange, Namami Gange; Nahin rukenge,
hum swachcha karenge!'

We have been benefitting from you, but now need to worship you,
We need to clean every wave, and in true sense rever you;
We need to bow down to you, we need to discharge our duty
Victory to Ganga, salutations to Ganga,

we will not stop till we clean all!

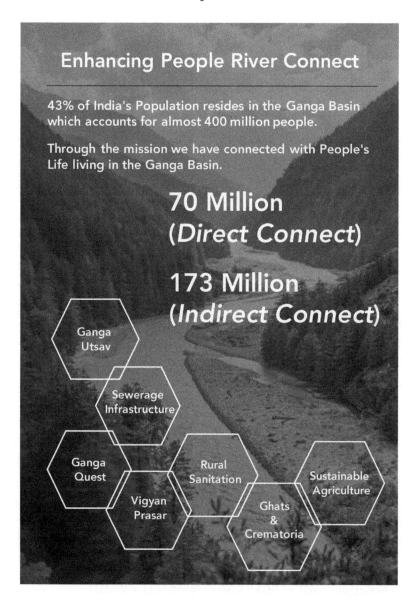

Enhancing People River Connect

43% of India's Population resides in the Ganga Basin which accounts for almost 400 million people.

Through the mission we have connected with People's Life living in the Ganga Basin.

70 Million (Direct Connect)

173 Million (Indirect Connect)

Ganga Utsav

Sewerage Infrastructure

Ganga Quest

Vigyan Prasar

Rural Sanitation

Ghats & Crematoria

Sustainable Agriculture

15

Many Firsts

The national experience of cleaning Ganga is unique in many ways. Firstly, it was much ahead of its time for a developing country to put this objective on its plate even before it had met its hunger and other economic goals. Never in the world, a country had taken up river conservation at this stage of development cycle—unlike India. Second, the type of public support to this programme has also been one of its kind, people have always supported this and politics has exempted from taking centre stage. Thirdly, the way the country has learnt from past experience, adopted a holistic and comprehensive approach to tackle the problem and committed a significant part of the budget to this cause under the Namami Gange Programme is unprecedented and is definitely more than bold. Such is our commitment to the national river. In course of its implementation, the programme has been able to achieve many a milestones which by themselves are first of their kind in their respective sectors, the country itself or in some cases internationally.

ALL-IN-ONE PLAN FOR THE RIVER AND ITS BASIN

By the time the Indian government declared Ganga as India's national river (in 2008), the country had enough first-hand experience of river conservation and its own quota of mistakes and limitations to realize the importance of a comprehensive planning if results were to be achieved. It was against this backdrop that the Ministry of Environment and Forests, assigned the task of preparing a GRBMP to restore and preserve the national river to a consortium of seven IITs. The outcome of the effort—the GRBMP—led to a seven-pronged action plan, with each pillar envisaged to be taken up for execution in a mission mode.

The GRBMP marked a radical departure from all earlier attempts at cleaning the Ganga because it was no longer about cleaning the river but covered a much wider canvas—the entire drainage area of 861,404 sq km—as well as preserving the wholesomeness of the river before the onset of degradation. Hence, the Ganga River Basin Management Plan (GRBMP) took into account the physical environment of the river, a complex combination of natural and manmade structures and processes and divided them into five main heads. These were: over-withdrawal of fresh water from the basin; discharge of pollutants into the aquatic environment; reduction in water-holding capacities and replenishment rates into water bodies, aquifers and ecosystems; mutilation of rivers by piecemeal engineering operations; changes in geological factors governing aquatic systems.

It described the aquatic system, which consists mainly of rivers, streams, groundwater and water bodies and its connection to the groundwater flow. In much of the basin, the GRBMP adopts the Ganga river system as the primary environmental indicator of National River Ganga Basin (NRGB). Hence, the GRBMP seeks ways and means to strengthen the basin environment against the identifiable adverse impacts.

The consortium defined the dynamics of the river basin through the lens of a hydrological-ecological system. Hydrological connections include groundwater flow, surface run-off, local evaporation transpiration-precipitation cycles and areal flooding, while ecological links are many and varied, such as biological agents. These linkages provide for extensive material transfer and communication between the river and basin, which constitute the functional unity of a river basin. Directly or indirectly, therefore, Ganga along with its tributaries and distributaries is a definitive indication of the health of the basin as a whole. Hence GRBMP adopted the Ganga River Network as the primary environmental indicator of the Ganga Basin. Again, the wholesomeness of the river may be defined in terms of four defining concepts: aviral dhara (continuous flow), nirmal dhara (unpolluted flow), geological and ecological integrity.

The restorative missions of the river, proposed for taking up, includes aviral dhara, nirmal dhara, ecological restoration (keeping the biodiversity of the river alive), sustainable agriculture, geological safeguarding (protecting the vulnerability of the basin from explosions, over-withdrawal of water), basin protection against disasters (like ensuring less harm to the community living on its banks) and environment knowledge-building and sensitization (building a comprehensive data bank to enable meaningful analysis and get quantitative data).

The GRBMP preparation had been a unique exercise in itself with coordination among not only the IITs but many other educational institutions and a pooling of knowledge and expertise so far unprecedented in the country. Both from concept to its implementation, the novelty is distinctly established and is expected to be useful not only for Ganga but for all other rivers in India and outside. This has given the country an expertise which will help us achieve international recognition.

MAKING GRBMP HAPPEN: RIVER GANGA (REJUVENATION, PROTECTION AND MANAGEMENT) AUTHORITIES ORDER 2016

Many of the well-intended and scientifically derived plans do not achieve implementation goals and remain statements of intent if they are not backed with a strong governance mandate. The wide-ranging objectives set forth by the GRBMP and initiatives taken by the NMCG could also meet the same fate. The risk has been mitigated to a large extent by notification of the River Ganga (Rejuvenation, Protection & Management) Authorities Order 2016 under Environment (Protection) Act 1986. This grants a statutory backing to the Ganga rejuvenation task by listing out the objectives and mandating NMCG to work on them.

This order lists that the Ganga shall be managed as a single system; chemical, physical and biological quality of the water of the Ganga will be maintained; continuity of flow of the Ganga will be maintained and longitudinal, lateral and vertical dimensions will be brought into river management practices. Further, the objective will be to restore and maintain the relationship between surface flow and sub-surface water, restoration of vegetation in the catchment area, conservation of aquatic and riparian biodiversity in the basin, regulation of activities in the floodplain zone and enhance public participation.

DOING IT FAST: A RACE AGAINST TIME

NMCG had realized that under Namami Gange Programme, success would depend upon an accelerated model for implementing sewerage projects, one of the more complex infrastructure projects due to congestion in cities, to catch up with the rising treatment gap. The mission focused on preparation of a pipeline of projects which could be implemented quickly on fund availability by simplifying its business processes. The mission, even with the limitations common to government organizations, has been able to establish a deep sense of involvement and project culture within the organizations to respect time as an essential factor in the entire process. Projects are intensely monitored at the highest level and the project management hierarchy has been kept flat with ease of access and seamless flow of information. The officials, mostly professionals, are encouraged to move beyond their domains and achieve project success, many a times handholding state agencies and suggesting solutions even if not strictly under their mandate. These hands-on methods have created an enabling environment and shown results which are one of their kind for any government programme and are recipe for a toolkit on project management.

Cities along the Ganga were mapped with a population of over

50,000, located within 5 km from the riverbanks. Post mapping, conditional assessment of the cities was scientifically conducted for assessing the sewage generation, treatment capacities, gaps and challenges. It indicated that despite the sewage generation of the basin being roughly over 2,900 MLD, the treatment capacity was just 900 MLD till 2014. Moreover, the STPs were plagued with various challenges, amongst which operation and maintenance was the primary cause of concern. Almost 350 projects including both sewerage and non-sewerage have been sanctioned under Namami Gange Programme at a cost of about ₹30,000 crore of which more than 150 projects have been completed and the remaining are at various stages of execution. This pace is phenomenal, never seen before. As many as 159 sewerage projects have been sanctioned to create treatment capacity of more than 4,900 MLD of which 56 projects to create 1,078 MLD treatment capacity have been completed. In 2014, only 28 projects existed for 462.85 MLD capacity on the main stem of the Ganga. This indicates a tenfold increase in the treatment capacity making us look forward to bridging the treatment gap for the first time ever. This will create adequate capacity for the coming 15 years. Projects have been taken up in tune with a comprehensive plan for all the 97 cities/towns along the Ganga including rehabilitation, upgradation of old plants after condition assessment. Subsequently, projects for tributaries have also been initiated. Major drains falling into Ganga have already been intercepted and diverted to STPs.

DOING IT RIGHT: HYBRID ANNUITY MODEL IN WASTE WATER MANAGEMENT

While the origin of the HAM can be traced back to the national highways sector, its implementation in the sanitation sector, however, came after much painstaking deliberations and heated discussions. When the officials of NMCG sat down to identify the causes for the failure of numerous STPs, they had to look no further than the financing model of these projects. In the Ganga Action Plan-I and Ganga Action Plan-II, the Centre would allocate funds to the concerned state authorities like UP Jal Nigam, for instance, both for the construction and maintenance of the STPs, but with little or no accountability and no guarantee against fund diversion. Secondly, even if the money was spent on constructing STPs, there was no surety that the project would be completed on time or would be properly maintained because of the lack of accountability.

In cases where the work of construction of the STPs and its O&M were given to different authorities, the challenges were of a different nature. When the STPs failed to function effectively, the different departments would blame each other for the non-functioning of the STPs. While the department, having left after constructing the STP, would refuse to take any responsibility, those tasked with the job of O&M would put the onus on the poor quality of the construction and therefore, account for their inability to manage the operations efficiently. Hence, a need was felt to make somebody accountable, not just in terms of time and cost overruns in project construction, but also for its upkeep and maintenance. That could only be possible through a private-public partnership model. So the NMCG officials decided to experiment with a new financing model—the HAM— despite the fact that it had faced difficulties and has mixed results in the case of road projects.

As the name suggests, HAM is a hybrid model, a mix of the EPC and build, operate and transfer (BOT) annuity models. The model argues that the same company, carrying out the construction activity, takes full responsibility for its O&M for the next 10–15 years. Under this model, only 40 per cent of the total construction cost is paid to the private operator in several tranches on the completion of the project. The rest—60 per cent of the construction cost—is paid over the total period of O&M of the project, along with the accrued interest. O&M charges are also paid as long the developer continues to meet the stringent water quality standards laid down under the bidding document.

The new financial model is a win-win situation both for the government and the private players. First, it reduces the financial risk on the concessionaire during the project implementation phase because he is assured of least 40 per cent of the project cost once the task is completed. The project developer also knows that the rest of the funds will also be made available over the 15-year O&M time period. Moreover, the payment is secured through International Bank for Reconstruction and Development (IBRD) guarantee in select projects like those in Agra, Meerut and Shaharanpur. The developer only has to take care of the construction and maintenance risk. Other risks, like land acquisition, obtaining permits and licenses for construction (the regulatory risks) remain the headache of the government in question. The model also takes care of an interest rate and inflation risks.

It also eases the initial cash flow pressure on the government because it has to pay only 40 per cent of the total project cost even after the project is completed and it ensures complete accountability and removes the blame game between the O&M player and the project developer. Moreover, not only the model and the bidding documents got endorsement from the government's think tank NITI Aayog, but projects are monitored by an independent project engineer appointed by NMCG, which also reduces the chances of uncertainty and controversy.

The first STP that was completed under the HAM model was the 68-million-litres-a-day sewerage treatment plant at Jagjeetpur, Haridwar, the state's biggest STP plant that takes care of 80 to 85 per cent of domestic discharge coming from five of the six different zones of the city. The project was awarded to HNB Engineers Private Limited at a cost of ₹171.53 crore. Others include the 14 MLD STP at Sarai, Haridwar, the 50 MLD STP at Ramana, Varanasi, etc.

Bidding for these projects is done in a transparent manner—e-bidding—on the basis of life-cycle costs, which includes not just the cost of construction of the STP and its O&M charges, but also the land cost as acquiring land is a major challenge in most parts of the country. A total of 28 projects have been sanctioned under the HAM model to create 1,801.5 MLD treatment capacity, including projects which are in the pipeline like the major projects in Meerut and Agra.

DOING IT RIGHT: 'ONE CITY, ONE OPERATOR' APPROACH

Suddenly, big names in Indian infrastructural industries seem to have developed a taste for dirty water. Companies like the Adani Enterprises, Shapoorji Pallonji, VA Tech Wabag, Triveni Engineering & Industries, Suez, to name just a few, are lining up not just to set up STPs and operate and maintain it for 15 years, but also to take complete charge of a city's wastewater management along the banks of the Ganges. Their enthusiasm has been fuelled not just by the introduction of new HAM-based PPP mode, but also with the announcement of the 'One City, One Operator' scheme, announced by the NMCG in 2018. This scheme not only ensures accountability, but provides a viable size of business allowing synergy of resource deployment and reducing costs in turn.

The novel scheme—where a single operator is given the responsibility of the entire city to maintain a certain quality of the water in the Ganga passing through this stretch—hopes to achieve better coordination among the different divisions and to ensure improved quality of water. The reasons for such optimism are that the operator will be forced to upgrade, operate and maintain existing STPs, pumping stations and even pipelines far more efficiently to ensure that the discharged wastes from households, industries and farms do not pollute the river. Of course, the long-term operator will have to build new STPs, operate and maintain it if and when required.

Interestingly enough, the concept of 'One City, One Operator' often stretches beyond the boundaries of a single city. For instance, the concessionaire is not just taking care of the raw sewage of Kanpur (total capacity 457 MLD), but also the 18 MLD of waste generated from Unnao, Shuklaganj and Pankha (adjacent to Kanpur). They are constructing a 15-MLD plant in Unnao, another 5 MLD in Shuklaganj and a 30-MLD plant in Pankha near the Pandu, thereby expanding the scope from 'One City, One operator' to 'One Cluster, One Operator'. And where the organization has not been able to provide a sewerage network, it has decided to provide every household with a septic tank for the collection of untreated waste. This waste is being collected, aggregated and carried to the Bingawan STP for treatment by private operators.

Similarly, another global leader has signed the first ₹1,477 crore project to operate, maintain and manage the sewage treatment network infrastructure in the cities of Agra and Ghaziabad for a period of 10 years, which can be extended by another five years under the 'One City, One Operator' model. They will be responsible for managing sewage treatment infrastructure of over 650 MLD, associated sewer networks and pumping stations, thus ensuring a cleaner and healthier ecosystem for the three million population of Agra and Ghaziabad. These steps will play a significant role in the rejuvenation of the Yamuna as this will ensure treatment of over 80 per cent of the sewage in both the cities. It will also mean that the government does not have to deal with five or six different operators.

KEEPING ENOUGH WATER IN THE RIVER: E-FLOW DETERMINATION AND NOTIFICATION

Shorn of its myriad definitions and complex jargon, the concept of environmental flows or e-flows, begs a simple question. How much water does a river need to sustain its social, cultural and ecological functions and how can this be determined? While the question may appear straightforward, finding the right solution can be a complex, contentious and an extremely difficult task. It is especially true for a river like Ganga. This is not just because it is the home to some of the most unique endangered species such as Ganges River Dolphin and the gharial (freshwater crocodile) and because it embodies the faith and spiritual ethos of millions of Indians, but also because it provides sustenance to 500 million people living on its basin.

So, any consensus about e-flows will call for a trade-off between the river's natural functions and its alternate uses—growing more crops using its water, generation of electricity, supplying towns with water for domestic and municipal purposes and its national and cultural importance. The challenge is also aimed at keeping at least some of the natural flow patterns along the whole length of the river, so that the people, animals and even plants downstream can continue to survive and use the river's resources. This is essential for the sustenance of the river itself as e-flows sustain various river functions.

Hence, to maintain a steady and healthy flow of the river, tributaries and floodplains along the entire course of the river, while supplying consumption needs of the people, requires a fine balancing act. 'Thus e-flows, aimed at fulfilling the ecological, social and spiritual needs of river users from the upper reaches to the sea, need to be factored into the integrated plan for supplying the water and removing the waste so that the equitable use of this priceless resource can be achieved,' as the World Wildlife Fund's report on 'Assessment of Environmental Flows for the Upper Ganga Basin' of 2012 points out. This again brings to the fore the age-old debate of development versus the long-term sustainability of the river.

As part of its overall task of preparing a detailed document for the effective abatement of pollution and conservation of the Ganga, the consortium of seven IITs were also asked to prepare and implement a Ganga River Basin: Environment Management Plan (GRB-EMP). The e-flow assessment, argued the report, is 'both a social and scientific process requiring expert knowledge of various fields, including but not limited to hydrology, hydraulics, geomorphology, ecology and biodiversity, socio-cultural, livelihood and water quality and pollution.' This is a complex task because it has no historical precedence.

In fact, e-flow assessment has now become an integral part of the modern approach to an 'Integrated River Basin Management' plan, which looks at both water and land management to ensure that river systems can be used and developed in a sustainable manner. As J. O'Keeffe and Le Quesne point out in their 2009 paper 'Keeping Rivers Alive: A Primer on Environmental Flows', flow is the main driver of biodiversity in rivers. It creates aquatic habitats, brings the food down from upstream, covers the floodplain with water during high flows and flushes the sediment and poor quality of the water through the system. Other experts refer to the flow regime in fresh water as a 'master variable' because of its strong influence on other key environmental factors like water chemistry, physical habitat, biological composition and interaction. Each component of a flow regime—ranging from low flows to floods—plays an important role in shaping the river ecosystem.

Even the National Environmental Policy (2006) of India on 'Freshwater Resources' has called for the promotion of integrated approaches on the management of the river basin by concerned river authorities, considering upstream and downstream inflows and withdrawals by season. It also promotes interface between land and water, and pollution loads and national regeneration capacities to ensure maintenance of adequate flows, in particular for maintenance of in-stream ecological values and adherence to water quality standards throughout their course in all seasons.

After much debate, the consortium agreed that environmental flows refer to 'a regime of flow that mimics the natural pattern of a river's flow that can perform its natural functions such as transporting water and solids from its catchment area, formation of land, self-purification and sustenance of its myriad systems. It also includes sustaining the cultural, spiritual and livelihood demands of people or associated associations—keeping the river and all its aspects functioning in a desired condition. It added that e-flows are not just about establishing a minimum flow level for rivers but it must also take into account floods, diurnal variations and droughts, as they are important with respect to silt transport and in controlling the characteristics of natural communities of water. These assessments are useful to know the environmental requirements before any development plans are made.

With World Wildlife Fund-India, the consortium agreed to the 'Building Block Model' to determine the e-flow requirement for 800 km along the main stem of the river—from Gangotri to Kanpur. The study of the Upper Ganga was important because that stretch of the river represents most of the problems facing the river such as diversions, hydropower, water abstraction from dams and barrages, agricultural and industrial pollution, sewage disposal from cities and the inflow from the most polluted tributaries, the Ramganga and Kali. In addition, the presence of endangered aquatic biodiversity in the form of two species of mammals (river dolphins, otters) crocodile (gharial and mugger), 12 species of turtles and 75 species of fish (including mahseer) make it a unique ecosystem. The IIT consortium also decided to develop a small-scale pilot implementation of e-flows in a small stretch, which would demonstrate the benefits and possibilities for e-flows in the short-term, and help replicate the concept in rivers across the country.

So, four delineated zones were earmarked: Gangotri to Rishikesh (Zone 1), upstream of Garmukteshwar to Narora (Zone 2), Narora to Farrukhabad (Zone 3) and Kannauj to Kanpur (Zone 4) to figure out the e-flow requirement. Once the different zones had been identified and described, at least one site was identified within each zone for which a detailed survey of the flow characteristics and biodiversity was undertaken. The information gathered at these sites would then be used to characterize the flow conditions that would be required to maintain the river zone. Hence, Kaudiyala was selected for the Gangotri to Rishikesh (Zone 1), Narora for upstream of Garmukteshwar to Narora (Zone 2), Kachla Ghat for Narora to Farrukhabad (Zone 3) and Bithoor for the Kannauj to Kanpur stretch. The study showed that Kaudiyala would require an e-flow of 400 cubic metre per second (m^3/s) as critical flow and a velocity of 0.64 metre per second (m/s) for January; e-flow of 3,250 m^3/s and velocity of 1.15m/s in August; and 290 m^3/s and 0.57 m/s during drought in January. Similarly, Kachla Ghat would require a flow of 300 m^3/s with a velocity of 0.38 m/s in January and 161.5 m^3/s and 0.33 m/s during the drought period.

Keeping the various reports in mind, the government in 2018 came out with a notification on e-flow, which stated that upcoming projects will have to ensure 20 per cent of the monthly average in the dry period (November-March), 25 per cent in the lean period (October, April and May) and 30 per cent in the high flow season (June-September) in the upper stretches of the river. The notification added that the government would 'ensure' that the river at least has the minimum-required environmental flow even after being diverted by projects and structures for purposes like irrigation, hydropower and domestic and industrial use. The notification ordered that the existing projects be tweaked in a way that they comply with the norms in three years.

It also outlined the total water that needs to be released from various barrages like Bhimgoda (Haridwar) 36 m^3/s during the non-monsoon months of October-May and 57 m^3/s during the monsoon season. Similarly, the Bijnor barrage is to release 24 m^3/s during the non-monsoon months and 48 m^3/s in the monsoon months. Similarly, conditions had been made applicable for the Kanpur and Narora barrage too. The Central Water Commission was made accountable for the supervision, monitoring, regulation of flows and reporting of necessary information to the appropriate authority and for taking necessary action in case of an emergency.

The government's notification came in the backdrop of the fast undertaken by Swami Gyanswaroop Sanand ji (Professor G.D. Agrawal, former professor of IIT Kanpur) who unfortunately left for heavenly abode in October 2018, after a long fast to seek continuity of flow, ban on the upcoming hydroelectric projects, mining in Haridwar areas and preservation of integrity of river Ganga.

Even if the steps taken may not meet the expectations of some of the environmentalists, the very fact that the paradigm of a prescribed environment flow in the country has been notified is first of its kind. As the e-flow determination models mature with experience the desirable states would be achieved in due course, till then the prospects are indeed encouraging.

BEYOND CLEANING: ENSURING ECOLOGICAL RESTORATION

If the objective of the NMCG, as defined by the IIT consortium, is to maintain the 'wholesomeness' of the Ganga, the restoration of its ecology assumes utmost importance. It is only through the preservation of biotic elements like flora, fauna, animals, microorganisms, other living things and its abiotic constituents like water, sand and other non-living things, that the river basin and the biodiversity that it fosters can be saved. The health of the basin depends on maintaining the continuing interplay of biotic and abiotic elements and their constituent ecosystems like rivers, wetlands, forests, grasslands, etc. Thus, the objective of 'Mission Ecological Restoration' is to restore the ecological balance of the river and provide an enabling environment for endemic flora, fauna and microorganisms to thrive on the Ganga's network. After all, the river basin is a 'geographical unit' enclosing an area drained by streams and channels that feed the river at a particular point.

Such an action plan is imperative because many important aquatic species (fish, dolphins, ghariyals and turtles) had either dwindled or disappeared from long stretches of the river over the past many decades. Given the fact that the river traverses through three different climatic-geographical zones—snow-clad alpine Himalayas to the tropical alluvial plains and finally to the estuarine zone—it is home to some of the most unique species of flora, fauna, animals and microorganisms.

Over the past two centuries, however, the Ganga network, especially in the upper reaches, has been considerably fragmented by dams for hydroelectric projects, barrages and other man-made structures. 'These obstructions slice the river into species, interrupting the flow of the river, nutrient, sediments and aquatic species of the river,' argues the IIT report. Besides, sediments are trapped behind the dams, thereby disrupting the downstream river's water-sediment balance and affecting nutrient flow and fertility of the downstream river.

Further downstream, Bhimgauda Barrage, Madhya Ganga Barrage and Narora Barrage intersect the river successfully to divert water to the Upper, Middle and Lower Ganga Canals. Further downstream, the Ganga is again clipped at Kanpur by Lav-Kush barrage. Finally, as the river heads for the estuarine reach, it is again bifurcated by the Farakka barrage in West Bengal, which diverts parts of the flow into the canal to feed the Bhagirathi-Hooghly River. So it is necessary to ensure a straight flowing path of the river, along with adequate water and sediment flows throughout the Ganga river network. The combined forces of irrigation, industrialization and urbanization have milked the mighty Ganga dry, so much so that it has been reduced to an emaciated stream with dry patches during the lean season in its downstream stretch and with damaging consequences for the river's abiotic and biotic systems.

In fact, the extinction of the Ganges dolphin from the middle Ganga stretching up to Allahabad may also be due to the diminished dry season flows in this stretch. Pollution from domestic and industrial wastes and agricultural run-off is extensive in the Ganga, downstream of Haridwar, and had assumed alarming proportions below Kannauj (after the confluence of the Ramganga and Kali rivers) at least up to Varanasi. Hence, a need was felt to check the pollution in the river for its ecological revival.

Another factor that is responsible for destroying the river's fragile ecological balance and for propagating new diseases and parasitic organisms, is the introduction of exotic and alien species of fish (like Talapia) into the river. It is, therefore, imperative that exotic species be eliminated and appropriate control measures be devised against invasion by any new alien species. Increased constructions on floodplains have also led to altered run-off patterns into rivers, increased pollution inflows, reduced groundwater recharge and hence, decreased flows into the river, which has curtailed the linkages between the river, its floodplains and floodplain wetlands. Moreover, riverbed irrigation with modern chemical pesticides has polluted the river bed, disturbing the breeding sites of higher aquatic animals.

Again, frequent disturbances in the Ganga river habitat by humans are a definite threat to riverine creatures. Dredging and plying of noisy ships, especially in the Hooghly river stretch, have affected major aquatic animals such as the Gangetic dolphin, which have vanished from these reaches. Frequent or intermittent dredging of the river for improving navigability in the river is harmful as well; it not only impacts the flora and fauna but also the aquatic animals that depend on the river bed and bank sediments for spawning, shelter, scavenging or other needs.

To conserve the ecological integrity of the Ganga and to reduce the direct dependency of the local communities on the river, the NMCG has given a project to the Dehradun-based WII called 'Biodiversity Conservation and Ganga Rejuvenation' to map and preserve the biodiversity of the river. The first phase of the survey carried out between 2017 and 2019, categorically stated that 28.6 per cent of the Bhagirathi's channels and 35.2 per cent of the Alaknanda's channels had turned into 'ecological channels' due to the 16 existing (14 ongoing and 14 other proposed hydroelectric projects) on the Bhagirathi and Alaknanda river basins—the tributaries of the Ganga. The study clearly states that these dams hamper the flow of the river and this can lead to the extinction of the Ganga Dolphin.

Their survey also revealed that 10 per cent of its high biodiversity areas fall alongside national parks and sanctuaries such as Rajaji National Park in Uttarakhand, Hashimpur Wildlife Sanctuary in UP and Vikramshila Gangetic Dolphin Sanctuary. The high biodiversity stretches have been divided into six zones: Devpprayag to Rishikesh (61 km), Makdumpur to Narora (147 km), Bhitura to Ghazipur (434 km), Chapra to Kahalgaon (296 km), Sahibganj to Rajmahal (34 km) and Behrampur to Barackpore (246 km). The WII report also stated that it had been tracking biodiversity through some key aquatic and semi-aquatic species, such as Gangetic Dolphins, gharials, otter turtles and various species of water birds. It also found that many species that used to be found in the main stem of the river that had disappeared, are now coming back. For example, they discovered nestling colonies of the Indian skimmer. Similarly, Seibold's, a species of the water snake, which had disappeared 80 years ago, has now resurfaced.

Through the project, the WII has involved members of the local community as guardians of the river who have been named 'Ganga Praharis'. The aim of this initiative is to establish a motivated cadre of Ganga Praharis to support local-level institutions and to monitor the quality of the natural resources of the river by mobilizing local communities at the grass-root level. This would be done by creating awareness about the benefits of a clean and vibrant Ganga and by forging a sense of belonging among the people towards Ganga. It would also link local communities and their livelihoods with the various agencies working for a clean Ganga and thereby, would create a convergence at grassroots level for undertaking such efforts.

LIFELINE OF THE RIVER: SCIENTIFIC AFFORESTATION ALONG THE RIVER

If India's holiest of the holy rivers continues to be the physical and spiritual lifeline of the nation, then forests too are the lifeline of any river, including that of the Ganges. Why is afforestation or development of degraded forests or grasslands so important? Afforestation controls the surface run-off during the monsoon season, helps in slope stabilization and enhances groundwater recharge. Forest cover also results in higher rainfall and raises water levels in the river. The abundant leaves, trees and forest cover decrease the speed of water diffusion, and support slow but greater infiltration of rainwater into the soil to ensure smooth functioning of the hydrological cycle.

Additionally, the presence of a healthy forest cover provides the self-cleaning ability to the river and it promises to strengthen the ecosystem, contributing to the cause of the Ganga rejuvenation. Realizing this linkage between the river and forests, the NMCG devised a 'forestry intervention' aimed at enhancing the productivity and diversity of the forests in headwater areas along the course of the Ganga and its tributaries. Bio-diversity conservation includes afforestation, conservation of flora, aquatic lives and wetlands. It also emphasizes on appropriate interventions through habitat management, catchment treatment-soil and moisture conservation, restoration of vital riparian forest buffer, improved livelihood of forest department communities and forest dwellers.

Hence, along with the Ministry of Water Resources, River Development and Ganga Rejuvenation, the NMCG appointed the Dehradun-based, Forest Research Institute of India, to conduct a survey of the biodiversity of the entire Ganga basin. They are to help with the rejuvenation of the river and its catchment area. The institute has consulted with various stakeholders, holding discussions at various levels and has been able to incorporate a scientific methodology for over a year. This includes the use of remote sensing and GIS technology for spatial analysis and modelling of a pre-delineated Ganga 'riverscape' covering 83,946 sq km out of a much larger Ganga river basin within the country.

Interventions in the Ganga riverscape includes the entire catchment of Bhagirathi, Alaknanda and Ganga sub-basins in the state of Uttarakhand and a 5 km buffer on either side of different tributaries of Ganga, except the Yamuna and its tributaries. The potential and treatment models of forestry and other conservation efforts can be divided into natural, agricultural and urban landscapes. This has led to extensive plantations by five participating states along the river course, besides other varied conservation interventions like soil and water conservation, bioremediation and bio-filtration, riparian wildlife management and wetland management. Supporting activities like policy and law interventions, concurrent research, monitoring evaluation and awareness are in progress.

The NMCG has provided ₹2,293.78 crore for a five-year project (2016-21). After a detailed study conducted over a year, the organization came out with a multi-disciplinary approach with potential plantation and treatment models. It also identified the nature of vegetation, soil conditions and agro-climatic zones of various types of treatment and plantation models. According to the report, around 134,000 hectares of land is to be used for plantations, but these plantations will have to be done in a scientific manner, conducive to the manner in Gangotri and Gangasagar. A detailed project reports that planting of plants worth ₹4 crore will be undertaken. Nearly 40 different plantations and treatment models have been selected for implementation for Uttarakhand, Uttar Pradesh, Bihar, Jharkhand and West Bengal. The project envisages the active involvement of two battalions of the Eco-Task Force in Uttarakhand and UP for raising plantations in difficult terrains. The State Forest Department in five states are also expected to involve the Indo-Tibetan Border Force, Nehru Yuva Kendra Sangathan and civil society organizations for various proposed activities, including monitoring and awareness campaigns. All these interventions will increase green cover, augment the water flow, beautify the river basin, enhance biodiversity and bio-filters in Ganga, and also educate the masses about the significance of keeping the river clean.

TRANSFORMING, PLANNING AND MONITORING: LIDAR MAPPING FOR GANGA REJUVENATION

This is a landmark project, the likes of which the country has never seen before. In association with the Survey of India, the NMCG is mapping, in unprecedented detail, the topography of the river and human settlements along the entire stretch of the Ganga. It is using state-of-the art Light Detection and Ranging (LIDAR) technology to pinpoint the network of drains and rivers of major cities releasing untreated sewage into the river, covering thousands of buildings, water bodies, aquifers and other natural elements that fall 10 km on either side of the river.

The process involves sending a fleet of aircraft or drones fitted with LIDAR technology across the whole course of the river to capture three-dimensional images of every metre of the land surrounding the river. These aircraft or drones send down laser pulses with light and depending on the time it takes to return from the surface, the digital elevation of the plain is mapped. When these data are combined with GPS data and other information, officials can identify hills, buildings, water bodies, drains, etc. with great accuracy and minimal human interference. These technologies help in mapping natural and man-made structure along the 10 km boundary on each side of the river over 5,252 km of the entire river.

Such mapping will not only help the NMCG officials to further identify the various sources of untreated waste entering the river through detailed modelling, but will also enable officials to design more effective pollution reduction strategies. It will also allow officials to discover long-hidden or destroyed water bodies, aquifers or streams that can be rejuvenated and nurtured for the health of the river. The GIS system will allow the users to view, understand, question, interpret and visualize data in different ways.

Government officials also hope to use the maps to improve their understanding of riverine city erosion, which will help local governments manage natural disasters such as floods. The NMCG and Survey of India have procured ₹86.84 crore for this project. The project will facilitate the GRBM by bringing in GIS support in the process of decision-making regarding different aspects of planning and implementation at the national, state and local levels. It will also help in monitoring the developmental work as well as real-time identification of critical hotspots. River Regulation Zones, if and when they come into being, will be far more implementable and be free from controversies with availability of this data set.

RIVER OF THE PEOPLE: CULTURAL MAPPING OF THE GANGA

Rivers and floods are metaphors of constant change. From philosophers to musicians, the river has inspired diverse groups of people and diverse cultures. Kelly D. Alley writes, 'Hinduism in India is a very strong example of how rivers may become central elements of religious and social life—and how a purely utilitarian policy may impair these structures. Losses of significant cultural ecosystem may exacerbate social conflicts.'

For the officials of Namami Gange, rejuvenating the 'wholesomeness' of the river means mapping and reviving the rich cultural heritage of different communities that live on the banks of the main stem of the river and its tributaries. This has called for the documentation of rituals, folklore, aesthetic sensibilities, narratives, religious practices, customary laws, dress patterns—the total cultural mileu in which they have thrived for thousands of years—to safeguard them.

Hence, the NMCG has asked INTACH to document the cultural heritage of the Ganga from Gamukh to Gangasagar. INTACH is one of world's largest heritage organizations with over 190 chapters across the country. The proposal seeks to develop an appreciation of the river as a cultural stream, embedded in the soul of India, by documenting its associated cultural narratives, including an annual calendar of events and rituals. This would cover archaeological heritage, intangible cultural heritage and environmental heritage. INTACH is currently engaged with documenting the built or architectural heritage, natural heritage and intangible cultural heritage aspects in districts along the main stem of the river.

In their earlier study on the historic city of Benaras, INTACH looked at the entire gamut of cultural heritage, including historical events of invasions and inhabitations, secular and spiritual influences. Each of these headings brought under it a plethora of tangible and intangible properties, social contracts and related norms of knowledge, traditions and customs. INTACH also looked at the complex identity of the city which has come about as a result of the collective memory of generations of communities settled here. 'The steadfast river Ganga, the famous galis, the magnificent ghats, the countless temples, kunds and pieces of religious interest, the historic Benaras Hindu University, the sadhus and their varied cults, the vitality of the Benaras gharana and the exponents in the field of music and dance, all add up to give Benaras its special place in the scheme of thing,' argued the report. Such an approach will be taken in the documentation of other settlements as well.

KEEPING A WATCH: REAL-TIME WATER QUALITY MONITORING STATIONS

'What gets measured gets managed' is age-old wisdom. Availability of real-time water quality data is not only an assurance of the state of the river but is also a ready tool for effective enforcement of prescribed standards. This also aids the planning process and facilitates mid-course correction of ongoing projects being the indicator of outcome. Ganga cleaning had mostly suffered on account of limited data availability since CPCB, with their limited resources, had not been able to generate the same.

Under the mission, a network of 36 real-time water quality

monitoring stations have been set up. These stations are operational since March 2017, out of which 18 stations are on the main stem of the river Ganga, nine stations are on its tributaries and nine are provided on the drains. A total number of 17 parameters are monitored which include temperature, pH, turbidity, water level, colour, total suspended solids, conductivity, nitrates, dissolved oxygen, chemical oxygen demand, ammonia, chloride, fluoride, potassium, TOC, biochemical oxygen demand and BTX. Installation of additional 40 stations is under progress. The stations are also tolerant to extreme environmental conditions and won't require manual intervention for at least 5 years, except for routine calibration and battery replacement. All the water quality monitoring stations have been fitted with GSM, GPRS for communication with the central receiving station. The pollution data is available at the headquarters of Namami Gange through online networking and in the offices of chief ministers of concerned states. This data sent by the stations is being calibrated by the scientists of CPCB before being made available in the public domain.

INFUSING DISCIPLINE AND FOCUS: GANGA TASK FORCE

Indian defence forces have been the benchmark of commitment, discipline and focus in our psyche, and the deployment of defence forces for any emergency or calamity has assured the citizens of performance. It was natural that the involvement of forces was considered as a unique way of looking at the problem and challenges. While defence forces had already had some involvement in environmental matters as part of Eco Task Force, NMCG conceptualized, for the first time, a uniformed cadre of soldiers committed to the cause of Ganga. Ministry of Defence responded by making available a battalion of the territorial army understanding the national priority. The move is a direct outcome of the vision of the Prime Minister to involve the ex-servicemen from the Ganga bank areas.

Ganga Task Force (GTF), a unit of the territorial army under the Ministry of Defence, was deployed in 2017. The force takes up different activities like afforestation, public awareness campaigns, patrolling of sensitive river areas for biodiversity protection, patrolling of ghats, monitoring of river pollution and also assistance during floods/natural calamities in the region. GTF is presently stationed at Prayagraj, Kanpur and Varanasi in the state of Uttar Pradesh and is actively involved in each and every sphere of the assigned tasks. A few of the activities carried out by the GTF during the year are undertaking the afforestation activities by using methodologies like conventional plantation of saplings, seed balling to increase forest cover, community plantation for public awareness, bank stabilization using biological means and food forest initiatives in Prayagraj, Varanasi and Kanpur. Micro forestry projects are also being undertaken by GTF. A seven-layer 'Model Food Forest' with 30 different location-specific native species has also been developed. GTF is also engaged in collecting water samples of Ganga and Yamuna from 20 identified locations which are being tested in the lab unit for 19 different parameters to understand the cumulative pollution from Prayagraj. The recent rejuvenation of Macferson lake at Prayagraj is an important and notable achievement of GTF. During the Ganga Utsav 2021, they undertook a unique 'Ganga Mashal' Yatra from Rishikesh to Bakkhali Beach, West Bengal connecting people on the way with message of healthy Ganga.

C-GANGA: KNOWLEDGE FOREVER FOR THE RIVER FOREVER

If the river has to be maintained forever, it needs to be cared with a complete focus and undivided attention. Knowing the river in its entirety is a challenge in itself. Our knowledge of the river and sustainability practices are mostly by traditions and local expertise and rightly so since the river is one and many at the same time. Ganga rejuvenation is also expected to serve as the model for other rivers and their rejuvenation programmes. To ensure replicability of the expertise obtained, the same needs to be documented and made easy for reference to one and many interested in the river. The efficacy of the efforts on rejuvenation would also depend upon simultaneous research and experimentations on the ground so that the Basin Management Plans keep getting refined day by day. Under the World Bank programme, a Ganga Knowledge Centre has already been envisaged. The IIT consortium also realized during the preparation of the plan that a much larger knowledge base was needed with the pooling of resources from many more institutions on a regular basis. That sowed the seeds of cGanga.

The Centre for Ganga River Basin Management and Studies (cGanga) was established at IIT Kanpur in 2016. This is the Centre of excellence for data collection, creation and dissemination of knowledge and information for the sustainable development of Ganga River Basin. The centre acts in the capacity of a comprehensive think tank to the NMCG, Ministry of Jal Shakti, Government of India. The Centre plays a crucial role in interacting with numerous national and international stakeholders including Central and state governments, regulatory authorities, industry, civil society, development finance agencies and investors. The purpose of such an interaction is to work on different research areas of river rejuvenation and also develop new eco-sensitive economic models for water management. One of the other mandates of cGanga is to act as a brain trust in the dynamic development and implementation of GRBMP prepared by the IIT consortium. The Centre also acts as a clearing house of knowledge and activities for new policies, governance and financial solutions along with the new technologies and innovations for the management of Ganga River Basin.

GLOBAL ATTENTION: INTERNATIONAL COLLABORATION FOR GANGA

Ever since the Namami Gange programme was launched, in no time it caught the international imagination. The whole world became curious to see how India would take up and handle this otherwise almost impossible feat. Quickly we started receiving statements of interest from many embassies and at one point we felt almost flooded with them. Many of them approached directly and few came through the ministry or different government departments. But it was clear that everyone wanted to be a part of this unique experience. But most of their eagerness to participate and contribute was overwhelming and at times even distracting. We got offers of technical support, financial support and many a time just experience sharing. Ganga had indeed gone global.

The World Bank had been a part of the Ganga experience even during GAP days along with few other countries. But a concrete international approach had been missing. However, The World Bank entered the scene in a big way with a $1 billion loan for the programme which also paved the way for the creation of the National Mission for Clean Ganga. Understanding the need for sharing of international experience NMCG started taking baby steps, in a measured manner and inked a partnership with a consortium of Canadian Universities in February 2014.

Post-launch of Namami Gange, major support came from Germany quite early on which extended elaborate technical support through GIZ, their development agency , after a systematic scoping mission led by Dr. Fritz Holzwarth, Director, Water and Marine, Germany, a well-known global expert on water and river basin management. Dr. Holzwarth travelled along Ganga and was fascinated by this great river and when I (Rajiv) had a chance to visit Germany as Joint Secretary in the Ministry of Housing and Urban affairs as part of a strategic Indo-German collaboration mission consisting of Joint secretaries from different sectoral ministries. An e-mail to Dr Holzwarth was enough for him to meet us at Bonn forgoing his weekend and take us to banks of Rhine to show its management. While we were on Rhine, we talked more of Ganga. Ms. Martina Burkard from GIZ and organizer of our visit listening to us never thought that she would also be some day joining Ganga rejuvenation project of GIZ in India and work with us. Neither did I expected that I would be getting another opportunity someday to work on Ganga project. Germany also extended financial assistance through Kfw, their funding agency to some projects in Uttarakhand and we are now working out some more collaborative activities.

Collaboration with GIZ and also India–EU water partnership has gained strength with pioneering work on e-flow determination methodology, river museums, River Basin Organisations, RBM Planning Cycle, capacity building, Ganga Box for innovative teaching, water quality monitoring, etc. This collaboration is also working for developing a policy for the reuse of treated wastewater.

Collaborations with several other countries such as the Netherlands, UK, Israel, Denmark, Norway, South Korea, Japan, Sweden, USAID, Australia, etc. are helping NMCG with technical support in a few specific projects. The Indo-Dutch Ganga Forum is active and several innovative ideas such as water as leverage and room for the river concepts are being explored. Centres of excellence for industrial clusters are being set up. There are specific activities with Israel as well including setting up centres of excellence on water and agriculture, improving water use, reuse, training programmes, etc.

Several technology-related collaborations are also being facilitated through cGanga, the collaborative platform established in association with the consortium of IITs. The cGanga has developed an Environmental Technology Verification process and has developed collaborations with universities, researchers and industries globally. A recent initiative of 'Ganga Connect'—an exhibition-cum-global interaction outreach in UK with cGanga evoked extremely positive response. Starting on the sidelines of COP26 at Glasgow, this continued at Cardiff, Birmingham, Oxford and London. Researchers, academics from several universities, technology providers, financial institutions, the Indian diaspora have given huge support and chapters have been formed of Ganga connect at Scotland, Wales, Midlands and London. Ganga Finance and Investment Forum has emerged out of this outreach. It is supporting NMCG in its international experience and helping them derive meaningful learnings for implementation in Ganga rejuvenation. It is laying good foundation for Ganga and River Knowledge Centre and a model for international alliance to rejuvenate our rivers and water ecosystem.

Many Firsts at a Glance

Institutional Strengthening *Empowered Institutional Framework for River Rejuvenation*	
NIRMAL GANGA	• *HAM in waste water management* • *'One city, one operator' approach* • *Real-time water quality monitoring*
AVIRAL GANGA	• *E-flow determination and implementation* • *Scientific afforestation plan along the River* • *Biodiversity survey of Ganga river and its tributaries* • *Organic corridors along the Ganga river* • *Small river and spring rejuvenation* • *Integrated mapping and conservation of fisheries along Ganga* • *Mapping and conservation of floodplain wetlands along the Ganga main stem*
JAN GANGA	• *Community-based structure and year-round activities* • *Ganga Task Force (GTF)* • *Linking livelihood and conservation by developing Arth Ganga model*
GYAN GANGA	• *Planning framework for river cities (Urban River Management Plan)* • *River-sensitive guidelines for preparing city master plan* • *Cultural mapping of Ganga river* • *LIDAR mapping of whole Ganga stretch* • *Microbial mapping for Ganga main stem*

16

Sustaining the Ganga in 2050: Clean, Free-flowing and Still the Goddess of Millions

'Will the Ganga survive its burden of human and industrial contaminants? Will dams and barrages strangle its flow one day with an unbearable burden of slit and detritus? Will it go the way of the great Yellow River of China, which dried up in 1997, at a staggering distance of 400 miles inland from the delta, sacrificed in the pursuit of industrial progress and in the name of modernity? The physical death of the most cherished river of India would be unthinkable for most people in India, who, despite the evidence of its endangered environment and ecology, still find solace in the idea of the Ganga as the maternal spirit of their civilization. The river, with its water and its valley that have sustained the imaginative life, material culture and daily subsistence of millions of inhabitants of the subcontinent over so many centuries, is now alas facing its most daunting challenges.'

This is how Prof. Sudipto Sen expresses his anguish for the sustainability of Ganga in his famous book *Ganga: The Many Pasts of a River*.

How do you sustain a divine and iconic river that symbolizes so many different things to so many different people, that holds multiplicity of meanings, rituals and practices for various sections of society, where faith and belief dominate every argument and which continues to be the epicentre of debates between development theorists and environmental activists? After all, the holy river means many different things to different people, and on different days, it is open to different interpretations and practices. It is the flow of liquid nourishment for individuals, agriculture and industry, a potential purveyor of hydroelectricity generation, a source of personal enlightenment and solace, a religious, social and cultural lifeline and a living goddess that needs to flow serenely to bestow her blessings upon anyone that comes calling.

Yet, the life of the river has never been short of ironies or challenges. Despite its reverential and iconic status, it has, over the years, become the depository of human and industrial waste from some of the largest cities of India. There are some 97 cities along the main stem of the Ganga that spew up domestic and industrial waste daily, and a substantial portion of it makes its way into the river in its raw and untreated form. As Chamman and Thompson wrote in 1995, 'Drained for agriculture on the one hand and filled with waste and toxins on the other, the Ganga struggles to maintain the ecological integrity and the self-purifying capacities for which it has been revered for centuries.'

Resuscitating and sustaining a river in such a state was never going to be easy for the mandarins of NMCG, tasked with this extraordinarily complex task. Finding the delicate balance between different pressures from varied forces of society on social, religious, cultural, or development planks and the diverse and logical arguments set forth by different protagonists call for a measured and nuanced approach. Thus, the interventions planned under the mission 'have dynamically expanded and adapted to include various aspects like river-sensitive urban planning, biodiversity mapping and management, historical and cultural considerations and reinforcing the people-river connect, among others'.

Why are we thinking of Ganga in the year 2050? In a technology-driven society, the pace of development almost doubles every decade, and so does the pace of destruction. For this reason, three decades are sufficient to extrapolate the levels of threat. On a different note, the period is also sufficient to show tangible improvements in socio-environmental indicators if serious efforts are taken. With Namami Gange, the efforts are indeed serious, and we look forward to continue seeing a Ganga—clean, free-flowing and having retained the faith of millions, which otherwise seemed impossible. Efforts on cleaning sustained during this period can outpace the destructive forces and lead to a rejuvenated state. The target is visibly on the horizon and, at its current state, is indeed achievable. Ideally, we are looking at the *'Ganga Forever'* target and want to make sure the same by 2050 rather than leaving it to speculations even then. In succeeding paragraphs, we touch upon some critical aspects that need to be taken into account if we do not intend to let this goal slip by.

The sustainability of the Ganga can be viewed from two different perspectives. The most natural way is to look at it as an independent entity and make sure that it exists in its most pristine form. The reality, however, is quite different. For that matter, any river, though existing as an otherwise distinct geographical form and an ecosystem personified most tangibly, does not exist in isolation. Water, the core element of a river, connects it inextricably to the other environmental phenomenon as a component of overall climate and environment itself. This makes it vulnerable to the threats common to the environment, especially emerging from climate change.

This relationship has been beautifully explained by Sudipto Sen in *Ganga: The Many Pasts of a River*. He writes, 'The river as a clearly defined object, with a beginning, a middle, and an end is, after all, a human fabrication. As a natural phenomenon, it is part of the earth's water cycle, the endless succession of clouds, rain, snow, and glacial melt that merges into other rivers, lakes, or oceans. This kind of reckoning was known to Indian philosophers of antiquity. For instance, a verse in the Prashna Upanishad, explaining personhood in terms of the specific and universal, gives an analogy of the river and the ocean. When the river reaches the ocean, it becomes the ocean, and its name and form are dissolved at that instant. The Buddhist text of the *Anguttara Nikaya* speaks of raindrops gathering on mountainsides and pouring down clefts, gullies and creeks, filling lakes and streams and replenishing the rivers that fill the oceans in the ceaseless play of the infinitesimal and the infinite.'

While the world is consistently realizing the threats from climate change and adopting the environmental-social-governance paradigm as a sustainability strategy, the latest approach is the Sustainable Development Goals (SDGs). The 17 SDGs are not isolated goals, but most of them are intricately connected. Environmental dimensions alone connect 86 of the 169 targets constituting these 17 goals. Water is an overarching aspect that connects not only many of the SDGs but also defines their interactions. A rejuvenated Ganga or any river is an easy-to-understand and quick mode of achieving a large chunk of the SDGs in the most tangible manner.

However, to argue that the biggest challenge to the river's free flow comes from the construction of high-altitude dams along the upper reaches of the Ganga will not be entirely wrong. It is true, especially in these trying times when climate change, a growing urban population in unplanned cities and rising domestic and industrial waste are already playing havoc with the river's ecosystem. Of course, some steps have been taken to resolve this challenge. For instance, on 26 August 2010, the Central government cancelled the last of the three controversial dams that were being built on the Himalayan portion of the Ganga on one of its headstreams known as the Bhagirathi.

Since work on two other upstream dams had been halted some months ago, the closure of the last one meant that all dam construction on the 135-km stretch from Uttarakhand to the Gangotri temple had been stalled. It meant the closure of phases I and II of the Bhairon Ghati, the Pala Maneri project and the Loharinag Pala project, each of which was capable of generating 380 MW, 480 MW and 600 MW of power, respectively. It also meant that the activists won round one of the battles between environmentalists and the state-owned power major, National Thermal Power Corporation. But the real question still remains: what stops future governments from overturning its position in the name of employment, development and ensuring a better standard of living for its citizens?

The succeeding paragraphs delve deeper into the issue and churn out some actionable plans. Still, insurance from the risk of development taking over the environmental concern and the river itself will come from some strong legislation—both at the national and state level.

With varied economic levels of basin states, arriving at a consensus is more than a challenge and would need a serious political push. Such legislation should prescribe the basic tenets around which all other secondary legislation should readjust themselves. The priority for 'Ganga Forever' should be established and its institutional mechanism mandated to prevent it from all future conflicts and manipulations. In the past, some efforts had been initiated by preparing draft legislation by the Ganga Mahasabha, an organization established by Madan Mohan Malaviya, another by Ganga Action Parivar led by Swami Chidanand Saraswati and the one prepared by a consortium of IITs. These drafts were compared and studied by the ministry and a composite draft was prepared that is under consideration.

The cancellation of the projects was part of an effort to honour the 'special features and unique status of the sacred Ganga in our (Hindu) culture and in our daily lives,' argued the government order, signed by the then Finance Minister, the late Pranab Mukherjee. The statement went on to add that the Ganga is the 'very foundation' and 'core' of Indian civilization. 'Our government is very conscious of the faith that crores of our countrymen and women have in this holiest of rivers, and it is in keeping with this faith that these decisions... have been taken.'

The scrapping of the dams was not only a critical step in ensuring the sustainability of the river, but it also showed a more balanced approach of the government to the pros and cons of hydroelectric projects. Despite pan-India protests, hydroelectric dams had always been a symbol of development and modernization from the days of the country's independence, with India's first Prime Minister, the late Jawaharlal Nehru, describing them as 'Temples of Modern India.' Such was the hold of these 'modern temples' that successive governments at the Centre and the state allowed the construction of the Tehri Dam, despite experts and environmentalists pointing to its threat in an ecologically-sensitive and seismically active zone.

The opposition to high-altitude dams has come largely from their adverse impact on the picturesque landscape, unique biodiversity and on the lives and livelihoods of the people both on the upstream and downstream cities and towns. As an article in 2008 in the environment magazine *Down to Earth* argued, locals objected to the extraction of water from the riverbed because the flow 'through a virtual cascade of tunnels would hinder groundwater recharge, withhold water needed to support biodiversity and potentially alter the river's ability to maintain a self-cleaning rate that is nearly three times as fast as other sacred Indian rivers such as the Yamuna.'

Other experts argue that once water flows are redirected to tunnels and trapped in reservoirs, it further reduces the prospects of agriculture and river-dependent livelihoods such as boating and fishing. Worse, establishing dams would result in the displacement and disruption of thousands of human lives, and their assessment calls for a 'thorough and careful assessment' before arriving at any decision on dam building. The aggressive stance of the activists and local populace against dam construction also led to a significant development—the creation of the National Ganga River Basin Authority (NGRBA), empowered planning, financing, monitoring and coordinating authority for the Ganga. Headed by the then Prime Minister, Manmohan Singh, its mandate was to ensure the effective pollution abatement and conservation of the river 'by adopting a holistic approach while keeping in mind the need for sustainable development goals. The first task of the NGRBA was to anoint Ganga, the status of a national river.

As Georgina Drew writes in her book *River Dialogues: Hindu Faith and the Political Ecology of Dams on the Sacred Ganga*, 'Like national birds and national flowers, the assumption and hope was that the Ganga would be granted more protection than other rivers. This distinction was important because the efforts to protect and preserve the river's ecological services, as well as the minimum flow needed to enable the sociocultural practices dependent on accessing that would ostensibly be difficult and costly to implement elsewhere.' The government also realized that if the same 'holistic approach' was advocated for other rivers, the nation's development agenda would take a major hit.

The first meeting on the NGRBA on 5 October 2009 saw the Ministry of Environment and Forests proposing a 'Mission Clean

Ganga 2020' programme to ensure that by the year 2020, not a single drop of untreated municipal sewage or industrial effluent would enter the river. A budget of ₹15,000 crore, argued the ministry, would be required to create the necessary treatment and sewage management infrastructure, with 70 per cent funding coming from the Centre and 30 per cent from the states. In the next few months, the Centre received a grant of $1 billion from the World Bank for renewed Ganga clean-up initiatives. 'The NGRBA has created a framework to ensure that all investments under the programme are well prepared, effective in reducing pollution, are socially and environmentally sustainable and proceed with transparent decision-making,' pointed out a press release from the World Bank office.

At its second meeting, some 14 months later, the NGRBA took two important decisions. First, it cancelled the three dams and secondly, it declared the stretch between Gaumukh and Uttarkashi as an eco-zone. And on 18 December 2011, the Ministry of Environment and Forests published the eco-zone notification. The official document included a commentary that addresses the boundaries of eco-sensitive zones, the 'zonal master plan for the eco-sensitive zones, the activities to be prohibited, regulated or permitted within the eco-sensitive and several provisions for the monitoring committee. The notification indicated that the e-zone will provide for the restoration of denuded forests; that it will aim to conserve water resources; that it will ensure that buildings, hotels and resorts follow the traditional concepts and architecture of the area; that it will not allow the change of land from green uses (such as horticulture, agriculture, tea gardens, parks to non-green uses) and the master plan will indicate areas on hill slopes where development shall not be permitted. Additional guidelines were also provided for the maintenance of springs, roads, natural heritage, man-made heritage and tourism.'

Yet, the unplanned construction of earlier dams on the ecologically sensitive hills had come at a great price. The first flash flood hit Uttarakhand in August 2013 after a cloudburst in the middle of the night. The deluge upturned bridges, roads, houses and killed hundreds. Only ten months later, in mid-June 2013, Uttarakhand was hit by an even more extensive series of floods. The swelling waters hit the Bhagirathi and the Alaknanda Valley, causing extensive damage to life and crops. And if the experience of flash floods from 2010 to 2015 is any indication, the Himalayas will likely suffer a number of cloudbursts and floods capable of destroying dam infrastructure and endangering lives.

SAVING THE RIVER FOR ETERNITY

The 17-member Chopra Committee headed by Ravi Chopra, set up by the Ministry of Environment and Forests under orders from the Supreme Court to look at safety measures after the flash floods left thousands homeless in Uttarakhand between 2010 and 2011, stated that the hydropower projects in the state aggravated the damage caused by flash floods. The report added that removing silt, sand, and boulders was responsible for the rushing waters to scour the riverbanks, destabilizing the land and destroying acres of agricultural lands and settlements. The report also noted that such dams change river flows and threaten to ruin riverine ecosystems. The committee further recommended that 'all but one of the 24 proposed power projects be scrapped because they have irreversible impacts on biodiversity'. The committee also suggested that a national Himalayan policy be developed to formulate a comprehensive plan to protect the region.

Maintaining the desired quantity for the ecological flow of the river was now handed over to the NMCG, which serves as the implementation arm as the National Council for Rejuvenation, Protection and Management of the River Ganga (after the dissolution of the National Ganga River Basin Authority) under the Jal Shakti ministry. The River Ganga (Rejuvenation, Protection and Management) Authorities Order of 2016 authorizes NMCG to take other measures which may be necessary for the continuous flow of water and abatement of pollution in the Ganga and its tributaries. The order also empowers the NMCG to 'issue directives to the state and district Ganga committees or local authorities in implementing the Ganga River Basin Management Plan and any other matter connected with the affairs of the Ganga and its tributaries.'

Hence, the NMCG, in its order dated 8 October 2018, stated that the different barrages along the main stem of the upper Ganga—from Haridwar in Uttarakhand to Unnao in Uttar Pradesh—have to mandatorily release a certain quantity of water to maintain a minimum environmental flow of the river downstream. For instance, the Bhimgoda barrage in Haridwar has to comply with its order of releasing at least 36 cubic metres of water per second (cumecs) in the non-monsoon months (October to May) and 57 cumecs during the monsoon months (June to September). This order is equally applicable for other barrages like the Bijnor, Narora and Kanpur barrages. Narora barrage, for instance, is expected to release 24 cumecs of water during the non-monsoon months and 48 cumecs in the monsoon months.

A study by the National Institute of Urban Affairs titled 'A Strategic Framework for Managing Urban River Stretches in the Ganga River Basin: Urban River Management Plan' argues that in order to ensure the sustainability of the river, three pillars of the river need to come together: policies which ensure that the river is 'environmentally responsible, economically beneficial and socially inclusive.' Environmental benefits include providing rich biodiversity, clean air, clean water, improved groundwater levels, while economic benefits bring livelihood opportunities, tourism growth and an attractive external investment. Social benefits include vibrant places of religious, cultural and recreational events and scenic picnic spots.

To ensure the sustainability of the river, it is imperative to incorporate river management into the overall city's master plan—the long-term strategic blueprint that outlines the broad contours of the city's development. Several policies/initiatives at the national and state level have direct implications on river management. These include the National Policy on Faecal Sludge and Septage Management 2017 (for on-site sanitation management); Swatch Bharat Abhiyaan 2014 (for both toilets and solid waste management); Jal Shakti Abhiyaan 2019 (for water bodies rejuvenation, water conservation, afforestation and groundwater recharge); Draft National Forest Policy,

2018 (for water management); National Water Policy 2012 (which has considerable river-related clauses); National Water Mission, 2011 (for climate change-related implications), Street Vendors Act, 2014, among others. The master plan should therefore have a river-centric approach to allow the customized implementation of these policies. Specific riverfront development projects like ghat development, large-scale river cleaning projects, eco-recreational sites, eco-tourism infrastructure can be identified as model projects within the master plan to develop river cities.

As the Prime Minister articulated in the meeting of the National Ganga Council on 14 December 2019, 'There is a need for rethinking for "River Cities". There is a need for the residents of these cities to ask what we can do for the rivers? Cities should be responsible for rejuvenating the rivers. It has to be done not just with the regulatory mindset but also with development and facilitatory outlook.'

RESPECTING RIVERS GEOMORPHOLOGY AND SUSTAINABLE MANAGEMENT OF SEDIMENTS

A river is a body of flowing sediment as much as one of flowing water[19].

Sustaining the river needs sustaining its ecology and creating conditions so that the river can continue to perform its ecosystem services. This means that we need to focus with systems approach and look at water, sediments, aquatic life, catchment area, etc. all taken together.

Sediment transport, bank erosion and associated channel mobility represent key physical processes of rivers, and their understanding is of crucial importance for defining river restoration and management strategies. Siltation process is subject to several factors including physiography, geology, meteorology, hydrology and flow characteristics of the particular reach along with river stage (childhood, youth, mature stage, old age).

Due to increased human activities along the river, this natural

---

[19]**Sediment Managament** [Web page] / auth. Bhaduri Amita : India Water Portal, 2019.

process of sedimentation has been accelerated. Changes in the amount and areal distribution of different sediment types are the cause of changes in river channel form and river habitat. Studies[20] indicate that the Ganga carries 262 million tonnes/year and the Brahmaputra carries 387 million tonnes/year of sediment, making their floodplains in the lower reaches one of the most fertile in the world.

Common practices carried out by river management agencies demonstrate that sediment management has rarely been based on best practices developed on the basis of scientific knowledge. For these reasons, a different approach to sediment management is desirable, incorporating knowledge and management of sediments at the basin scale and a wider application of available scientific knowledge. A systematic data collection and analysis needs to be carried out to study the aggradational and degradation behaviour of rivers, especially with respect to rivers carrying large quantities of sediment load.

In view of these challenges, an exercise has been undertaken in the ministry to develop a sound policy on this aspect. This draft on sediment management has identified the following basic principles that need to be followed for the silt management of Indian rivers.

- Sediment management should become a part of integrated river basin management plans. This is a significant aspect which GRBMP has also pointed out as strategic intervention.
- Erosion, movement and deposition of sediment in a river are natural regulating functions of a river. The river stream has to complete its geo-morphological cycles from youth, maturity to old age. A stable river is able to constantly transport the flow of sediments produced by the watershed such that its dimensions (width and depth) pattern and vertical profile are maintained without aggrading (building up) or degrading (scouring down).
- Justification for removal or disturbance of silt must be evidence-based. Where justified, silt management actions

---

[20]**Suspended Sediment Transport in the Ganges-Brahamputra River System, Bangladeh** [Report] by Rice Stephanie Kimberly, The University of Mississippi, 2007.

must follow best practices to minimize damage to the environment/river morphology.

- Annual silt requirement at fast-developing infrastructure project may be estimated and critically aggrading river reaches and their sections in the vicinity may be analysed in their physical mode for supplementing. The same can be clubbed with silt removal wherever possible.

- There is a need to pursue the schemes with utmost care backed by scientific study, mathematical model study and detailed physical model study in identifying the rapid aggrading areas, suitable sites for mining, the requirement of construction material, suitability of silt/sand to be mined for a specific purpose and accordingly take corrective measures for controlled dredging in PPP mode.

There are two types of methods to minimize the siltation in rivers—one that is required for the catchment and the other is in the river itself. Effective methods in the catchments area to reduce soil erosion can be afforestation, forest management, improved cultivation practices, riparian buffer management and minimizing anthropogenic activities on floodplains. Methods that can be adopted in the river itself to control soil erosion are storage reservoirs, desilting basins, bank protection and local sediment control. Many of these methods have been adopted in the GRBMP too, incorporated in Namami Gange mission and interventions such as scientific afforestation, floodplain demarcation are under implementation.

In order to study the impact of sand mining on the river morphology and geology, a project has been taken up under the mission with IIT Kanpur to provide assessment, analysis and mitigation strategies on the geomorphic and ecological impacts of sand mining in large rivers as revealed by high-resolution historical remote sensing data and drone surveys. This project would involve a comprehensive assessment of the impacts of sand mining in the upper reaches of the Ganga river and its tributaries where the extraction of river sand and gravel is significantly higher than natural replenishments and is

Sewerage Projects in Uttarakhand

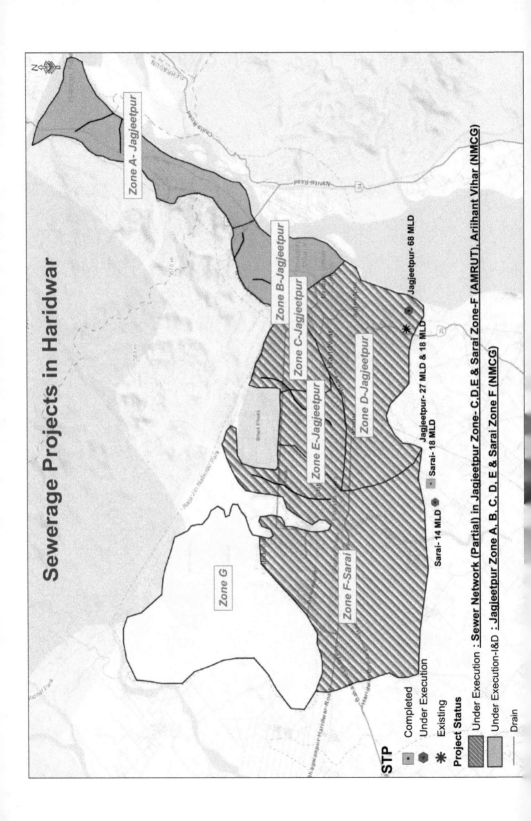

Sewerage Projects in Haridwar

Zone A- Jagjeetpur

Zone B-Jagjeetpur

Zone C-Jagjeetpur

Zone E-Jagjeetpur

Zone D-Jagjeetpur

Zone F-Sarai

Zone G

STP
- Completed
- Under Execution
- Existing

Project Status
- Under Execution : Sewer Network (Partial) in Jagjeetpur Zone- C,D,E & Sarai Zone-F (AMRUT), Ariihant Vihar (NMCG)
- Under Execution-I&D : Jagjeetpur Zone A, B, C, D, E & Sarai Zone F (NMCG)
- Drain

Sarai- 14 MLD
Sarai- 18 MLD
Jagjeetpur- 27 MLD & 18 MLD
Jagjeetpur- 68 MLD

Sewerage Projects in Uttar Pradesh

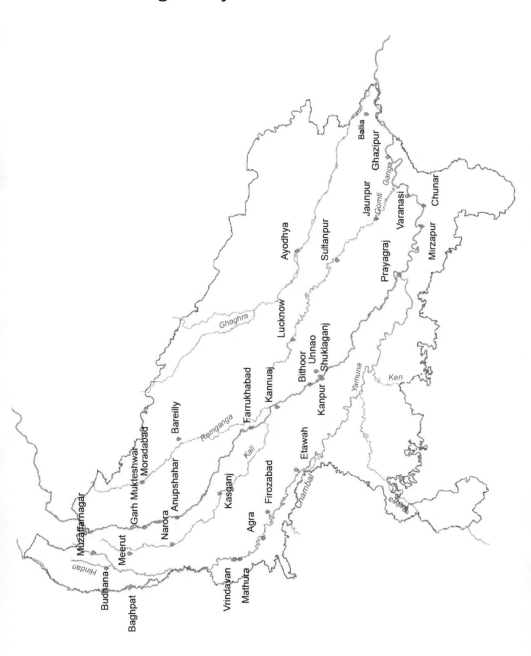

Sewerage Projects in Prayagraj

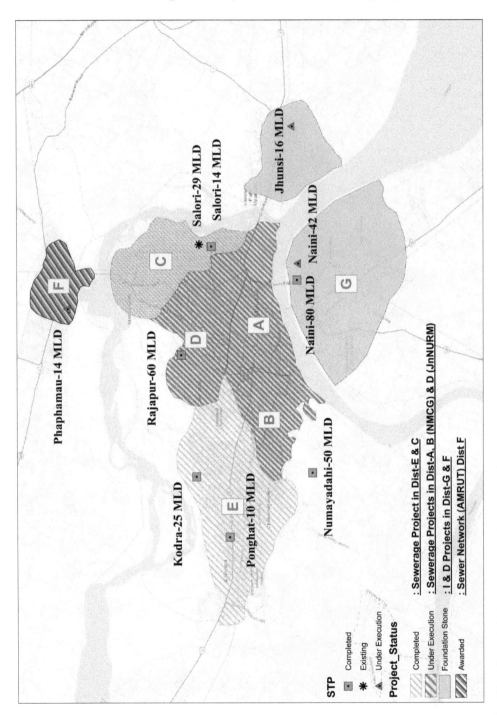

Sewerage Projects in Varanasi

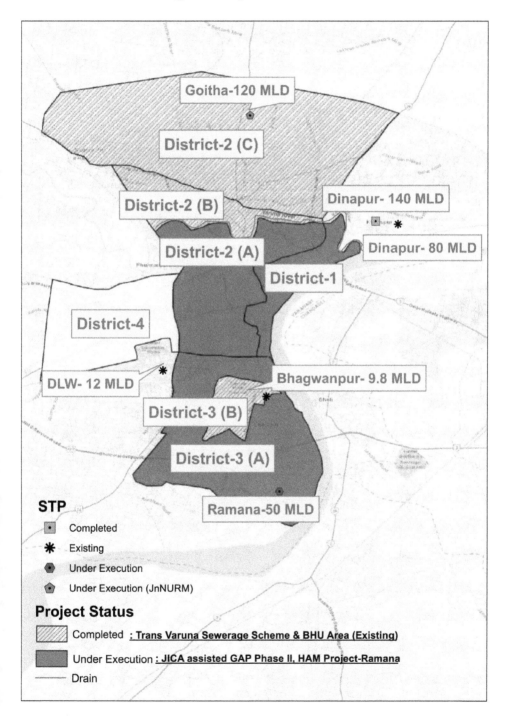

Sewerage Projects in Bihar

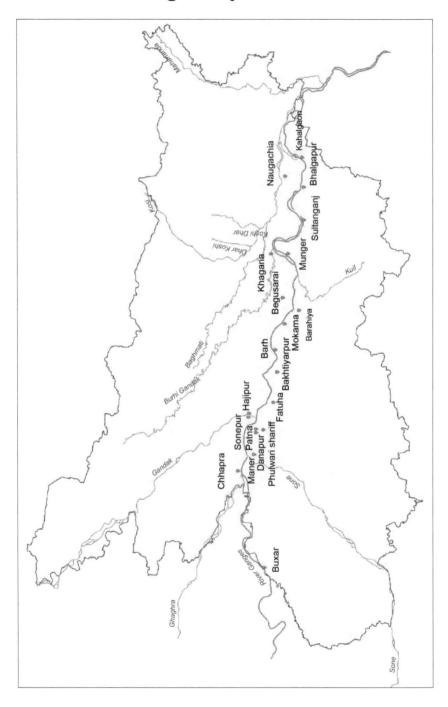

Sewerage Projects in Patna

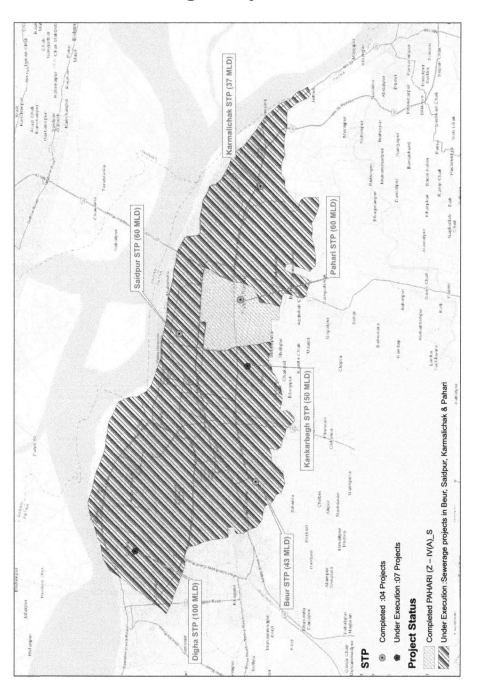

Karmalichak STP (37 MLD)

Saidpur STP (60 MLD)

Pahari STP (60 MLD)

Kankarbagh STP (50 MLD)

Beur STP (43 MLD)

Digha STP (100 MLD)

STP

    Completed :04 Projects

    Under Execution :07 Projects

Project Status

    Completed PAHARI (Z – IV(A)_S

    Under Execution :Sewerage projects in Beur, Saidpur, Karmalichak & Pahari

Sewerage Projects in Jharkhand

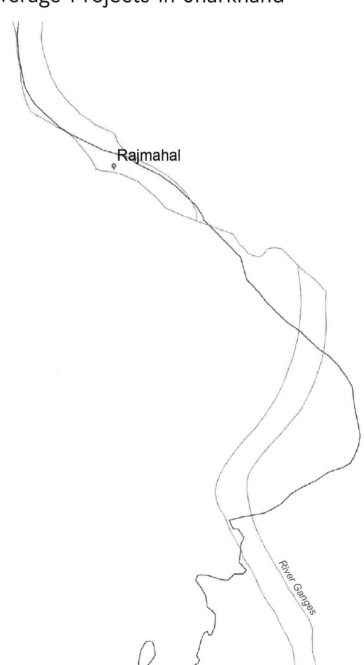

Sewerage Projects in West Bengal

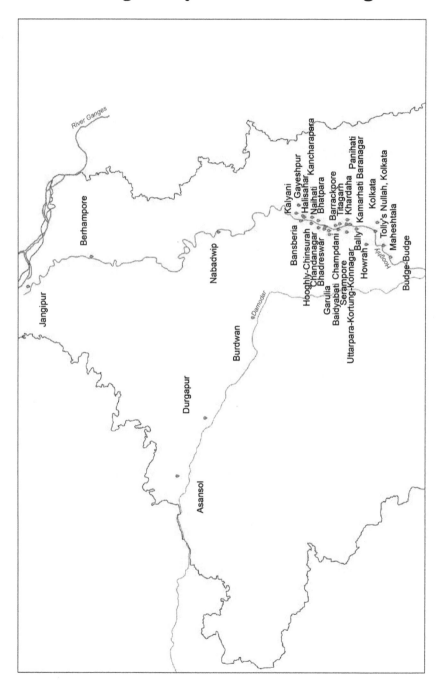

Sewage Treatment Capacity on Ganga Main Stem

Year 2014

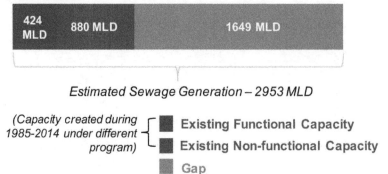

Estimated Sewage Generation – 2953 MLD

(Capacity created during 1985-2014 under different program) ▮ **Existing Functional Capacity**
▮ **Existing Non-functional Capacity**
▮ Gap

Year 2021

Estimated Sewage Generation – 3148 MLD

Total Capacity Creation - 3363 MLD
(Including additional capacity to take care of future need)

▮ **Capacity Created**
▮ **Capacity Under Creation**

45 projects for 13 Major Tributaries under progress to create treatment capacity of more then 2800 MLD

Ganga: A Natural Wonder

Birth of Ma Ganga on the snow-capped Gaumukh Mountains

Source: Wildlife Institute of India (WII)

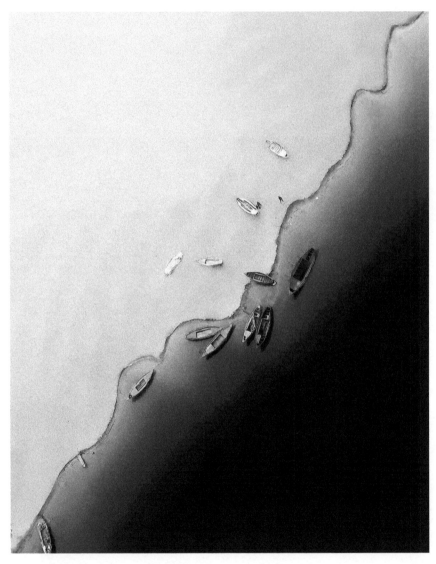

The curls and colours of the divine: Ganga landscape

Source: NMCG, obtained from Shutterstock

The bridge between divine and us: Lakshaman Jhula at Rishikesh

Source: NMCG, obtained from Shutterstock

Pristine view of Ganga at Haridwar

Source: NFDC

Living with the ebb and flow of the river

Source: NFDC

Adding colour to the ancient: Murals at Varanasi by the confluence of local and international artists.

Source: NFDC

In the twilight zone: Howrah Bridge stands as a sentinel on Ganga

Source: NFDC

A young Ganga in all her exuberance

Source: Rag Rag me Ganga Team

Creating a flutter: Haiderpur wetlands, a safe nesting abode for migratory birds

Source: Rag Rag me Ganga Team

The glow of the flow

Source: Water Digest

A bend in the river: Ganga as a waterway

Source: NFDC

Ongoing celebration of reverence

Source: Rag Rag me Ganga Team

Ek shaam Ganga ke naam

Source: NMCG, obtained from Shutterstock

A kaleidoscope of colours perennial river, eternal city

Source: Abhishek Kumar Singh through WII

Civilizations will come and go, Ganga will stay

Source: Saurav Gawan through WII

Making of a divine river: Sangam of Alaknanda and Bhagirathi at Devprayag

Source: Upma Manral through WII

Cradle of civilization: Uttarkashi in the curls of Ganga
Source: Uday Bhattacharya through WII

Ghats of Ganga, making millions move
Source: River from the Sky, National Geographic

River of the People

The ripples of a holy dip in Ganga

Source: Water Digest

The lights of gratitude to Ganga: evening arti at Varanasi

Source: Abhishek Kumar Singh through WII

An ode to Ma Ganga: the dance of the faithful's

Source: Water Digest

Making the mark of existence

Source: Water Digest

Ganga Aamantran Abhiyan (River rafting expedition)

Source: NMCG, obtained from Shutterstock

It's playtime folks

Source: Water Digest

Invoking the Sun god on the banks of Ganga: Chhath puja in the morning

Source: Water Digest

Bowing to the Sun god: Chhath Puja in evening

Source: Water Digest

Sailing the boat of faith

Source: NMCG, obtained from Shutterstock

Pristine lap of mother Ganga: Har ki Pauri

Source: Jyotirmoy Gupta

Chandi Ghat at Haridwar

Reimagining the ghats: increasing space, adding colours

Source: NMCG

Sweating it out for the river

Source: NMCG

Celebration time: The myriad colours of Ganga Utsav

Source: NMCG

Committing support to the national lifeline: participants of Ganga Marathon at JLN stadium, New Delhi

Source: NMCG

Jalaj: Adding awareness, generating livelihood through boat rides

Source: River from the Sky, National Geographic

Inside Jalaj

Source: River from the Sky, National Geographic

The complete makeover: Har ki Pauri

Source: NMCG

Celebrating the river city relationship: An aerial view of Kolkata

Source: Dhritiman Mukherjee through WII

God's view of Ganga: An aerial landscape of Haridwar

Source: Rag Rag me Ganga Team

Multicoloured sea of humanity at Sangam, Prayagraj

Source: NMCG, obtained from Shutterstock

Ready to do anything for Ganga: Union Minister participating in a cleaning drive
Source: NMCG

Celebrating river and culture: Ganga arti at Dashashwamedh Ghat in Varanasi

Smile of the river

Unlocking the locks

Circle of life: meeting point of Ganga and the ocean at Gangasagar

Source: Uday Bhattacharya through WII

Path to salvation: The line-up for a holy dip during Kumbh Mela at Prayagraj

Source: Pramil Dwivedi through WII

A view of Triveni Sangam during Kumbh in Prayagraj

The calm before the spiritual awakening

Source: Pramil Dwivedi through WII

Young Ganga, Ganga for Young

Source: Nilanjan Chatterjee through WII

Ganga, the goddess, leaving Gangotri for her winter home at Mahhwa on Yam Dwitiya

Source: Kamal Joshi through WII

Creativity inspired by Ganga

Source: River from the Sky, National Geographic

Ganga brings smiles

Source: River from the Sky, National Geographic

The force of Namami Gange: Ganga Task Force in action

Source: River from the Sky, National Geographic

Culture along the Ganga

Source: River from the Sky, National Geographic

Making Nirmal Ganga Possible

In the lap of Ganga: safe and sound

Source: River from the Sky, National Geographic

**KANPUR CITY
SISAMAU NALA
FLOWING INTO GANGA RIVER**

Proof of action: Preventing flow of 140 MLD sewage in Ganga from more than a century-old Sisamau drain at Kanpur

Source: NMCG

Joshimath 1.08 MLD STP

Srinagar 3.5 MLD STP

Srinagar 1 MLD STP

1 MLD STP Badrinath

Making Nirmal Ganga possible: small-scale STPs in Uttarakhand

Source: NMCG

Making Nirmal Ganga possible: 37 MLD STP at Karmalichak, Patna

Source: NFDC

Making Nirmal Ganga possible: a top view of 140 MLD STP at Dinapur, Varanasi

Source: NMCG

Making Nirmal Ganga possible: a view of 80 MLD STP at Naini, Prayagraj

Source: NMCG

Making Nirmal Ganga possible: a view of 14 MLD STP at Salori, Prayagraj
Source: NMCG

Modern saviour of the ancient river: STP at Jagjeetpur, Haridwar

Source: NFDC

Making Nirmal Ganga Possible: 27 MLD STP at Jagjeetpur, Haridwar

Source: River from the Sky, National Geographic

Overcoming the terrain barrier: 7.5 MLD STP at Rishikesh

Source: River from the Sky, National Geographic

Making Nirmal Ganga Possible: 5 MLD STP at Sahibganj, Jharkhand

Source: NMCG

A colorful approach to a Nirmal Ganga: 43 MLD STP at Beur, Patna

Source: NMCG

Making Nirmal Ganga Possible: 58 MLD STP at Moradabad, Uttar Pradesh

Making Nirmal Ganga Possible: 4 MLD STP at Vrindavan, Uttar Pradesh

Making Nirmal Ganga Possible: 31 MLD STP at Bhatpara, West Bengal

Source: NMCG

Making Nirmal Ganga possible through organic farming

Source: Rag Rag me Ganga Team

Making Nirmal Ganga possible through organic farming

Source: Rag Rag me Ganga Team

River for Everyone

Colours and birds both are back

Source: NFDC

Smooth-coated Otter, once considered extinct, are back on a rejuvenated Ganga

Source: WII

Small clawed, big impacts on the nutrient life cycle

Source: WII

Nirmal Ganga is our objective too

Source: Abhijit Das through WII

Back from the brink: Ganga Dolphins are no longer a rare sight in the river

Source: Ganesh Chowdhury through WII

We love Ganga too!

Source: Dhritiman Mukherjee through WII

Roaring through the woods. Improved habitation of Bengal Tiger on the banks of Ganga

Source: Dhritiman Mukherjee through WII

The gold of Gangetic biodiversity: Golden Mahseer

Source: J A Johnson through WII

Sharp and focused: Snow leopard in Gangotri National Park

Source: Dhritiman Mukherjee through WII

imparting serious offsite and on-site impacts. This has led to changes in channel form, physical habitats, food webs and engineering structures associated with river channels and their watershed. As these adverse effects become increasingly recognized and understood, instream sand mining/aggregate extraction has invited increasing scientific scrutiny. Excessive sedimentation in channels, however, also pose serious threats in terms of channel instability, bank erosion and frequent flooding. Therefore, all such activities must be carried out with utmost care. This would be essential to sustain river, its ecosystem as well as the habitations along the river.

PAYING FOR ITS OWN UPKEEP

Riverfront development presents a unique opportunity to bring the river to the 'front yard' of the city from the generally neglected state in which they are usually found. 'Every new investment along the rivers encourages activity, unleashes vitality and increases land value while providing places for people to enjoy,' argues the National Institute of Urban Affairs report. It also provides the poor urban local bodies and municipal authorities a chance to earn some revenue through the entry and parking fees, which could go a long way in the upkeep of these riverfronts.

While there has already been a burst of riverfront development projects in India, there has also been criticism that these have been focused more on the economic aspects, side-lining its ecological importance. Hence, it is important that all the three pillars of sustainable development—environment, economic and social issues—are taken into consideration while designing the projects. NMCG, in collaboration with the World Resource Institute, has recently published a guidance note for urban riverfront development. The note provides details about the protocols for the design, implementation and governance of riverfront developments. It also outlines mechanisms to ensure smooth operation and maintenance for riverfront development projects further away from the river. Hence, in recent years, there has been a burst of riverfront development projects across Indian cities. Examples include Sabarmati Riverfront (Ahmedabad), Dravyavati Riverfront (Jaipur) and Ganga Riverfront (Patna), among others. Most of these projects are conducted on a large scale, requiring significant funding and budgets. However, small and medium cities may not have access to that kind of funding but can always come up with smaller projects.

Setting up biodiversity parks in floodplains to recreate self-sustaining ecosystems with native flora and fauna is another example of helping the river protect itself. Floodplains are fertile areas, and therefore a good quality of fauna is already available within them. Biodiversity parks not only conserve natural resources of an area but also have an educational and cultural value—especially for environmental sustenance in urban centres.

River markets (or floating markets) have traditionally been an integral part of river cities, serving as a centre for trade and commerce and contributing to the city's economy. They have also helped to strengthen the connection between the city and the river. However, with time, these markets have begun to be replaced by other larger markets further away from the river. Today, it may be difficult for the river markets to be the main source of trade and commerce, but as is evident in many cases around the world (Bangkok, Ayutthaya and Chang Mai in Thailand; Lokbaintan and Banjarmasin in Indonesia; Colombo in Sri Lanka) these markets can serve as a secondary source.

Such river markets exist in India as well. There is a floating market in Jammu and Kashmir on the Dal Lake that operates daily with vendors selling produce on the riverbanks. A similar market called 'Floating Triveni Super Store' operates in Kerala, offering subsidized rates on sale. In 2018, a floating market was opened in Patuli, Kolkata, on a canal adjacent to the Eastern Metropolitan Bypass. It features more than 200 vendors and 100 boats selling fish, fruit and vegetables. Such unique concepts can be replicated in other cities located on riverbanks or where large water bodies exist. In addition to fruits and vegetables, these markets could also support aquaculture activities, given that the Ganga is home to 143 species of fish. A vibrant river market is a top tourist attraction in many cities, thereby boosting the local economy.

However, the growth of such riverfronts and heightened public interaction on banks will give rise to new challenges, encroachments, unhindered land usage, indiscriminate economic activity, and increased solid waste. In time, we will have to think of some form of 'River Regulatory Zones' on the lines of Coastal Zones already established for the management and regulation of coastal areas.

Rejuvenating water bodies and wetlands can go a long way in reducing the stress on rivers because they are intrinsically connected to rivers either through their drainage patterns or groundwater flow. They improve groundwater recharge, thereby augmenting the water supply of a city. Similarly, rejuvenated wetlands are natural 'wastewater treatment plants that can significantly mitigate the river's pollution load'. The recreational benefits that these two interventions offer are an added incentive for the river. Setting up of a riparian buffer—a longitudinal 5- to 15-metre stretch of the rich, continuous buffer of vegetation—on either bank of the river can act as a shock absorber for the river and its aquatic ecosystem from detrimental development activities. The buffer zone protects the urban area from the impact of floods. Similarly, saving the floodplains—defined as an area inundated by floods that occur once in a fixed number of years—can also go a long way in saving the river.

There is a huge potential for water sports and related activities in the Ganga basin. Examples of prevailing activities include the Rishikesh city in Uttarakhand. Studies have shown that 36 km of the stretch from Kaudiyala to Rishikesh cities with 12 major rapids provide ideal natural conditions for exciting water sports activities. Similarly, there is an enormous potential to develop inland waterways for commercial efforts and tourism, which have not been taken up on a large scale. River tourism is a lucrative trade with the potential to significantly contribute to the local economies through employment on cruise ships, pleasure boats, parks, and recreational facilities along the riverbanks.

USE, REUSE AND FURTHER REUSE: THE ENDLESS CYCLE TO SAVE EVERY DROP

There are, however, a host of less critical but no less important steps to save the river. Measures to limit extensive water reuse can both be a cost-effective and long-term sustainable solution to the looming threat of water scarcity. Increased use of reused water—wastewater from domestic and industrial units treated through different processes—can significantly reduce the gap between the water supply and wastewater disposal and help save the environment. As experts point out, 'it provides a dependable and locally-controlled water source that result in less groundwater extraction or diversion from other freshwater sources, pollution abatement and creation, rehabilitation, or improvement of wetlands and riparian habitats.' Even the Water Reuse Association advocates treating wastewater for beneficial purposes, such as agricultural and landscape irrigation, industrial processes, toilet flushing or replenishing a groundwater basin.

As water shortages grip the nation and states start demanding more and more water to meet the needs of its ever-burgeoning population, industries will have to settle for reused water either on their own or through legislation focusing on water conservation and environmental compliance. Thermal power plants would be ideal for reuse because of their large water requirements for cooling, ash sluicing, rad-waste dilution and flue gas scrubber requirements (Metcalf and Eddy, 2003 and 2007). Petroleum refineries, chemical plants, and other industrial facilities will benefit from reclaimed water not only for cooling but also for processing its inputs.

For most industries, reclaimed water is ideal for providing cooling facilities for the plant because advancements in water treatment technologies have allowed industries to use poor quality water successfully. Additionally, the reuse of treated wastewater for irrigation and industrial purposes can be an effective tool for saving freshwater for domestic use and improving the quality of river waters used for drinking purposes by reducing effluent disposal into rivers (the United States Environmental Protection Agency, 2003). Moreover, industries should no longer just focus on reducing their own water usage through concepts like zero water discharge but also help their vendors find effective solutions to cut water usage.

Similarly, farming, which uses nearly 90 per cent of the country's total water needs, is ripe for some serious reforms. Growing water-guzzling crops like rice, wheat and sugarcane in wrong agro-climatic zones, like dry zones, need to be stopped. 'Unregulated and free access to groundwater has resulted in unlimited rural, urban and industrial extraction—which has resulted in widespread shortages in rural and urban areas including large metropolitan centres,' argues Mandakini D. Surie, a development practitioner in her paper, 'Will Coronavirus Force India to Face up to the Water Crisis.'

In the Indian context, water-related issues are varied and far more complex than in many other countries in the world. It is not just about having a limited supply of freshwater—18 per cent of the global population only has 4 per cent of the total freshwater—along with wrong government policies fuelled by vote bank policies, but also the near absence of proper water management, lack of proper data and continued use of outdated technology. According to experts, it has resulted in huge wastage and only a 38 per cent water use efficiency. One of the broad strategies to address this challenge for satisfying irrigation demand under conditions of increasing water scarcity in both developed and emerging countries is to conserve water and improve water use efficiency through better water management and policy reforms. In this context, water reuse becomes a vital alternative resource and an essential element of integrated water resource management at the catchment scale.

For those living in urban areas, recycled water can be used for non-drinking purposes such as irrigation of public parks and recreation centres, watering athletic fields, schoolyards and playing fields, construction of highway medians and shoulders and landscaped areas surrounding public buildings and facilities. Urban reuse can be expanded to include vehicle washing facilities, laundry facilities, window washing and mixing water for pesticides, herbicides, liquid fertilizers, toilet and urinal flushing in commercial and industrial buildings. Reclaimed water can also be used in dust control and all construction activities.

TURNING WASTE INTO WEALTH: THE BUSINESS OF MONETIZATION

Perhaps the best example of the use of reclaimed water comes from Surat in Gujarat, a model that many other states can follow in India. By setting up state-of-the-art STP to ensure that every drop of wastewater is treated and reused for purposes other than drinking, the city's entire industrial water requirement is met through treated or recycled water. From March 2019 onwards, the Surat Municipal Corporation has been supplying 115 MLD treated water to industries within the city. It remains the first city in the country to start selling recycled water to industries in 2014.

The other by-products of treated wastewater too should not be allowed to go to waste. The sewage sludge—solid, semi-solid or as residual slurry material—coming out of the STPs, can be dried and sold as organic fertilizer to farmers, which is currently being given out for free. It is not just a great example of not turning waste into wealth but also monetizing existing assets, a practice that is gaining significant importance in the Narendra Modi government. Similarly, biogas, another by-product of an STP, can be used for generating electricity. The Dinapur STP in Varanasi is one such example where 40 to 60 per cent of the electricity consumption is met by the biogas generated within the treatment plant itself.

One approach to sustainability is through the decentralization of the wastewater management system. This system consists of several smaller units serving individual houses, clusters of houses or small communities. Black and greywater can be treated or reused separately from the hygienically more dangerous excreta. Non-centralized systems are more flexible and can adapt easily to the local conditions of the urban area, and can grow with the community as its population increases. This approach leads to the treatment and reuse of water, nutrients and by-products of the technology (i.e. energy, sludge and mineralized nutrients) in the direct location of the settlement.

PRICING OF WATER

Water pricing is regarded as the most efficient way to improve water resources allocation and water use efficiency. Pricing is the most attractive water management instrument and is often at the centre of water policy reform but is rarely implemented to its full potential. Though pricing of water has been a topic of debate from the early 1970s during the second irrigation commission report, little has been achieved so far. Constitutionally, water is a state subject, and it is the writ of the state government that runs. In the irrigation sector, Kerala was the first state to impose irrigation water charges in 1974. (S.K. Sarkar 2019) But other states are yet to follow through.

Interestingly enough, the Central government came out in 2016 with a National Water Framework Bill, which lays down the principle of water pricing. For example, it says that water used for commercial agriculture and industry should be priced on a full economic pricing basis. For domestic use, a graded pricing system may be adopted. After all, water pricing remains a highly politically-sensitive issue, and few political parties are willing to disturb the existing status quo.

High pricing of freshwater for industries and the construction sector will help in increasing the demand of recycled treated wastewater. By 2050, the water demand is expected to exceed supply. Moreover, per capita water availability has been declining over the years, and it has now touched the scarcity benchmark of 1,000 cubic metres annually.

As large water users, water polluters and potential customers, the industry as a partner can help bring circular economy solutions to scale. Increasing awareness of environmental risk means industry leaders are increasingly looking for ways to reduce their water footprint and minimize environmental degradation. After all, water reuse brings tremendous environmental benefits, such as decreasing water diversion from or wastewater discharge to sensitive ecosystems, reduction and prevention of pollution, creation, rehabilitation, or improvement of wetlands and riparian habitats. Water reuse is regarded as a sustainable approach and can be cost-effective in the long term.

However, what provides the best hope for the river is the decision of various political parties to save the river. As the BJP's manifesto of 2019 states that the party is committed to ensure a clean and uninterrupted flow of the Ganga from Gangotri to Ganga Sagar. 'We will ensure that the sewerage infrastructure to deal with 100 per cent of the wastewater from the Ganga towns is completed and is functioning, and take steps to enhance the river flow. The villages located on the riverbanks, which are already open defecation free, will be taken up under special project to ensure complete sustainable management of solid-liquid waste,' said the BJP manifesto.

Even in its 2014 manifesto, the BJP promised to 'ensure the cleanliness, purity and uninterrupted flow of Ganga and take all measures, legal and administrative, in this regard. Necessary financial and technical assistance will be provided on priority. In addition, a massive "Clean Rivers Programme" will be launched across the country with the participation of voluntary organizations.'

Similarly, the Congress manifesto of 2019 promised to double the budget allocation for cleaning rivers, including the Ganga. 'Congress promises to review the current methodology for cleaning rivers and strengthen efforts by employing the latest advances in science and technology. We will convert the Ganga Action Plan into a people's programme and implement the same.'

The management of water resources, including rivers, has to be looked at through a more holistic lens where water is not 'just a resource to be exploited, but one that sustains economies and ecosystems into the future. The integrated management of both surface and groundwater and how they interact with society and the economy is a starting point towards water security and sustainability of the river. There is also an urgent need for states to come together to discuss, analyse and strategize their water management plans, and is perhaps the first step in this direction. Secondly, the job of sustaining the river should become the responsibility of both the urban local bodies and residents of the state, which calls for a bottom-up approach to the whole issue.

In recent times, the role of the government is changing from providing development to providing regulatory and oversight services. Infrastructure and legacy water laws, prices, rules and tenure, transparency for water allocations can come from an improved water governance paradigm. Governance will be the ultimate tool to ensure the achievement of these objectives, which itself will have to be evolved in such a way that these priorities are made an integral part of the governance priority and get enforced naturally. It is nobody's case that effective city governance ensuring proper management of sewage and solid wastes and prompt restrictions on industrial waste discharge could have avoided compounding of the problems and allocation of huge funds in the name of Ganga to meet the same objectives.

Moving forward, the sustainability of Ganga forever would be critically linked to the sustainability of NMCG itself as the overall custodian of this cause with adequate strength and ability. Its role would also have to evolve to meet the evolving nature of the challenges, as global experience has shown. The trend worldwide is for the river conservation bodies to gradually adopt a river-basin approach and emerge as River Basin Organizations, responsible for the basin level planning, development and regulatory responsibilities with appropriate financial, management and legislative backing. This is no more an option but a compulsion, and we would be wise to move in this direction sooner than later. This will also meet the need to align the goals of government agencies, urban local bodies, various stakeholders, environmentalists and those working on social development and economics for governing India to ensure a clean, free-flowing river that remains the goddess of millions of Indians across the length and breadth of the country.

As an institution, NMCG did not have the benefit of a greenfield start, as it had to carry the baggage of its predecessor organizations. But starting from zero, this actually became easier to handle, as it allowed fresh thinking and improvisations. Whether by design or by sheer chance, many may call it a compulsion as well, NMCG had to adopt the strategy of identifying the objective, getting into operation and improvising on the way. The pressure to get into action and show results being the guiding factor, one hardly had the time to learn, especially in areas where there was no expertise. Gradually this became a habit first, and then the organizational culture to keep learning. In retrospect, this has added to the strengths of the organization to adapt and remain relevant in changing contexts. The popular concept of limits to growth for organizations by Peter M. Senge is relevant: doing the same things will not bring the same results forever. The only option to remain sustainable is to remove the limiting factors and reinitiate the growth curve through learning as an organization. NMCG would need to evolve structurally and at the same time culturally to ensure its own sustainability while ensuring that for Ganga. This will be possible when NMCG consciously will try to remain a learning organization.

गंगोत्री की निर्मल धारा
में जो कल-कल छल-छल शब्द बहें
काशी की पावन लहरों में
पल-पल विश्वास का अर्थ मिले।
कहीं अतुकांत-सी बहती हो
कहीं छोर नहीं, कोई ओर नहीं
कहीं बहती हो हर तुक में तुम
हर शब्द, अर्थ का भाव लिए।
गंगा तुम स्वयं वो कविता हो
जिसमें कविता का अर्थ मिले।[21]

The mellifluous sound that flows with the serene stream,
emanating from Gangotri, provides the truest meaning of faith,
in form of its holy waves, as it reaches Kashi. Sometimes,
unbound of boundaries or any end, you keep flowing as carefree as
one could be, and sometimes as meaningful as describing the entirety
of our existence.

Ganga, you yourself are the verse that provides the depth,
continuity and purity to poems.

---

[21]Tiwari, P. (2021). *O Ganga Behati Rehna.* New Delhi: Swapan Publications.

GANGA REJUVENATION EFFORTS: COMPARATIVE STUDY

Previous Efforts	Namami Gange
River-wise Programme: (GAP-I, Gap-II, YAP-I, Action Plan, etc.)	Comprehensive integrated program and empowered institutional framework for implementation
Centrally Sponsored	Central Sector (100% federal funding for new projects)
O&M was not taken care of	Long-term O&M (15 years) included in project cost
Inadequate and uncertain funding	Five years of dedicated budget allocation
Hybrid Annuity Mode: Performance-linked payments	Hybrid Annuity Mode: Performance-linked payments
Focus only on major towns	Comprehensive programme including rural sanitation, urban river connect and basin approach
Main focus was on STP construction	Focus on biodiversity, environmental protection, afforestation, wetland conservation, solid waste management, sustainable agriculture along with STP construction and maintenance
Lack of community involvement	Dedicated cadres of locals, ex-servicemen, youth, science clubs to increase community participation in river rejuvenation
Lack of research and scientific data	Evidence-based planning and policy formation
No integration of urban planning and river rejuvenation	Paradigm shift towards integrating the rivers in city planning to make it a river centric planning
Piecemeal approach	Basin approach

IMPACT ON WATER QUALITY

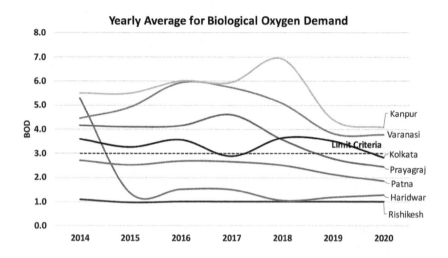

Yearly Average for Biological Oxygen Demand

Increased Dissolved Oxygen (DO) levels indicate improvement in the quality of water. The criterion of minimum DO level >5 mg/litre is now met throughout Ganga

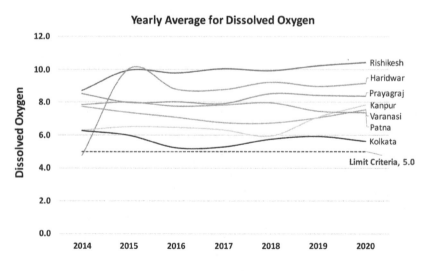

Yearly Average for Dissolved Oxygen

Decreasing levels of Biological Oxygen Demand (BOD) indicates momentum gained for Nirmal Ganga.

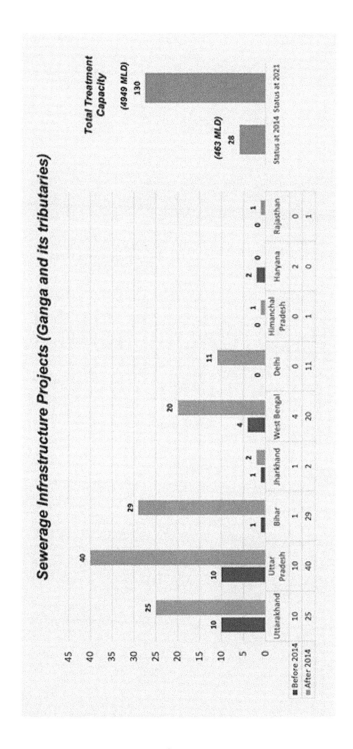

Sewerage Infrastructure Projects (Ganga and its tributaries)

	Uttarakhand	Uttar Pradesh	Bihar	Jharkhand	West Bengal	Delhi	Himanchal Pradesh	Haryana	Rajasthan
Before 2014	10	10	1	1	4	0	0	2	0
After 2014	25	40	29	2	20	11	1	0	1

Total Treatment Capacity

(463 MLD) 28 — Status at 2014

(4949 MLD) 130 — Status at 2021

Sanctioned Projects

2014 (6 PROJECTS)

- 43 MLD, Beur
- 179 km, Beur
- 37 MLD, Karmalichank
- 16 MLD, 227 km, Halishahar
- 21 MLD, 46 km, Kalyani
- 31 MLD, 125 km, Bhatpara

2015 (5 PROJECTS)

- Restoration works, Gangotri
- Restoration works, Devprayag
- Restoration works, Uttarkashi
- 60 MLD, 55 km, Saidpur
- 172 km, Saidpur

2016 (7 PROJECTS)

- 43 km, Prayagraj
- 1.6 km, Prayagraj
- 8.6 km, Delhi
- 7.61 km, Delhi
- 204 MLD, Delhi
- 5.09 km, Delhi
- 182 MLD, Delhi

2017 (36 PROJECTS)

- 3.78 MLD, 2.5 km, Joshimath
- 1.01 km, Badrinath
- 26 MLD, 3 km, Rishikesh
- 4.38 MLD, 1 km, Chamoli
- 82 MLD, Jagjeetpur, Sarai
- 3.5 MLD, Rishikesh
- 2 MLD, Uttarkashi
- 17 km, Haridwar
- 0.5 MLD, 7.2 km, Rudraprayag
- 0.35 MLD, 5 km, Karnaprayag
- 4.5 MLD, 2.3 km, Srinagar
- 0.06 MLD, Kirtinagar
- 12.5 MLD, 4 km, Muni ki Reti
- 0.15 MLD, 0.38 km, Nandaprayag
- *(Later bifurcated into 6 projects)* 140 MLD, 28 km, Varanasi
- 72 MLD, 13 km, Prayagraj
- 50 MLD, Ramana
- 2 MLD, Bithoor
- 15 MLD, 3 km, Unnao
- 10 MLD, 0.44 km, Ramnagar
- 30 MLD, Mathura
- 5 MLD, 0.15 km, Shuklaganj
- 60 MLD, Pahari
- 96.5 MLD, Karmalichak
- 116 km, Barh
- 87.69 km, Pahari
- 100 MLD, 288 km, Digha
- 50 MLD, 150 km, Kankarbagh
- 9 MLD, Naugacia
- 10 MLD, Sultangaj
- 26 MLD, 114 km, Tolly Nullah
- 3.5 MLD, 34 km, Rajmahal
- 6.42 km, Delhi
- 9.6 km, Delhi
- 94 MLD, Delhi
- 564 MLD, Delhi

2018 (26 PROJECTS)

- 45 MLD, Jagjeetpur, Sarai
- 3.6 km, Haridwar
- 30 MLD, Paudi Gharwal

Awarded Projects

2014 (3 PROJECTS)

- 14 MLD, Prayagraj
- 58 MLD, 46.3 km, Moradabad
- 21 MLD, Kalyani

2015 (12 PROJECTS)

- Restoration and Rehabilitation, Gangotri
- Restoration and Rehabilitation, Uttarkashi
- 2.5 MLD, 59 km, Anupshahar
- 1.4 MLD, Devprayag
- 4 MLD, 21.03 km, Narora
- 134.2 km, Prayagraj
- 241.6 km, Prayagraj
- 140 MLD, Varanasi
- 10 MLD, 0.44 km, Varanasi
- 72 MLD, 13.21 km, Budge - Budge
- 16 MLD, 227 km, Halishahar
- 9.3 MLD, 132 km, Budge - Budge

2016 (2 PROJECTS)

- 214.8 km, Prayagraj
- 24 MLD, 247.14 km, Barrackpore

2017 (24 PROJECTS)

- 2 MLD, Gyansu
- 0.15 MLD, 0.38 km, Nandaprayag
- 0.06 MLD, Kirtinagar
- 3.5 MLD, Srinagar
- 1 MLD, 2.23 km, Srinagar
- 3.5 MLD, Tapovan
- 3 MLD, Pauri Gharwal
- 17.1 km, Haridwar
- 1.01 MLD, Badrinath
- 27 MLD, Jagjeetpur, 18 MLD Sarai
- 4.38 MLD, 1.04 km, Chamoli
- 3.78 MLD, 2.5 km, Joshimath
- 0.53 MLD, 6.69 km, Rudraprayag
- 0.35 MLD, 4.73 km, Karnaprayag
- 82 MLD, Haridwar
- 1.63 km, Kanpur
- 42.66 km, Prayagraj
- 401 km, Kanpur
- 43 MLD, Beur
- 179.7 km, Beur
- 60 MLD, 55 km, Saidpur
- 94 MLD, Najafgarh
- 8.49 km, Delhi
- 7.71 km, Delhi

2018 (32 PROJECTS)

- 3.65 km, Haridwar
- 12.5 MLD, 3.5 km, Muni ki Reti
- 26 MLD, 2.5 km, Rishikesh
- 2 MLD, Bithoor
- 160 MLD, 16 km, Kanpur
- 6 MLD, 0.15 km, Shuklaganj
- 13 MLD, 3.3 km, Unnao
- 72 MLD, 13.21 km, Prayagraj
- 80 MLD, Prayagraj
- 10 MLD, 0.44 km, Varanasi

Top labels (above timeline):
67.5 MLD, Mathura
4 MLD, Vrindavan
5 km, Ayodhya
172.5 km, Saidpur
115.9 km, Pahari
87.69 km, Pahari
60 MLD, Pahari
96.54 km, Karmalichak
11 MLD, Barh
10 MLD, Sultanganj
32 MLD, 18.95 km, Chapra
17 MLD,114 km, Begusarai
9 MLD, Naugachia
3.5 MLD, 34.21 km, Rajmahal
13 MLD, 11.38 km, Jangipur
3.5 km, 5.25 km, Behrampore
318 MLD, Delhi
204 MLD, Delhi
8.13 km, Delhi
5.09 km, Delhi
6.16 km, Delhi
182 MLD, Delhi
0.01 MLD, Chunar
30 MLD, Jaunpur
15 MLD, 2.8 km, Kasganj
2.55 km, Firozabad
44.95 MLD, 2.2 km, Etawah
14 MLD, 2.35 km, Baghpat
6.5 MLD, Maner
100 MLD, 288 km, Digha
50 MLD, 150 km, Kankarbagh
3.5 MLD, Sonepur
10 MLD, Bakhtiyarpur
8 MLD, Mokama
20 MLD, 4 km, Nabadwip
18 MLD, 2.5 km, Kanchrapara
40 MLD, Bally
65 MLD, Howrah
46.24 MLD, North 24 Parganas
564 MLD, Okhla
1.72 MLD, Paonta Sahib
8.5 MLD, 1.7 km, Ramnagar
31 km, Dehradun
Budhana
100 MLD, 288 km, Digha
54.5 MLD, 5.91 km, Muzzafarnagar
32 MLD, 18.95 km, Chapra
25 MLD, 7.3 km, Danapur
13 MLD, Phulwarisharif
7 MLD, Fatuha
13 MLD, 11.38 km, Jangipur
3.5 MLD, 5.25 km, Behrampore
Chandannagar, Bansberia
Uttarpara, Kotrung & Konnagar
21 MLD, 1.2 km, Ghazipur
18 MLD, 2.07 km, Mirzapur
6 MLD, Baidyabati and 7 MLD, Bhadreshwar

2019 (21 PROJECTS)
2020 (13 PROJECTS)
2021 (3 PROJECTS)

Ganga

Completed Projects

2014 (2 PROJECTS)

13.5 km, Haridwar

18 MLD, Haridwar

2015 (1 PROJECTS)

1.02 km, Rishikesh

2016 (9 PROJECTS)

Restoration and Rehabilitation, Devprayag-

1.4 MLD, Devprayag

27.7 km, Joshimath

3.5 MLD, 11km, Devprayag

Restoration and Rehabilitation, Gangotri-

85 MLD, 10.8 km, Prayagraj

20 MLD, 9.24 km, Prayagraj

109 km, Prayagraj

14 MLD, Prayagraj

2017 (7 PROJECTS)

7.5 km, Badrinath

0.22 MLD, 7.6 km, Devprayag

35.6 km, Gopeshwar

1 MLD, 2.8 km, Gangotri

Restoration, Uttarkashi

8.2 MLD, 61 km, Gayeshpur

21 MLD, 46.3 km, Kalyani

2018 (15 PROJECTS)

3.5 MLD, Tapovan

3.65 km, Haridwar

2 MLD, Uttarkashi

0.06 MLD, Kirtinagar

3 MLD, Pauri Gharwal

42.6 km, Prayagraj

140 MLD, 28 km, Varanasi

9 MLD, 69 km, Garhmukhteshwar

1 MLD, 62.5 km, Kannuj

4 MLD, 21.03 km, Bulandshahar

SEWERAGE PROJECTS IN THE GANGA STATES

Epilogue

Letter to the Readers

To build a great institution, we must operate with the heart of an entrepreneur, the discipline of an athlete and the intellect of a scholar. Building great institutions require time, energy and the engagement of every stakeholder. I was determined to create that kind of ecosystem.

Whether I succeeded in building a model institution for the rejuvenation of Ma Ganga will only become clear over time as the organization and the mission is still a work in progress. But when I look back on those nearly six years of my tryst with the river, first as a Mission Director in the government, and then as Director General of the NMCG, I can only say with some confidence and satisfaction that I have achieved certain milestones and traversed some ground in this hugely daunting task of cleaning and rejuvenating India's longest and holiest of holy rivers, its tributaries and its ghats.

It has been a labour of love. I have always revered, respected and loved Ganga since my childhood; its waters have continued to provide me with much happiness, succour and it continues to keep me grounded. I will forever remain indebted to the river for all that it has taught me, and hopefully, all that it has changed in me for the better.

I must admit that I was fortunate enough to lead a wonderful team of people who displayed exemplary spirit and courage, seized every opportunity to learn and grow and overcame every challenge that was thrown at us during my stint at the NMCG. I can assure you, dear readers, that the task at hand was mammoth, complex and a long-drawn-out one. It called for close cooperation and coordination not just between the Centre and the state governments, but also among different ministries, departments and local urban bodies spread across the 11 states whose borders touch the river's edge.

Early on, I realized that the support and spirit of partnership and cooperation with the most important stakeholder of this mission—the crores of people living in the riverine cities and along its banks—was going to be critical, a sine qua non for its success. I also understood that saving and rejuvenating Ma Ganga is not a task for the faint-hearted or for those unwilling to take risks, to learn every day and to change with every new experience. The mission posed a wicked problem that had many different solutions and it needed a flexible mindset.

The ongoing mission calls for a deep understanding of different technologies, processes and designs of STPs, drains, the ecosystem and of flora, fauna, microorganisms and animals that call this river their home. It requires comprehending various issues that impact the river ecosystem, including the lakes, water bodies and aquifers, forests, irrigation practices and industry-specific pollutants.

A CIVILIZATIONAL CHALLENGE

This mission also demands that we make sense of Indian customs, traditions, religious sentiments, beliefs and practices among different people living in the riverine states. All these factors have a direct bearing on the purity and the ecological flow of the river. Our job is also to change the mindset, thinking and behaviour of the people, impressing upon them the centrality and importance of the river and water in their daily life. It is a civilizational challenge that needed to be solved with a sense of urgency.

This has also meant taking a stand on critical development issues—finding the right balance between the demands of growth and employment, while at the same time ensuring the long-term ecological health of the place. Should the establishment of new hydroelectric projects and dams be allowed even though it will mean restricting the natural flow of the river or force it to change its natural course with consequent adverse impact? No. Not only will such projects inundate acres of land along its banks, but they may also turn into drains during the dry seasons because of the ecological flow. These and such other questions haunted me for years, but I had to make a decision.

The NGRB, incidentally, is the largest and the most water-rich basin in the country, supporting an estimated 46 per cent of the Indian population. It houses a large number and variety of wetlands, lakes and other water bodies spread across the basin, supporting a large and diverse ecological system, which fulfils crucial social, ecological and economic functions such as nutrient recycling, water purification, flood attenuation, groundwater recharge and the buffering of shoreline against erosion. It also provides freshwater fish, fodder and recreational space on its banks to our society.

Its protection, therefore, is of paramount importance, I concluded. As a well-known sadhu once remarked on the ghats of the river: 'If Ganga dies, India dies. If Ganga thrives, India thrives.' The lives of 1.3 billion people are in some way or another connected to the well-being of the river. Hence, my fervent appeal to you, dear readers, is that you try to save the river for your own survival, if not for the sake of the Ma goddess. Today, she needs all your help and support. She will continue to need it as she travels from the upper reaches of the Himalayas to her final resting place in the Bay of Bengal. She will keep providing economic sustenance to millions of Indians along the way.

SAVING THE RIVER AND ITS TRIBUTARIES

How do you save the river—simply by respecting its right over its own water, land and by learning to cohabit with it through its different moods. You must refrain from extracting too much water for selfish needs and make sure you leave enough for the river to sustain itself or its inhabitants—plants, animal and other organisms—that are dependent on it. Secondly, you must respect the right of the river over its own land by allowing the river's water to spill over into the adjoining areas during the monsoons and to contract when the flow recedes during the summer months or in the dry season.

Encroaching on its land for farming or to set up industries or hotels is a sure-fire recipe for disaster because no embankment or temporary barricade can calm the fury of a river in its full spate. Destruction of life, livestock and property will follow, which can cost the nation and humanity thousands of crores in relief and rehabilitation. It must be ingrained in our consciousness that we are not to take away the river's last drop. It is not humanly possible to police every inch of such a huge ecosystem and take necessary action against the wrongdoers. Self-regulation is the only answer.

Thirdly, it is important to remember that the health of a river reflects a society's philosophical and physical state. A pure, free-flowing river is a sign of a progressive, environmentally conscious and a caring society. The health of the Ganga reflects on a society that revers all water bodies. The leaders of India must realize their commitments and responsibility to the river and to the ecosystem at large. Profitable business practices cannot thrive at the cost of the environment because a degraded environment will not only have a damaging impact on the health of the workforce (and on their families) but will also add to the industry's losses. It will not only cost them in terms of time and resources but also impact their future.

Today, most industries only pay lip service to environmental concerns and minimally comply with legal requirements. Commitment towards nature is lacking even though issues of environmental, social, governance (ESG) and sustainability of businesses have increasingly become important for regulators and investors at home and abroad. Thus, taking charge of cleaning and maintaining water bodies, lakes and stretches of the river can go a long way in nurturing and sustaining them for the future and will also help reduce the carbon footprint of the country.

THE COVID-19 EXPERIENCE

The devastation wrought by the COVID-19 pandemic shook all to the core. Recuperating at the hospital, I was hurt and pained by photographs and recurring images of half-burnt bodies floating on the Ganga on television screens. The bodies had been dumped by people unable (or unwilling) to pay for the last rites of their near and dear ones. Defiling and polluting a river is not part of our age-old traditions, rituals. Nor is it a part of any religious practice. Such a practice should be shunned because it only harms those living downstream.

Dear readers, you must learn to live with the river, build with nature, make room for the river and maintain its sanctity and purity at all costs. Even religious texts and scriptures have outlined a set of rules to follow; follow them in letter and spirit and the river will give back more in return.

Despite the enormity of the challenge ahead of us and many failed attempts, we should not lose hope and let our spirits sag because there are many success stories today. We have successfully cleaned up the Ganga in the Uttarakhand stretch, meeting and at times doing better than the international standard on maintaining DO, BOD, COD and other parameters. Similarly, certain ghats today sport a clean, aesthetic and smart look, and many cities are no longer eyesores with open drains, toxic pollutants and domestic wastes flooding the river and its tributaries. The clean-up journey is very much on its way to completion.

How did we achieve our success when many others had failed in the past? The answer is long and has been described in great detail in the chapters. I would just like to describe our approach in a few words, quoting William Arthur Ward, the American motivational speaker: We listened before we acted, thought before we reacted, earned before we spend, waited before we criticized, and tried very hard before we quit.

A LONG-TERM SOLUTION

This cannot be a one-time effort. We need to take up measures to build on continuous processes of maintaining the drains and the STPs, reducing the pollution of the cities, increasing forest cover and sustaining the water bodies. The true cost of ensuring a free-flowing and healthy river is the efficient use of water, reduction of wastage and eternal vigilance by the people. This has to be ensured long after I am gone, or even after the NMCG has ceased to exist.

In fact, I have believed in the simple advice expounded by the sixth American President, John Quincy Adams, who said: 'If your actions inspire others to dream more, learn more, do more and become more, then you are a real leader.' I hope I can inspire and create a sense of ownership among the people, who will zealously guard the river's health and well-being as if it is a member of their own family.

More importantly, it is time for you, readers, to sensitize and teach your children and others, about the need to safeguard the purity and usage of the river. Once polluted and defiled, it can cause immense damage to the whole ecosystem, especially since climate change is already playing havoc with nature. The cost of negligence is too high a price for all of us to pay.

The revival of the river has also seen the return of certain aquatic life, long declared dead or extinct. For instance, the Ganga Dolphin, which had gone missing for sometime now, has suddenly become visible near Benaras and other stretches of the Ganga. The Ganga Praharis in Kolkata, West Bengal have reported sightings of the Bengal shark, not seen since 1965. And as the objective of the mission reaches completion, I am sure that many other extinct animals and plants will make their re-appearance.

The message is clear: the river belongs to all, even the smallest microorganisms—not human beings alone—and thus, we have no right to pollute it and destroy the habitations of others. It is a question we all need to ponder on.

But the most important lesson that the river teaches you is that if you don't disturb, pollute, defile or block its path, it will always remain pure, it will then bring all the goodness of nature and help you live a happy, healthy and prosperous life. This cannot be too much to ask for.

Bibliography

1. Consortium, IIT, *Ganga River Basin Management Plan,* New Delhi: National Mission For Clean Ganga, 2015.
2. Britannica, *Ganges River,* 6 March 2009.
3. The Kuppuswami Sastri Research Institute, *Bhagvadgita,* Chennai, 2007.
4. Khandelwal, K.N., *Jawaharlal Nehru The Discovery of India,* Lakshmi Narain Agarwal, 2017.
5. Commission, Member (Water Resources) Planning, *Report on Utilization of Funds and Assets Created through Ganga Action Plan in States Under GAP,* Environment & Forests Division and Water Resources Division Planning Commission, 2009.
6. CPCB, *Annual Report 2014-2015,* Delhi: CPCB.
7. MoEFCC, 'The Environment (Protection) Act, 1986'.
8. NMCG, *Annual Report 2018-19,* New Delhi: NMCG.
9. Government of India, *Report of the Inter-Ministerial Group on Issues Relating to River Ganga,* New Delhi: GoI, 2013.
10. Reichard, James S. *Environmental Geology.* McGraw-Hill Science Engineering, 2nd edition, 2013.
11. MoEF, 'Public Accounts Committee (2014-15)', Eighth Report, New Delhi.
12. *India Budget,* 10 July 2014, https://www.indiabudget.gov.in/doc/bspeech/bs201415.pdf.
13. Disaster Mitigation and Management Centre, Department of Disaster Management (Government of Uttarakhand), 'Disaster Response and Management', *Disaster - Response and Management Journal Vol. 4,* 2016.

14. SANDRP, *Report of Expert Committee on Uttarakhand Flood Disaster & Role of HEPs: Welcome Recommendations*, 29 May 2014.

15. Aayog, NITI, *Inventory and Revival of Springs in the Himalayas for Water Security*, New Delhi, August 2018.

16. NGT, 'NGT Judgement Ganga', New Delhi, 17 July 2017.

17. 'MoU with Power Ministry', New Delhi: Government of India, 28 January 2016.

18. Twain, Mark, and Clemens, Samuel L., *Following the Equator*, Connecticut: Biblioteca Virtual Universal, 2008.

19. Mehrotra, Rahul, *Mapping the Ephemeral Mega City: Kumbh Mela*. Hatje Cantz Verlag, 2015.

20. Prayagraj Municipal Corporation, 'Prayagraj Kumbh Mela 2019', Administrative Report, Prayagraj, 2019.

21. The World Bank, *Building Resilience for Sustainable Development of the Sundarbans through Estuary Management, Poverty Reduction, and Biodiversity Conservation*, Strategy Report, Washington: The World Bank, 2014.

22. CEE, *Ganges River Dolphin*, Project Report, New Delhi: CEE, 2017.

23. WII, *Forestry Intervention for Ganga*. Detailed Project report, New Delhi: NMCG, 2016.

24. Acciavatti, Anthony, *Ganges Water Machine: Designing New India's Ancient River*, Oro Editions, 2015.

25. Bhat, Akash, *Kumbh Mela: Historical And Cultural Background*, March 2021.

26. Mehrotra, Rahul, and Vera, Felipe, *Reversibility Disassembling the Biggest Ephemeral Mega City*, August 2015.

27. Eck, Diana L., *Banaras City of Light*. Penguin India, 2015.

28. Black, George, *What It Takes to Clean the Ganges*. New York, 18 July 2016. Accessed 2020. www.newyorker.com.

29. Albinia, Alice, *Empires of the Indus: The Story of a River*, John Murray, 2012.

30. Otto, Frei, *Occupying and Connecting: Thoughts on Territories and Spheres of Influence with Particular Reference to Human Settlement*. Edition Axel Menges, 2008.

31. *Branding Patna*, 2017, Accessed 2020. http://brandingbihar.com/.

32. Rodgers, Dennis, and Satija, Shivani, *Understanding the tipping point of urban conflict: the case of Patna, India*. Working Paper, Manchester: Urban Tipping Point, 2012.

33. Lall, Nishant, 'Creating a Civic Realm: Ganga Riverfront Revitalization, Patna', Patna & New Delhi, 1 September 2016.

34. PIB. *Project Dolphin announced by PM Modi to be launched in 15 days: Javadekar.* New Delhi, August 2017.

35. Memorial Gates Trust, 'Participants from the Indian subcontinent in the First World War', 2002.

36. Ivermee, Robert. *Hooghly: The Global History of a River.* London: C Hurst & Co Publishers Ltd, 2020.

37. IPE Global, *DPR For Development of Sewerage Syatem in Halishahar Municiplity Under NRGBA ESAMP*, Detailed Project Report, New Delhi: IPE Global, 2016.

38. Secretariat, The Ramsar Convention, 2014, Accessed 2020. https://www.ramsar.org/.

39. Ghosh, Amitav, 2016, *The Hungry Tide*, Noida: Harper Collins.

40. Gopinath, Girish, and Seralathan, P., *Rapid erosion of the coast of Sagar island, West Bengal -India*, October 2005.

41. CSE, *Living with changing climate.* Research Report, New Delhi: CSE, 2012.

42. L.Goodbred Jr., Steven, and A. Kueh, Steven, *Controls on facies distribution and stratigraphic preservation in the Ganges-Brahmaputra delta sequence*, 2 May 2002.

43. TEEB for National and International Policy, 'The Economics of Ecosystems and Biodiversity for National and International Policy Makers', Research Report, 2009.

44. Prevention Web, *World Disaster Report*, 2002.

45. Mallet, Victor, *River of Life, River of Death: The Ganges and India's Future*, New Delhi: OUP Oxford, 2017.

46. Colopy, Heryl, *Dirty, Sacred Rivers: Confronting South Asia's Water Crisis.* New Delhi: Oxford University Press, 2012.

47. Rangathan, Priya, *Amphan in the Sundarbans: How Mangroves Protect the Coast From Tropical Storms*, May 2020.

48. UNESCO, *Securing the Future of Mangroves*, Policy Brief, UNESCO, 2012.

49. The World Bank, *Ganges Strategic Basin Assessment-A Discussion of Regional Opportunities and Risks*, Washington: The World Bank, 2014.

50. Rasul, Golum, *Water for Growth and development in the Ganges, Brahmaputra and Meghna basins: An economic perspective*, Kathmandu, 24 March 2015.

51. DDA, *Delhi Master Plan 2041*, Master Plan, New Delhi: DDA, 2021.

52. NEER Foundation, *The NEER Foundation*, Accessed 2020, http://www.theneerfoundation.org/.

53. Shinde, Victor R., 'Reviving "the connect" between river, City and its People', *The Journal of Governance*, 107-120, 2020.

54. NMCG, *National Mission for Clean Ganga, 2013*, nmcg.nic.in.

55. Drew, Georgina, *River Dialogues: Hindu Faith and the Political Ecology of Dams on the Sacred Ganga (Critical Green Engagements: Investigating the Green Economy and its Alternatives)*. University of Arizona Press, 2017.

56. Modi, Narendra, *Mann Ki Baat, 2015*. Accessed 2020. www.pmindia.gov.in.

57. Ministry of Jal Shakti, *Jal Shakti Abhiyan, 2016*. https://ejalshakti.gov.in/.

58. *BJP Manifesto 2019*, New Delhi.

59. *BJP Manifesto 2014*, New Delhi.

60. *Congress Manifesto 2019*, New Delhi.

61. Metcalf, and Eddy, *Wastewater Engineering: Treatment and Reuse*, Hong Kong: McGraw Hill Companies, 2003.

62. EPA, US, *United States Environmental Protection Agency, 2003*, cfpub.epa.gov.

63. Surie, Mandakini D., *Will coronavirus force India to face up to its water crisis?*, 2020.

64. Government of India, *Report of the Irrigation Commission*, 1972.

65. O'Keeffe, Jay, Nitin Kaushal, Luna Bharati and Vladimir Smakhtin, *Assessment of Environmental Flow for the Upper Ganga Basin*, Assessment Report, WWF, 2012.

66. WWF, *Keeping Rivers Alive-A primer on Environmental Flows and their Assessment,* Primer, WWF, 2009.

67. MoEF, 'National Environment Policy', 2006.

68. Banerjee, Bidisha, *Superhuman River-Stories of the Ganga.* Aleph Book Company, 2020.

69. Doron, Assa, Richard Barz, and Barbara Nelson, *An Anthology of Writings on the Ganga: Goddess and River in History, Culture, and Society,* Oxford University Press, 2014.

70. Colopy, Cheryl, *Dirty, Sacred Rivers: Confronting South Asia's Water Crisis,* Oxford University Press, 2012.

71. Iqbal, Iftekhar, *The Bengal Delta: Ecology, State and Social Change, 1840-1943 (Cambridge Imperial and Post-Colonial Studies Series),* Palgrave Macmillan, 2010.

72. Douglas, Ed. , *Himalaya: A Human History.* Bodley Head, 2020.

73. Hollick, Julian Crandall, *Ganga,* RHI, 2007.

74. Times of India, *Polluted Ganga river can treat infections: Scientists,* New Delhi, 3 october 2016.

75. Bagla, Pallava, and The Economics Times, *Is Ganga water special because of an enigmatic X-factor?* New Delhi, 22 November 2015.

76. Darian, Steven G., *The Ganges in Myth and History.* Motilal Banarsidass Publishers, 2001.

77. Jal Shakti Ministry, *Jal Manthan.* New Delhi, July 2017.

78. Pandey, Sugandhaa, *Saddle up to read about Kanpur's iconic leatherworking tradition that has put it on the world map,* June 2021.

79. Mundy, Captain, *The Journal of A Tour in India,* London: William Clowes, 1858.

80. Federici, Cesare, *The Voyage and Travaile Into the East India: London 1588,* New York: Theatrum Orbis Terrarum, 1588

81. Chaudhuri, Prasun, *On the Trails of the Vanishing Waterways of India,* New Delhi, June 2019.

82. Acciavatti, Anthony, *Ganges Water Machine: Designing New India's Ancient River.* Oro Editions, 2015.

83. *Census India, 2011,* Accessed 20 September 2020. https://censusindia.gov.in/.

84. British Indian Empire, 2017. *http://dutchinkerala.com/*. Accessed 20 September. http://dutchinkerala.com/imperialgazetteer.php?id=07.

85. MoHFW, *Ministry of Health and Family Welfare,* Accessed 21 September 2021. https://mohfw.gov.in.

86. MoHUA. n.d. *Ministry of Housing and Urban Affiars.* Accessed 21 September 2021. https://mohua.gov.in/.

87. *Swachh Bharat Urban,* 2014, Accessed 17 August 2021. http://swachhbharaturban.gov.in/.

88. *Swachh Sarvekshan 2020.* Accessed 20 August 2021. http://www.swachhsurvekshan2020.org/Rankings.

89. NMCG. n.d. *Namami Gange Mission.* Accessed 21 September 2021. https://nmcg.nic.in/.

90. NWDA, *National Water Development Agency.* Accessed 23 August 2021. http://nwda.gov.in/.

91. WHO. 2020. *World Health Organization.* Accessed August 17, 2021. https://www.who.int/.

92. MoEF. n.d. *Ministry of Environment and Forest.* Accessed September 21, 2021. https://mpforest.gov.in/.

93. IIT consortium, *Ganga River Basin Management Plan.* New Delhi: National Mission For Clean Ganga, 2015.

94. Britannica, *Ganges River,* 6 March 2009.

95. The Kuppuswami Sastri Research Institute, *Bhagvadgita, 2007,* Chennai.

96. Maker, TEEB for National and International Policy. 2009. 'The Economics of Ecosystems and Biodiversity for National and International Policy Makers.' Research Report.

97. NMCG, and NIUA, *Urban River Management PLan.* A Strategic Framework for Managing Urban River Stretches in the Ganga River Basin, New Delhi: NMCG, 2020.

98. NMCG, and SPA Delhi, *Urban Wetlands/Water Bodies Management Guidelines.* Guideline/toolkit for local stakeholders, New Delhi: NMCG, 2019.

99. Mishra, Rajiv Ranjan, 'Special Issue on Namami Gange.' *The Journal of Governance* 3-18, 2020.

100. Government of India, Namami Gange, New Delhi, 2021.

101. WII, Ganga River State of Biodiversity at a Glance, Research Report, New Delhi, 2018.

102. PIB, *PM inaugurates Six Major Projects in Uttarakhand to make River Ganga Nirmal and Aviral.* New Delhi, 29 September 2020.

103. Mallet, Victor, *River of Life, River of Death.* New Delhi: OUP Oxford, 2017.

104. Gorakhpur, Geeta Press, *Matsya Puran (Sachitra Hindi Anuvaad Sahit).* Gorakhpur: Geeta Press Gorakhpur, 2017.

105. Vinay, *Padma Purana,* Diamond Books, 2007.

106. Pandey, Raj Bahadur, *Rigveda,* New Delhi: Diamond Pocket Books, 2005.

107. Joshi, K.L., *Narasimha Purana.* Delhi: Parimal Publications, 2005.

108. IIT consortium, *Ganga River Basin Management Plan, Mission 1: Aviral Dhara.* Management Plan, New Delhi: NMCG, 2015.

109. IIT consortium, *Ganga River Basin Management Plan, Mission 2: Aviral Dhara.* Management Plan, New Delhi: NMCG, 2015.

110. IIT consortium, *Ganga River Basin Management Plan, Mission 3: Ecological Restoration.* Management Plan, New Delhi: NMCG, 2015.

111. IIT consortium, *Ganga River Basin Management Plan, Mission 4: Sustainable Agriculture.* Management Plan, New Delhi: NMCG, 2015.

112. IIT consortium, *Ganga River Basin Management Plan, Mission 5: Geological Safegaurding.* Management Plan, New Delhi: NMCG, 2015.

113. IIT consortium, *Ganga River Basin Management Plan, Mission 6: Basin Protection against Disasters.* Management Plan, New Delhi: NMCG, 2015.

114. IIT consortium, *Ganga River Basin Management Plan, Mission 7: River Hazards Management.* Management Plan, New Delhi: NMCG, 2015.

115. IIT consortium, *Ganga River Basin Management Plan, Mission 8: Environmental Knowledge-Building and Sensitization.* Management Plan, New Delhi: NMCG, 2015.

116. NEERI, *Assessment of Water Quality and Sediment to understand the Special Properties of River Ganga*. Assessment Report, New Delhi: NMCG, 2020.

117. Indira Gandhi National Open University, *History of India,* New Delhi: Indira Gandhi National Open University, 2020.

118. The World Bank, *The National Ganga River Basin Project,* 23 March 2015.

119. SANDRP. 2019. *Decoding the Economics of Ganga Waterway (National Waterways-1).* February 8.

120. NITI Ayog, *Inventory and Revival of Springs in Himalayas for Water Security,* 2019 Working Group Report, New Delhi, 2019.

121. The Print, *How industrial waste, govt apathy are killing the Ganga in Kanpur,* New Delhi, 7 January 2018.

122. NGT, *M.C. Mehta vs Union of India.* New Delhi, 13 July 2017.

123. The New Yorker, *What It Takes to Clean the Ganges,* New Delhi, 18 July 2016.

124. The Economic Times, *Rejuvenating Ganga: Project to make the river clean & uninterrupted may cost Rs 1 lakh crore,* New Delhi, 27 July 2014.

125. Britannica, *Job Charnock,* 6 January 2021.

126. Britannica, *Battle of Plassey Indian history [1757],* 16 June 2021.

127. Goodberg, S.L., and S.A. Kuehl. 1999. *Holocene and modern sediment budgets for the Ganges-Brahmaputra river system.*

128. Rudra, Dr. Kalyan. 2016. 'State of India's Rivers for India Rivers Week.' Status report.

129. Government of Bihar and World Bank, *BIHAR KOSI FLOOD (2008),* Need Assessment Report, 2010.

130. Sarkar, S.K., The Hindu (Business Line), *It's time to overhaul water pricing norms,* New Delhi, 8 May 2019.

131. Low, Sir Sidney, *A Vision of India,* Seema Publications, 1975.

132. Government of Jharkhand, Sahibganj, accessed on 15 August 2021 at https://sahibganj.nic.in/history/.

133. Forrest, Lieutenant Colonel, A picturesque tour along the rivers ganges and jumna in India, 1920.

134. Mahajan, Jagmohan, Ganga Trail: Foreign Accounts and Sketches of the River Scene, Books from India (U.K.), 1984.

135. Sediment Managament by Amita Bhaduri, India Water Portal, 2019.

136. Rice, Stephanie Kimberly, Suspended sediment transport in the Ganges-Brahmaputra River System, Bangladesh, Texas A&M University, 2007.

137. Tiwari, P., O Ganga Behati Rehna, New Delhi: Swapan Publications, 2021.

138. Ministry of Water Resources, RD & GR, Draft Policy on Sediment Management, New Delhi, Government of India, 2017.

Ingram Content Group UK Ltd.
Milton Keynes UK
UKHW012124060323
418148UK00014B/471/J

WHAT'S THE WEATHER?

IT'S SNOWING!

Written by
Azra Limbada

©2021
BookLife Publishing Ltd.
King's Lynn
Norfolk PE30 4LS

All rights reserved.
Printed in Malaysia.

A catalogue record for this book is available from the British Library.

ISBN: 978-1-83927-193-9

Written by:
Azra Limbada

Edited by:
William Anthony

Designed by:
Chris Cooper

PHOTO CREDITS

All images are courtesy of Shutterstock.com, unless otherwise specified. With thanks to Getty Images, Thinkstock Photo and iStockphoto.
Front Cover – Echunder, A3pfamily, Mike Mareen, Evgeny Atamanenko, Libor Fousek. Character throughout – yusufdemirci. 4 – By Aluca69. 5 – Creative Travel Projects. 7 – Carlos Horta. 8 – Sunny Forest. 9 – Tita77. 10–11 – Sthapana Sriyingyong. 12 – Triff. 13 – Jefunne. 14 – Evgeny Bakharev, yusufdemirci. 15 – Bobkov Evgeniy, cuppucino. 16 – Ipedan. 17 – bibiphoto. 18 – Delbars. 19 – Gecko1968. 20 – Smit. 21 – Max Topchii. 22 – Barbara_Krupa. 23 – aleksandr4300.

CONTENTS

Words that look like <u>this</u> can be found in the glossary on page 24.

WHAT CAN YOU SEE?

Take a look outside. What can you see? Are the trees swooshing in the wind or is there a big rainbow in the sky?

Weather is what you can see in the sky and feel in the air outside. There are lots of types of weather, such as rain, sunshine, wind and snow.

Hi! I'm Snowy the Snowball.

5

SEASONS

Winter

Spring

Autumn

Summer

In many countries, there are four seasons in every year. They are called spring, summer, autumn and winter. Each season has different kinds of weather.

Winter is the season when everything gets very cold. This means you will have to wrap up in lots of warm clothes before going outside.

You might even get to make me!

IT'S SNOWING!

Look at all the snow covering the winter forest!

Snow may fall down from the sky when the weather is very cold. It is made up of lots of tiny <u>ice crystals</u>.

If the <u>temperature</u> is cold enough, the snow will fall as powder. This means it will cover the ground like a big, white blanket.

Snow angels

Brrr! Can you make snow angels too?

THE WATER CYCLE

The water on our planet never goes away. We always have the same amount of water on Earth. It moves around in a big <u>cycle</u>.

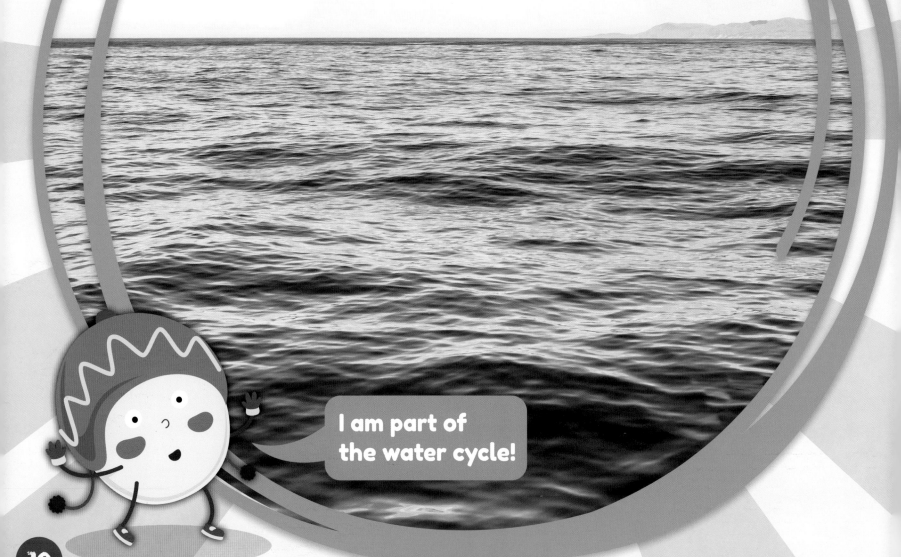

I am part of the water cycle!

When the sunlight heats water up, some of it rises into the sky. It cools down and makes clouds.

UP IN THE CLOUDS

All the fluffy clouds that you see in the sky are made of air and lots of tiny <u>droplets</u> of water.

When the temperature is at <u>freezing point</u> or below, the water droplets in the clouds stick together to make little snowflakes.

I am made from lots of tiny ice crystals!

13

SNOWFLAKES

Snow may fall from clouds like these.

The little snowflakes will keep getting bigger until they are too heavy to stay in the sky. That's when they fall down from the clouds.

BLIZZARD!

Look at how much snow there is!

A blizzard is when certain types of cold weather come together to make a <u>storm</u>. Blizzards are made up of strong winds and lots of heavy snow.

This car is trying to drive through a blizzard.

Blizzards are very dangerous. They can make it hard to see. Because a blizzard happens when it is very cold, it can also give you <u>frostbite</u>.

ANIMALS

Deer are a type of animal that can live in the snow.

Some animals are able to live in snowy weather.
This is because they are <u>adapted</u> to the cold weather.
They are able to find food and stay warm.

Polar bears live in the snowy Arctic. Their thick fur helps them to stay warm and blend in with the snow.

This mother polar bear and her cub love playing in the snow!

SNOW FUN

Playing in the snow can be lots of fun. Some children make people out of snow and dress them in hats and scarves. Children may also go skiing.

It is important to dress warmly and play safely in the snow, even if you are just throwing snowballs at each other!

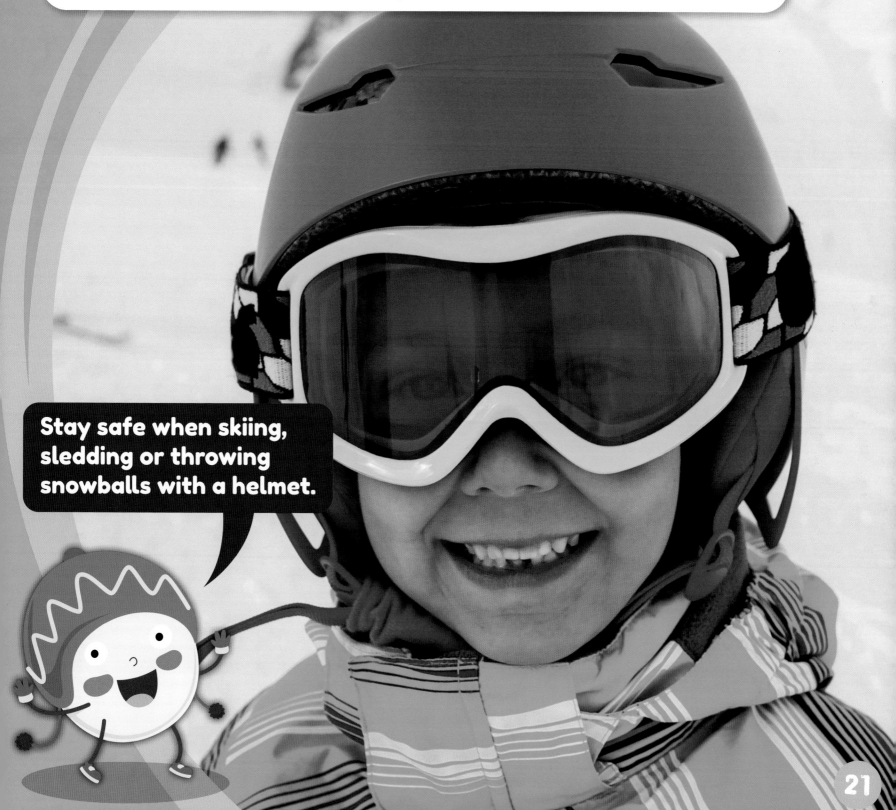

Stay safe when skiing, sledding or throwing snowballs with a helmet.

MELTING AWAY

The sunlight has melted this snow.

As the weather gets warmer, snow melts away and turns back into water. Some of the water seeps into the ground and helps plants to grow.

Some of the water goes back into the sky. It makes new clouds and becomes part of the water cycle again.

Watch me disappear into the air and become a new cloud!

23

GLOSSARY

adapted — able to exist in a certain environment because of changes that have happened over time

cycle — a set of events that happen again and again in the same order

droplets — very small drops of liquid, such as water

freezing point — the temperature at which water turns to ice, which is 0 degrees Celsius

frostbite — when very cold weather freezes and hurts the skin

ice crystals — small, special shapes made of frozen water

storm — strong weather such as heavy rain and wind

temperature — how hot or cold something is

INDEX

24